Praise for

The Big Brain & Body Regulation Toolbox for Kids & Teens

"After three decades in clinical practice, I've seen many resources come and go, but *The Big Brain & Body Regulation Toolbox for Kids & Teens* stands out for its clarity and cross-disciplinary utility. Jen Wilke-Deaton has created a guide that is simple to navigate and even simpler to read, without sacrificing clinical depth.

I particularly appreciate the strengths-based lens she applies to ADHD, autism, and mood disorders. It offers a compassionate, actionable perspective for educators while maintaining a firm footing in evidence-based practice. While this is a must-have desk reference for therapists and supervisees, its practical language makes it a powerful tool for teachers and community members. It is a perfect bridge between clinical diagnosis and classroom support."

—**Tony Miller, LPCC-S,** OW/OP clinical director, Mustard Tree Counseling

"*The Big Brain & Body Regulation Toolbox for Kids & Teens* by Jen L. Wilke-Deaton offers a comprehensive and highly practical resource for clinicians working with children and adolescents. The book draws from a wide range of evidence-based approaches, but what stands out most is the way these models are brought together in a cohesive and accessible format. The interventions are clearly explained, with thoughtful attention to the 'why' behind each strategy, making it easier for clinicians to apply them with intention. The book also provides guidance on adapting interventions across school, clinical, and community settings, which adds to its practicality.

Clinicians working with youth experiencing anxiety, depression, ADHD, autism, or broader behavioral challenges will find this book especially useful. It serves as a well-organized, integrative resource—bringing together multiple therapeutic approaches and tools in one place while maintaining a respectful, neurodiversity-affirming lens. This is a valuable addition for both new and experienced clinicians looking to strengthen their work in supporting regulation and overall well-being in children and teens."

—**Christina Sullivan, LCSW,** owner and clinical director, Broward Therapy Group

"Once again, Jennifer has knocked it out of the park in creating interventions for some of children's most difficult struggles. As a fellow clinician and longtime conference attendee, I have found her tools to be practical, effective, and fun for both clinician and client. This workbook goes a step further by extending into school systems and treatment facilities as a go-to guide from which all personnel can benefit. She very thoughtfully encompasses school tier systems and provides techniques for multiple modalities. For parents, she also includes mind-body strategies for improving sleep, limiting screen time, and refining nutrition. This is especially helpful as access to mental health resources can be limited for families. If you have a child experiencing difficulties with ADHD, ASD, anxiety, or depression and need more relevant approaches to today's symptoms, this is your guide!"

—**Jaime Taylor, LPC,** children's therapist, author, and school counselor

The BIG Brain & Body Regulation Toolbox for Kids & Teens

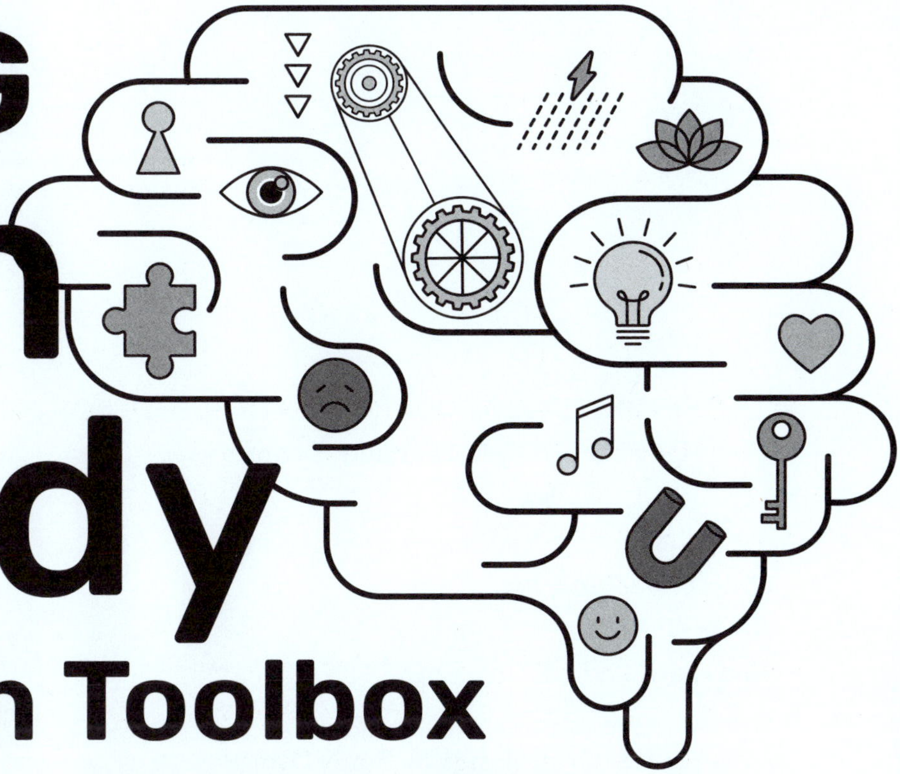

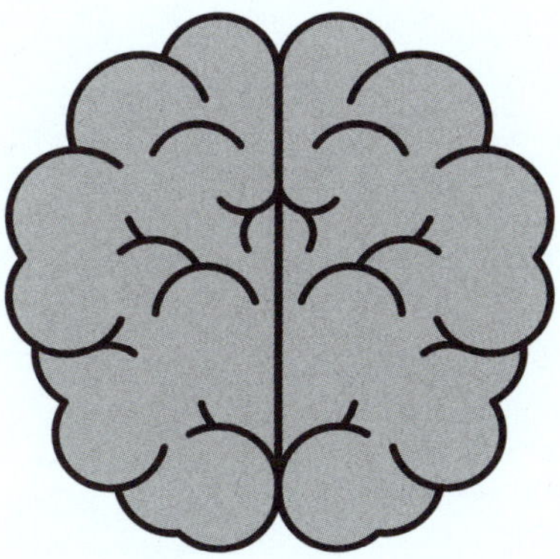

117 Neuroscience-Informed Interventions for **Anxiety, Mood Management, Executive Function, Coping & Social Skills**

Jen L. Wilke-Deaton, MA, LPA

THE BIG BRAIN AND BODY REGULATION TOOLBOX FOR KIDS AND TEENS

Published by
PESI Publishing, Inc.
3839 White Ave
Eau Claire, WI 54703

Cover and interior design by Emily Dyer
Editing by Kate Sample

ISBN 9781683739364 (print)
ISBN 9781683739371 (ePUB)
ISBN 9781683739388 (ePDF)

Printed in the United States of America.

PESI Publishing
pesipublishing.com

Contents

Introduction 1

1. Building a Functional Foundation: "The Big Five" 5

Sleep 6

Handout: 5 Essentials for Healthy Sleep Hygiene 8

Worksheet: Smooth Sleep Cycling 10

Technology 12

Handout: Healthy Screen Use 14

Handout: Five-Week Nighttime Technology Titration 15

Movement 17

Handout: Our Brains Love Movement! 19

Worksheet: Active Body, Peaceful Mind 20

Nutrition and Hydration 22

Handout: Food and Mood: What Helps, What Hurts 24

Nervous System Regulation 25

Handout : My Autonomic Nervous System 27

Handout: Understanding Your Child's Autonomic Nervous System Threshold 28

Worksheet: Big Five Check-In Sheet 29

2. Anxiety 31

Case Example 33

Anxiety Key Concept: Reinforcement 34

Crystallized Coping Skills 35

Handout: Active Coping Skills 37

Handout: Passive Coping Skills 38

Worksheet: Crystallized Coping Skills 39

Coping in All Your Places and Spaces 40

Worksheet: Coping in All Your Places and Spaces 42

The Stress and Worry Tree 43

Template: Stress and Worry Tree 45

Template: Worry Leaf 46

Anxiety Appointments 47

Advanced Anxiety Appointments 49

Worksheet: Your Thoughts and Your Body 51

Anxiety Anchors 52

Handout: Anxiety Anchors 54

Play Dough Magic ... 55
Handout: Play Dough Recipes ... 58
Anxiety Sunglasses ... 60
Worksheet: Anxiety Rating Scale ... 62
Tactile Grounders / Weighted Objects ... 63
Handout: Weighted Grounding Objects: Examples, Ideas, and Tips ... 65
The Existential Oak Tree ... 66
Handout: Existential Oak Tree Script ... 69
Transitional Objects ... 70
Handout: Transitional Objects ... 71
Transition Hallways for Separation Anxiety ... 73
The Five Senses Scavenger Hunt / Sensory Soothing Box ... 75
Worksheet: The Five Senses Scavenger Hunt ... 77
Quiet Time (QT) ... 78
Say What You Mean and Mean What You Say ... 80
Handout: The Four Steps of "I" Statements ... 82
Worksheet: "I" Statement Practice Scenarios ... 83
Your Support Net ... 85
Worksheet: Who Will Be in Your Support Net? ... 88
Template: Your Support Net Calendar ... 89
Passcode Word (Younger Ages and Stages) ... 90
Worksheet: Making a Passcode Word ... 92
Passcode Word (Older Ages and Stages) ... 93
Worksheet: Communication Contract ... 95

3. Depression ... 97
Case Example ... 99
Depression Key Concept: Validation ... 100
Depression Beast ... 101
Worksheet: Depression Beast ... 103
Is Your Depression Beast Nearby? ... 104
Worksheet: Is Your Depression Beast Nearby? ... 105
Flip the Switch (Opposite Action) ... 107
Handout: What Is Opposite Action? ... 109
Worksheet: Flip the Switch ... 110
OAs for All the Days and All the Ways ... 111
Worksheet: OAs for All the Days and All the Ways ... 113
The Reality Journal ... 115
Handout: What Is Suffering? ... 117
Worksheet: Reality Journal Comic Book ... 118
Self-Esteem Gift Box ... 119
Template: Something Great About You ... 121

Automatic Negative Thoughts 122
Worksheet: Automatic Thoughts 123
Personal Love Letters 125
Handout: How to Write a Personal Love Letter 127
Template: Your Personal Love Letter 128
The Cathartic Letter 129
Magic Mirror 131
Worksheet: Magic Mirror 133
Personal Art Gallery 134
Worksheet: Your Personal Art Gallery 136
Wise Mind 137
Handout: Wise Mind 139
Wise Mind Detective 140
Worksheet: Wise Mind Detective 142
Handout: How to Get to Wise Mind 144
ACCEPTS: Coping in a Crisis 145
Worksheet: Your ACCEPTS Skills 147

4. ADHD 149
Case Example 151
ADHD Key Concept: Dual-Hemisphere Processing (Part 1) 152
ADHD Key Concept: Dual-Hemisphere Processing (Part 2) 154
Handout: Understanding Executive Function 155
Fidget or Distractor? 157
Handout: Fidgets 159
Fabric Sticks for Focus 160
Resistance Bands 162
Pacing Runways 164
Visual Movement Boxes 166
Line-Up Lists 168
Stripping the Environment 170
Effective Classroom Seating 172
Visual Checklist 174
Handout: Visual Checklist: Examples and Guidelines 176
Template: Visual Checklist 177
The 20/10 Rule 178
Altering Verbal Antecedents 180
Handout: Antecedent-Response Cycle 182
Handout: Altering Verbal Antecedents 183
Priming the Cognitive Pump 184
Thoughts Don't Have to Become Behaviors 186
Worksheet: Impulse Control Decision-Maker 188

5. Autism ... 191
Case Example ... 193
Autism Key Concept: Differentiating Masking and Social Skills ... 194
Bull's-Eye for Boundaries ... 195
Handout: Four Kinds of Relationships ... 198
Worksheet: Bull's-Eye for Boundaries ... 200
Being an Effective Social Detective ... 201
Worksheet: Being an Effective Social Detective ... 203
Handshakes, Fist Bumps, and More ... 204
Handout: Intensity of Touch ... 206
Eye Contact ... 207
Worksheet: Eye Contact Checklist ... 210
Tone, Tempo, Volume, and Inflection for Prosodic Speech ... 211
Handout: Emotions List ... 213
Gestures and Posture ... 214
Template: Body Parts ... 216
Template: Message Cards ... 217
Sharing the Conversation ... 218
The Actors' Faces ... 220
Emotion Charades ... 222
Template: Emotion Charades ... 224
Chronemics: Time Blindness ... 225
Worksheet: Understanding Time ... 227
Chronemics: How Long Do I Wait? ... 228
Handout: How Long Do I Wait? ... 230
Cheat Sheets for Difficult Interactions ... 231
Worksheet: Tricky Situations Cheat Sheet ... 233
What You Like to Talk About ... 234
Worksheet: What You Like to Talk About ... 237
Therapist Worksheet: Making Bigger Connections with Preoccupational Interests ... 239

6. Behavior Management ... 241
Case Example ... 243
Behavior Management Key Concept: Realistic Intervention Timelines ... 244
Behavior Management Key Concept: Consequences ... 247
Life Skills Resume ... 250
Worksheet: My Life Skills Resume ... 251
Self-Concept Cake ... 253
Worksheet: Self-Concept Cake Part 1 ... 255
Worksheet: Self-Concept Cake Part 2 ... 256
Example Worksheet: Self-Concept Cake Part 1 ... 257
Example Worksheet: Self-Concept Cake Part 2 ... 258

Punishment vs. Growth-Based Models of Intervention 259
Worksheet: Punishments vs. Growth-Based Interventions 262
Example Worksheet: Punishments vs. Growth-Based Interventions 263
Breath Training for Self-Regulation 264
Music for Stress Reduction 267
Handout: How to Check Your Heart Rate 269
Worksheet: Your Calming Music 270
The Anger Volcano 271
Handout: The Anger Volcano 273
Wise Compromises 274
Worksheet: Wise Compromises 276
Boundary Word or Phrase 278
Handout: Boundary Word or Phrase 280
Processing Aggressive Media Content 281
Worksheet: Processing Aggressive Media 284
Advanced Processing and Whole-Brain Problem-Solving 285
Worksheet: Choose Your Own Adventure 288
Example Worksheet: Choose Your Own Adventure 289
Praise/Correct/Praise 290
Get Out of Trouble Free Passes 292
Handout: Get Out of Trouble Free Passes 294
Delayed Gratification 295
Worksheet: Delayed Gratification 297
Assigned Participation Tasks 298

References 301
Acknowledgments 303
About the Author 305

Introduction

The Big Brain and Body Regulation Toolbox for Kids and Teens was created with you—the clinician or educator—in mind, to help reframe how to understand and respond to the increasingly complex challenges children face today. This resource is rooted in the realities of the modern world, including the influence of technology, the pervasive role of social media, and the ongoing impact of COVID-related isolation on children's social, emotional, and developmental well-being.

What sets this toolbox apart is its emphasis on delivering practical, immediate-use worksheets, activity sheets, and structured strategies that are designed to help you meaningfully engage with any child in your care while also equipping the adults around them with effective support.

While many stand-alone interventions offer short-term relief, they often lack the structure and depth necessary for long-lasting change. In contrast, *The Big Brain and Body Regulation Toolbox for Kids and Teens* provides a collection of evidence-based practices that are intentionally interconnected, creating a scaffolded framework to help children build essential life skills and to promote long-term growth.

This resource also serves as a guide through the research and data, empowering you to understand the "why" behind each intervention and to advocate confidently for the needs of the kids you work with. Drawing from a multimodal, multidisciplinary perspective, the book begins with a foundational chapter on five universal skills necessary for developmental success.

From there, the following chapters focus on some of the most common mental health concerns that you see in your practice with young clients. Each chapter starts with fundamental building blocks, which can be easily adapted and expanded into more advanced applications. The interventions provided have practical implementations and immediate, easy-to-use multimodal tools. You'll find clear goals outlined for each technique, along with step-by-step guidance, implementation tips, and troubleshooting strategies to help you tailor each approach to the individual needs of the children you serve.

How Does Each Chapter Focus on Improving Your Skill Set?

- **Chapter 1: Building a Functional Foundation: "The Big Five":** Explore and review universal therapy skill sets for immediate effectiveness
- **Chapter 2: Anxiety:** Develop graduated exposure exercises, practical coping strategies, and mindfulness and self-regulation techniques
- **Chapter 3: Depression:** Increase self-esteem, self-concept, and motivation; develop techniques of validation; decrease suffering

- **Chapter 4: ADHD:** Improve autonomy; decrease environmental dependency; develop task transitions; grow executive functioning skills and aligned cortex connections (i.e., time management and personal organization); create proactive and engaging environments
- **Chapter 5: Autism:** Create scaffolded skills of verbal and nonverbal communication, affective awareness, expression, boundaries, and self-advocacy; promote acceptance in peer sets
- **Chapter 6: Behavior Management:** Coach effective self-regulation; develop whole-brain problem-solving; establish safety

Who Is This Book For?

While primarily written for mental health therapists, this book is for all people who work with kids—social workers, occupational therapists, speech-language pathologists, treatment center staff, juvenile detention or probate officers, caregivers, educators, school administrators, and more. This book is for any and all of you, whether you're new to the field, intermediate, or advanced! Everyone is eager to find practical application tools and techniques, and this book aims to provide you with an overflowing toolbox for success, no matter your milieu.

How to Use This Book

This book is designed to help you build a stable foundation for a child's growth as well as provide quick access and specific tools for some of the most pressing issues when working with kids, including:

- Mood regulation and distress tolerance
- Anxiety
- Impulsivity
- Low motivation
- Hopelessness
- Self-worth and efficacy
- Autonomy
- Empathy and personal responsibility
- Positive social skills and community engagement
- Focus, attention, and effort
- Executive functioning, time management, and organization
- Acting-out behaviors and noncompliance with requests

We must endeavor to have flexible, brief, and evidence-based interventions—not only in therapy settings, but also in schools, homes, and treatment facilities. Those of you who are theoretically familiar will hear the voices from acceptance and commitment therapy (ACT), attachment theory, behavioral intervention, cognitive behavioral therapy (CBT), dialectical behavior therapy (DBT), mindfulness, and neurodevelopmental/neurophysiological, sensory, social, and trauma-informed approaches.

Many times, a single intervention can work for a number of different concerns and moments—that's the goal! I aim to show you how this can work with examples and vignettes to help you operationalize the tools and feel confident in applying techniques. If you are trained in sand tray therapy, art therapy, or other expressive forms, you'll find that most of the interventions in this book can be adapted to fit your specific modality. The interventions in this book are labeled with the categories that they pertain to for easy identification. The following table provides the key to the symbols for each category.

A	Acceptance and Commitment Therapy
At	Attachment
B	Behavioral Intervention
C	Cognitive Behavior Therapy
D	Dialectical Behavior Therapy
M	Mindfulness
N	Neurodevelopmental/Neurophysiological
S	Sensory
Soc	Social
T	Trauma-Informed

For those of you working in a school system or treatment facility, you will also find embedded in this book multiple tier 1 (universal), tier 2 (preventive), and tier 3 (individualized) interventions easily applied in your environment. Like the category, the tier is also marked on each intervention.

1

Building a Functional Foundation: "The Big Five"

While it's natural to seek quick, easy-to-use strategies with kids, the reality is that these tools are only truly effective when built on a solid foundation. We can bring out every technique we know, but if the underlying structure is crumbling, we're ultimately setting our clients up for failure—often reinforcing their negative core beliefs about themselves (and about the therapeutic process).

That's why, in this chapter, we'll focus on five key areas—the "Big Five"—that significantly influence how receptive children's brains and bodies will be to therapeutic intervention: (1) sleep; (2) screen and technology exposure; (3) physical movement; (4) nutrition and hydration; and (5) nervous system regulation. The development of healthy habits in each of these interconnected areas is crucial to a child's mental health and well-being. Therefore, this is exactly where you begin laying a solid, functional foundation.

As professionals, our job is to guide our clients. But we cannot force a caregiver to put their child to bed at a reasonable hour or make an adolescent practice yoga. We can, however, provide the client or their caregiver with psychoeducation, offer them actionable strategies, and troubleshoot their challenges *on a consistent basis*. A one-time psychoeducational session won't do much, but regular check-ins and active engagement during *each contact* with clients will go a long way, building a solid foundation that sets them up for long-term success in therapy and in life.

All individuals, families, and environments are different, and habits that have been crystallized through years of repetition are hard to break (unfortunately, the 21-day habit change theory is a fallacy—darn!), but working with kids and their families to create small daily changes in these five areas *can* lead to dramatic improvement in mood, thoughts, school performance, and behavior.

Sleep

We will start with sleep for two reasons: first, because the quality of a person's sleep impacts *everything* in their life (more on that later); and second, because even small changes to a child's sleep routine can have a tremendous and rapid positive impact on mood and behavior. In other words, a little bit can go a long way, and seeing results can help clients and caregivers feel empowered to keep going with the changes.

Quality of sleep impacts so many things: mood, hormones, appetite, executive function, and digestion. At a developmental stage when kids are bombarded with new information, sensory exposure, and hormones daily, sleep is a crucial reset for the brain and body to rest and recoup. When kids don't get enough rest, or the rest is inconsistent or interrupted, it's common to see a lack of concentration, poor linear functioning, delayed executive functioning skills, slower information processing, irritability, increased internal rumination, and excessive psychomotor movement. Or, as some might call it, a moody, irritated child who struggles to focus or stay on task at school, instead "zoning out" or bothering other students with excessive talking, movement, and noisemaking. Sounds a lot like attention-deficit hyperactivity disorder (ADHD), anxiety, or depression, doesn't it?

While sleep can't act as a cure-all, we do know that when a child's circadian rhythm becomes regulated, many issues with attention, mood dysregulation, rumination, irritability, lethargy, and fatigue resolve.

In many homes where sleep is an issue, families are struggling to navigate extracurricular activities, childcare, homework, work schedules, and the like. As a parent myself, I know how a late baseball game on a Monday can throw my family's routine off-kilter, the effect of which we feel as it plays itself out through the week. Prioritizing sleep can be challenging in busy households! It's possible that something has to give so that sleep can take precedence over other activities. It's that important.

Note: Prescription medications (e.g., Clonidine), hormones (e.g., melatonin), and antihistamines (e.g., Benadryl) usually offer short-term relief to sleep difficulties. If needed, it's important to pair them with routine and environmental changes for long-term success. Of course, clients should only use these while in the care of a medical professional.

What's Happening in the Brain?

When we create and follow a regular routine of getting to sleep and staying asleep, our brains develop with more regulated neurotransmitter function, which in turn improves our ability to process, encode, and retrain neural connections in the brain. This makes learning (academically and therapeutically) much easier and helps to "hardwire" skills with more long-term effects.

Tier 1

School, Treatment, and Community Settings

Issues with sleep are often revealed when kids are falling asleep during instructional or therapeutic programming. If this is an ongoing issue, consider allowing designated resting or napping time, at least initially, rather than endlessly and fruitlessly prompting them to stay awake.

Share the *Five Essentials for Healthy Sleep Hygiene* handout with parents and caregivers via all-district communication, during conferences, or as part of a treatment plan.

Resources

- *Five Essentials for Healthy Sleep Hygiene* handout
- *Smooth Sleep Cycling* worksheet

Handout

5 Essentials for Healthy Sleep Hygiene

1. **Create a sleep schedule.** Have your child go to bed and wake up around the same time each day if possible. Choose a routine you can stick to most of the time, even on non-school days, like weekends and school breaks. A good rule of thumb is to try not to deviate by more than an hour from your routine. When a sleep routine is "out of whack," it can take up to three days to get back into rhythm!

Note: Kids who live in two homes (e.g., separated parents, extended family) often struggle with dysregulated circadian rhythms due to differing sleep routines between homes. No two routines will ever match perfectly; however, the more they align, the better it will be for the child.

2. **Allow enough time to meet the recommended hours of sleep for your child.** Base your child's hours of sleep on their age and stage of development. While some individuals function on less sleep than others, you'll generally want to follow the recommendations of the National Sleep Foundation (2025):

Age Group/Stage	Recommended Hours of Sleep*
Newborn (0–3 months)	14–17 hours
Infant (4–11 months)	12–15 hours
Toddler (1–2 years)	11–14 hours
Preschool (3–5 years)	10–13 hours
School Age (6–13 years)	9–11 hours
Teenager (14–17 years)	8–10 hours
Young Adult (18–25 years)	7–9 hours
Adult (26–65 years)	7–9 hours
Older Adult (65+ years)	7–8 hours

* There is no exact amount of sleep that will satisfy an entire age group. Sleep times outside the recommended range (1–2 hours, based on stage) may be appropriate for some individuals.

3. **Eliminate sugar and caffeine *at least* one hour before bedtime.** Both sugar and caffeine, along with nicotine, are common stimulants that interfere with sleep, even several hours after consumption. Take note of the types of snacks and drinks your

child consumes after dinner. Many foods and drinks have more sugar and caffeine than expected, so be sure to check labels if you are unsure.

Note: While we are finally seeing a downward trend in tobacco usage in young people from pre-2020, likely due to laws regulating accessibility and marketing to youth, research still shows that upwards of 34 percent of high school students have used or experimented with a tobacco product (Gentzke et al., 2022). If you smoke or vape, be sure to keep your devices with you at all times, and consider using them only outside the home to reduce the likelihood that your child will smoke or vape, even into adulthood.

4. **Create a nighttime pro-sleep routine.** Perhaps you turn the lights low, read a book together (avoid tablets and backlit e-readers), and give your child a gentle hand massage before saying goodnight. A regular bedtime routine like this is enough to cue your child's brain that it's time to sleep. Other ideas might be giving your child a warm bath, brushing their hair, or quietly humming a song together. Remember, the key is consistency, not the "perfect" routine.

5. **Turn off backlit technology *at least* one hour before bedtime.** Screens (e.g., TV, tablets, phones, laptops, backlit e-readers) cause stress to the nervous system in a way that's difficult to turn off, and it can leave your child "on edge," their mind anxious and overthinking and their body unsettled. Not exactly great conditions for sleep.

   Even better, aim to get technology out of the bedroom completely. Removing devices from the room will eliminate sleep-disrupting notifications—dinging, vibrating, lighting up the room—throughout the night. Furthermore, the late hours of the night and early hours of the morning are the times you are least likely to be supervising your child's technology use. Combined with a tired brain, the risk of poor decision-making, misunderstandings, impulsive responses, boundary testing, and aggression increases significantly.

A gentle reminder: Vicarious, or modeled, learning is the most powerful learning. If you can do the behavior you're asking of your child (or even better, make it a norm for everyone in your household), they are more likely to comply.

Worksheet

Smooth Sleep Cycling

How you sleep has a big impact on how you feel! When you get good sleep regularly, it feels like you are riding a bike with nice round wheels: The ride is smooth, you are in control, and you can overcome small bumps in the road. When your sleep is inconsistent or disrupted, the wheels on the bike cannot maintain their round shape: The ride becomes unpleasant, it's difficult to steer, and small bumps in the road can feel catastrophic.

Let's think about how you feel when you have good sleep and when you don't. Place a check mark on any of the statements that match your experience. There is also space for you to add your own examples.

How do you work when your wheels are filled and functioning?

- ❒ I feel focused.
- ❒ I am in a good mood.
- ❒ It is easy to make decisions.
- ❒ I can think clearly.
- ❒ It is easier to solve problems.
- ❒ Life feels manageable.
- ❒ I am open to new ideas.

What else?

____

____

____

____

How do you work when your wheels are flat?

- ❒ My temper flares up.
- ❒ I feel irritable.
- ❒ I find it hard to focus.
- ❒ I cannot think straight.
- ❒ I find it hard to let things go.
- ❒ I am easily annoyed by others.
- ❒ I am easily overwhelmed.

What else?

____

____

____

____

What are three things you could do differently to get better sleep?

1. ____

2. ____

3. ____

Technology **C, N, S**

Most of the children and teenagers you work with can be referred to as "digital natives"—part of a generation that has grown up surrounded by ever-present technology, never knowing a world without it. As this is still a recent phenomenon, the negative consequences of a screen-saturated childhood are only beginning to surface. Yet their impact is already widely felt. Just ask any caregiver how their child behaves after excessive screen time, or what the most frequent conflict at home tends to revolve around.

At one time, screen time recommendations were based on time limits only; current recommendations now differentiate between "structured" and "unstructured" screen time. *Structured* technology use—such as school-based instruction and telehealth services—is considered acceptable for up to four to five hours per day. In contrast, *unstructured* screen time—like video games, social media, YouTube, and similar activities—carries the recommendation of being limited to one to two hours daily (Brodersen et al., 2022; Gath et al., 2026; Kar et al., 2025).

Kids and teens are using 300 percent more than that—up to fourteen hours a day!

Exposure to backlit screens can increase chemicals in the brain that interfere with attention, processing, and retention, and it may also lead to agitation, mood and sensory dysregulation, and memory issues. (Remind me why these devices are a good thing?) The good news is that even small changes can help kids' brains heal and recover from the effects of excessive screen exposure.

As highlighted in the sleep section, backlit screen exposure should be discontinued at least one hour before bedtime, but many families share the common misconception that their child "can't sleep" without it (usually the TV). While this may feel true for them, the reality is that the screen is doing more harm than good, and with the right approach, children *can* learn to sleep without it. However, abruptly removing a familiar sensory routine like falling asleep with the TV on can lead to increased difficulty falling and staying asleep, along with heightened frustration, power struggles, and other negative behaviors. If a child has already developed a dependency, a gradual approach—such as reverse titration (or weaning)—is a more effective and compassionate strategy. The *Five-Week Nighttime Technology Titration* handout provides a week-by-week plan to do this.

What's Happening in the Brain?

Excessive screen time, particularly social media use, contributes to "dopamine hunger," the constant chase of a burst of the feel-good chemical that occurs when viewing novel information, like getting approval (e.g., a "like") online. Aside from that, it alters norepinephrine, serotonin, and cortisol, affecting impulsivity, executive function, mood, sleep, and agitation.

Tier 1

School, Treatment, and Community Settings

Share the *Healthy Screen Use* handout with parents and caregivers via all-district communication, during conferences, or as part of a treatment plan.

Resources

- *Healthy Screen Use* handout
- *Five-Week Nighttime Technology Titration* worksheet

Handout

Healthy Screen Use

Screens are a part of life—and that probably won't change. This handout breaks down the most important things you need to know about them, along with recommendations for decreasing the negative impact screen time can have on your well-being.

Reduce Unstructured Screen Time

More than two hours per day of unstructured time on screens can have a negative impact on memory, sleep, and the processing and understanding of new information. *Unstructured* means time spent doing things that aren't related to your schoolwork—like playing video games, watching YouTube or Netflix, scrolling on social media, or chatting on Discord.

Tips and Fixes

- Track the time you are spending with unstructured screen time using your phone timer, a stopwatch, or even the timer on the stove.
- Take movement breaks every 10 to 15 minutes to help your brain rest.
- Conserve your unstructured time to play games with friends, either in person or online.
- Ask a trusted adult for a reminder or cue for when your screen time is running out. (Your maximum amount of time should be around two hours total each day.)

Reduce Blue Light Exposure

Devices like phones, tablets, TVs, and computers give off a specific kind of light called *blue light*, and this is one of the biggest reasons screens are so problematic for your brain. As if the content you're viewing isn't stimulating enough, blue light exposure causes chemicals in the brain to ramp up anxiety, excitability, and irritability and cause trouble with attention.

Tips and Fixes

- Increase your distance from backlit screens.
- Adjust the brightness or use screen light limiters on laptops, monitors, tablets, and TVs.
- Wear blue blocker glasses when using screens.
- Use "night/dark mode" settings on devices whenever possible.

Handout

Five-Week Nighttime Technology Titration

If you or your child uses a TV or another backlit screen as part of their nighttime ritual, it may be affecting their quality of sleep. The approach provided in this handout is an effective way to reset sleeping habits gradually over a five-week period.

If sleeping without technology may make it difficult for the child to maintain sleep, due to outside noises or other family members, introduce a white noise machine or some other consistently repetitive sound, such as a ceiling or box fan, nature sounds (no animal sounds), or low-decibel sound machines (less than 50 dB). Any sounds that include language (e.g., audiobooks, podcasts) are not recommended, as they have an inconsistent audio pattern that can increase, rather than decrease, brain activity.

Note: When choosing an alternate device, consider different "colors" of noise: White noise includes all audible frequencies equally, while brown noise consists of mostly low audible frequencies.

Complete the following steps to create a new nighttime routine. Each week will build on the previous weeks, creating habits that will slowly become normal without overwhelming a child's system.

Week 1: Allow the child to have the TV on as normal but cover it with a towel, as the flashing light of the screen will still engage the brain even with closed eyes. Then decrease the volume of the TV by one bar or number each night.

Week 2: Continue covering the screen with a towel and decreasing the volume by one bar or number each night; engage a white or brown noise machine if needed.

Week 3: Continue to cover the screen. Turn off the TV 20 minutes before sleep initiation. Introduce non-technology-based activities, such as reading, drawing, or doing word puzzles.

Week 4: Repeat week 3, but turn off the TV 40 minutes before sleep initiation. Continue non-technology-based activities.

Week 5: Repeat week 4, but turn off the TV 60 minutes before sleep initiation. Continue non-technology-based activities.

Five-Week Nighttime Technology Titration

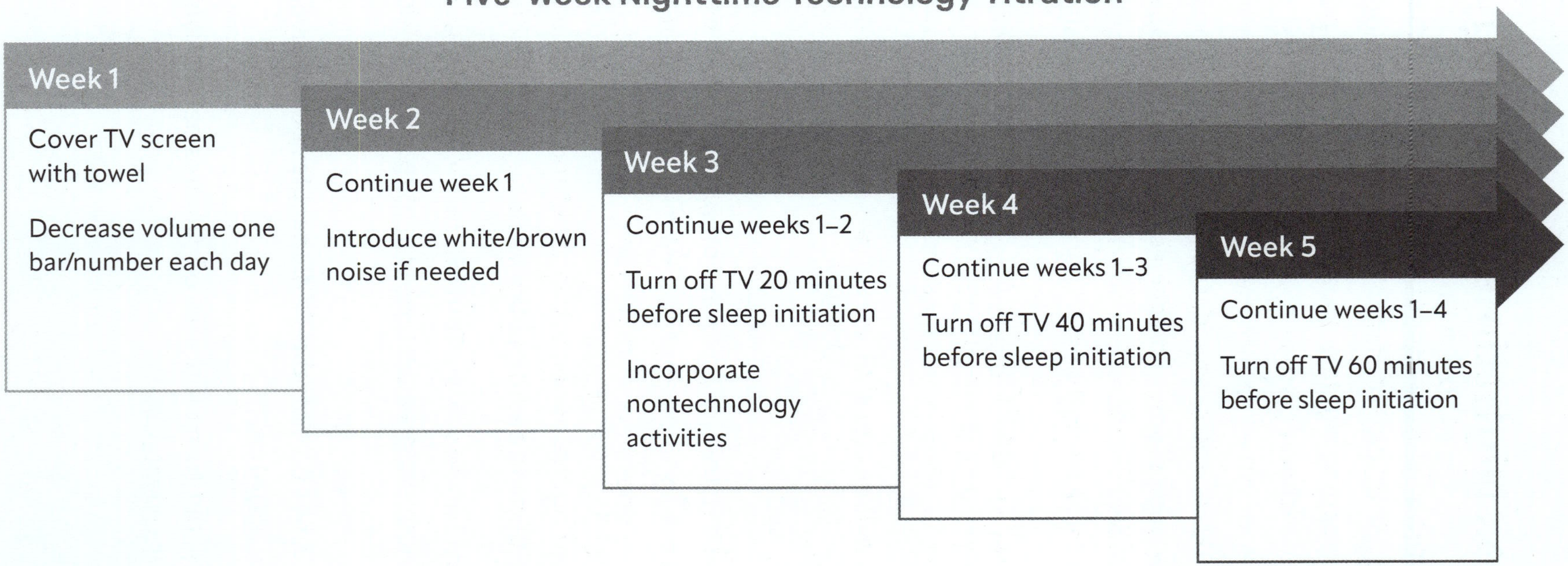

Movement **N, S**

The benefits of brain health and mood management should be a regular focus of attention with the kids and families you see. The research on the connection between movement and mental health is abundant. For example, people who experience anxiety, panic attacks, and posttraumatic stress disorder have significantly more cortisol (i.e., the stress hormone) flooding through their system, especially following a panic/anxiety attack or triggered physiological/psychological response. Increasing physical activity levels helps the body process that cortisol more effectively and increase production of endorphins, leading to decreased anxiety and improved mood, energy, and concentration. Similarly, an active lifestyle is a key intervention for depression, bipolar disorder, attention-deficit/hyperactivity disorder, and more. Physical movement can also improve vestibular awareness—the sense of balance, spatial orientation, and movement—which is linked to improved focus, attention, and emotional regulation.

When helping clients increase their activity level, it's important to be flexible and creative about what counts as exercise, especially for kids with limited access to green space or families who are less active. Things like taking a load of laundry up the stairs count! Kids with more rigid dispositions who fall prey to "all-or-nothing" thinking may struggle to recognize that even five minutes of movement a day is better than none. Circumvent this thought by setting small goals that are within reach to build up some engagement and momentum. It's up to you to reinforce even the tiniest increments of progress for these kids.

One of the best ways I've found to get my clients moving is to walk the walk myself, so I bring movement into my sessions, such as session-opening and closing stretches or yoga poses, walk-and-talk therapy (with safety and confidentiality top of mind), and movement-based therapy games. This applies to telehealth sessions too. Even behind a camera, clients can get moving with activities like posture checks or even walking on a treadmill.

Note: Be aware of clients' physical limitations and mobility concerns; encourage them to consult their healthcare provider before engaging in new physical activities.

What's Happening in the Brain?

Exercise increases the release of feel-good hormones (endorphins and dopamine) and promotes oxygenation to the brain, which helps with regulation and improved mood. It also decreases the reactivity of the sympathetic nervous system and the hypothalamic-pituitary-adrenal axis, allowing you to handle stress more effectively.

Tier 1

School, Treatment, and Community Settings

If organized physical activity isn't available in your setting, remember that even basic movement can improve mood regulation and stability. Regularly taking "brain breaks" or adding simple stretching to transition times can garner enough physiological impact to mitigate mood, attentional, and behavioral disturbance.

Share the *Our Brains Love Movement!* handout with parents and caregivers via all-district communication, during conferences, or as part of a treatment plan.

Resources

- *Our Brains Love Movement!* handout
- *Active Body, Peaceful Mind* worksheet

Handout

Our Brains Love Movement!

Movement is important for healthy bodies, but did you know it's just as important for healthy brains? Let's look at the benefits of regular movement on the brain.

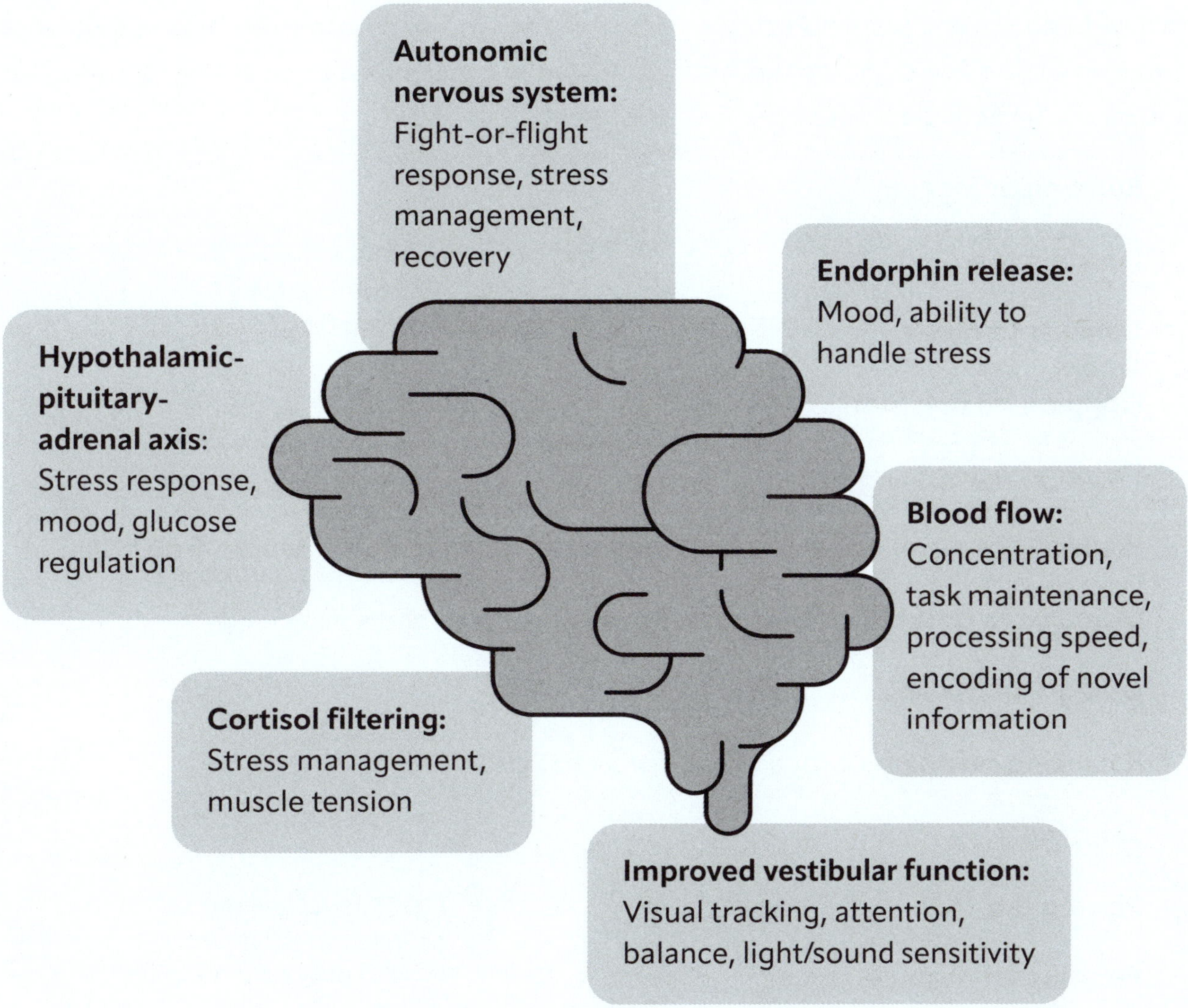

Worksheet

Active Body, Peaceful Mind

Did you know that when you move your body, you're not just helping your muscles? You're also helping your mood and your brain! When you do things like run, jump, and stretch, your brain makes more of the chemicals that help you feel happy, calm, and focused. Movement can help you turn a bad day around—and can even help you do your homework! The key is finding the kinds of movement *you* enjoy! Look at the following list and circle the activities that sound fun or interesting to you.

Running or jogging

Jumping rope

Dancing to music

Hopping on one foot

Doing jumping jacks

Walking like an animal walks (e.g., crab walk, bear crawl, inchworm, frog hops)

Doing yoga poses (e.g., tree pose, downward dog, child's pose)

Doing wall sits or chair squats

Balancing on one foot (or a pillow for a challenge!)

Skipping

Playing tag

Running an obstacle course

Biking or riding a scooter

Climbing (e.g., playground, climbing wall)

Kicking a soccer ball

Shooting a basketball

Playing catch

Tip: Get outside! The sun gives us vitamin D, which helps us feel more energized and happier.

Tip: Set movement reminders on your phone (or ask a grown-up to)!

Tip: Try a new activity every day!

Jumping on a trampoline

Swinging

Swimming

Walking

Skating or rollerblading

Playing frisbee

Hula hooping

Stretching

Jumping over lines

Playing hopscotch

Do you have any other ideas?

Tip: Even five minutes of movement helps us feel better. You can do it!

Tip: Choose three to five activities on the list. Set a timer and do each activity for one minute. Then do it all over again!

____

____

____

____

Nutrition and Hydration

C, N, S

Just like regular sleep and physical activity, good nutrition plays a powerful role in supporting mood, emotional well-being, and academic performance. What we feed our bodies directly affects our mood and mental health. Poor nutrition has been linked to issues like low mood, irritability, fatigue, anxiety, difficulty focusing, and impulsivity. There are many reasons why kids may not get the nutrition they need—cost, limited access, location, lack of education or awareness, and cultural factors, to name a few. The problem is compounded by the ease of accessibility of cheap, highly processed foods.

Dehydration can also affect kids in similar ways to poor nutrition, leading to irritability, low mood, trouble concentrating, tiredness, and slower thinking. And like nutrition, it can be impacted by similar challenges.

While you can't eliminate every barrier, you *can* make a difference by educating, supporting, and advocating for the kids and families you work with.

Note: The recommendations in this section are not aimed at clients with eating disorders, pediatric feeding disorders, or disordered eating in general. Please refer clients to the appropriate specialists as needed and follow their recommendations.

Children who rely heavily on simple carbohydrates (e.g., bread, pasta, sugary foods)—particularly those experiencing depression—may engage in what is often referred to as *carbohydrate boosting*, in which they use these foods to temporarily improve their mood. While this can lead to a short-term increase in neurotransmitters like serotonin and dopamine, it is frequently followed by a mood and energy "crash" due to rapid fluctuations in blood glucose. A practical initial intervention for these clients is to encourage pairing carbohydrates with protein and healthy fats. For example, if a child tends to eat bread on its own, adding a nut butter can help slow glucose absorption and promote more stable mood and energy levels.

Textures of foods can also have an impact on good nutrition for the brain. Some children are so resistant to crunchy, mushy, or gelatinous foods that they will not ingest foods like raw veggies or oatmeal (which are good sources of fiber). At times, gustatory resistance can result in very limited food selections, which may warrant accessing liquid nutritional drinks or suspension vitamins to improve nutritive intake.

If a client uses alcohol (or you suspect they might), do mention that not only is it a known depressant, but it is also inflammatory to the brain and body, causing gastrointestinal issues and disrupted sleep.

What's Happening in the Brain?

Good nutrition provides the building blocks needed for neurotransmitter production, protects the brain from the impact of oxidative stress, and improves the opportunity for the brain to make new hardwired connections (especially omega-3 fatty acids, vitamin B / folate, and essential nutrients for learning and memory). Good hydration practices are necessary to improve neurotransmitter function, blood flow, attention, and short-term memory.

Tier 2 or 3

School, Treatment, and Community Settings

Food insecurity—the lack of consistent access to enough nutritious food or the uncertainty of being able to obtain it—is a significant factor when it comes to assessing and addressing nutritional health. When possible, include food access in 504 plans or Individualized Education Programs (IEPs), discharge or aftercare planning, or family work. Consider keeping water and healthy snacks in your office or group space to offer kids as needed, particularly for after-school sessions when they might be low on "gas" for therapeutic work.

At minimum, share the *Food and Mood: What Helps, What Hurts* handout with parents and caregivers via all-district communication, during conferences, or as part of a treatment plan.

Resources

- *Food and Mood: What Helps, What Hurts* handout

Handout

Food and Mood: What Helps, What Hurts

Foods That Help (Eat these *most* of the time)

Food Group	Examples
Fruits	Blueberries, apples, kiwi, oranges, cherries
Vegetables	Asparagus, kale, spinach
Lean meats	Chicken, turkey
Dairy products	Milk, yogurt, cheese
Whole grains	Quinoa, brown rice, whole-wheat bread, oats
Fish	Salmon, tuna
Healthy fats	Avocados, olive oil, coconut
Healthy starches	Sweet potatoes, squash
Seeds	Sunflower seeds, flaxseed
Nuts	Almonds, peanuts, cashews
Legumes	Black beans, kidney beans, chickpeas, lentils
Other	Mushrooms, eggs, dark chocolate

Foods That Hurt (Eat these *some* of the time)

Food Group	Examples
Frozen/ready-made meals	Pizzas, hot pockets, frozen dinners
Baked goods	Brownies, cookies, cakes, donuts, muffins
Processed cheese products	Nacho cheese sauce
Salty snacks	Potato chips, pretzels
Sweets	Candy, milk chocolate, ice cream, frozen desserts, sugary cereals
Dressing	Sauces, salad dressings, syrups, jams
Fast food	French fries, burgers, hot dogs
Sweetened beverages	Juice products, soft drinks, sports drinks (in excess)

Tip 1: Aim to drink 64 oz. of water each day to stay hydrated.

Tip 2: "Eat the rainbow"—choose a fruit or veggie for each color of the rainbow!

Tip 3: Start simple. Too many changes at once can be overwhelming.

Nervous System Regulation

C, N

Every brain, young and old, is constantly scanning for safety, danger, or threat—an unconscious process known as *neuroception*. Our brain activates the autonomic nervous system (ANS) accordingly with the goal of keeping us alive and safe, a process that is being increasingly recognized for its critical role in regulating our internal environment.

Often referred to as our "reptilian brain," the ANS is made up of two main systems: the sympathetic nervous system (SNS) and the parasympathetic nervous system (PNS). The SNS is responsible for our "fight/flight/freeze/fawn" response to stress, danger, or intense activity. When the SNS is activated, our capacity to process information, learn, and focus diminishes almost completely as the brain prioritizes immediate survival over higher-order thinking, making problem-solving and rational decision-making nearly impossible. When the stressful situation has subsided, the PNS helps the body and brain recover and return to homeostasis. When the PNS is activated, we can think, listen, decide, and act in ways that are logical and meaningful.

This complex process is why, when in a life-threatening situation, we react without thinking about what we're doing. For example, if a bear is suddenly charging at us in the woods, we don't stand there and think about why the bear is charging, deliberate on our best course of action, or consider the supplies we need to gather. No, we react: We fight, run, hide, whatever we need to do to survive. Not until later do we think about the circumstances, the why, or what we wish we would have done differently. Under stress, the logical brain is offline while our survival brain—the seat of our primal instincts—takes over.

A client in a highly emotionally escalated state is no different. Sure, there's no bear, but their brain doesn't know that. It perceives stress (more on this later) and triggers the SNS. This is why talking to, instructing, or attempting to reason with someone in this state is ineffective. The logical part of the brain simply isn't available. This is where many caregivers, educators, and other adults can unintentionally worsen the problem. With matching intensity, an adult might tell an escalated child to "use their words" or ask them to make better choices, which only serves to frustrate and invalidate the child's experience, further fueling the escalation and extending the length of the dysregulated state. The better response is for the adult to model regulation themselves (e.g., pausing, taking a deep breath, and stepping away to return in one minute) and then communicate to the child's ANS that the situation is safe through a soothing tone, disarming body language, and breathing—this is called *co-regulating*.

Teaching kids (and their adults) self-regulation skills that soothe the nervous system is an excellent *preventive* way to decrease behavior escalation, emotional outbursts, and other stress responses before they can even present. When incorporated into a routine consistently (there's that word again), a minimum of five times each day, self-regulation skills are remarkably effective at helping kids engage, respond, and process stress more effectively and calmly.

Tier 1

School, Treatment, and Community Settings

It is important to recognize that not every little nervous system that enters your space is regulated and ready to learn. Starting your time together with a brief regulation activity (they are widely available online) will pay off tenfold in focus, calming energy, and decreased disruptive behavior.

Share the *Understanding Your Child's Autonomic Nervous System Threshold* handout with parents and caregivers via all-district communication, during conferences, or as part of treatment planning with families.

Resources

- *My Autonomic Nervous System* handout
- *Understanding Your Child's Autonomic Nervous System Threshold* handout

Handout

My Autonomic Nervous System*

Sympathetic Nervous System

- Stress response
- Prepares you to fight, take flight, or freeze up
- Fast heartbeat; shallow, fast breaths
- Pupils of eyes expand (light sensitivity)
- Digestive system shuts down (digestion slows)
- Blood flows away from your brain and to your skeletal muscles (hard to think clearly)
- Stress hormones rush through the body (feels like anxiety or adrenaline)
- Uses lots of energy

Parasympathetic Nervous System

- Relaxation response
- Prepares you to calm, rest, think, and restore
- Slow, rhythmic heartbeat; full, slow breaths
- Pupils of the eyes shrink
- Digestive system is active (can digest food and nutrients)
- Blood flows to your digestive system, lungs, and brain
- Calming hormones rush through the body (lifting mood and helping with relaxation)
- Conserves energy

* Adapted from *Applied Mindfulness: Approaches in Mental Health for Children and Adolescents* (Morgan & Jacobson, 2019).

Handout

Understanding Your Child's Autonomic Nervous System Threshold

If you've ever wondered why your child's behavior seems to go from 0 to 100 in under a second, understanding their nervous system's stress threshold is a great place to start. This handout will help you better understand what's happening internally when behaviors seem to come out of nowhere, and when to proactively add in self-regulation practices to help soothe their ANS.

Above the Threshold

High escalation; expectation or external trigger has become too distressing

Looks like:

- **Fight:** Aggression, arguing, threats
- **Flight:** Running, avoiding, AWOL attempts
- **Freeze:** Shutting down, staring blankly, refusing to engage
- **Fawn:** Giving up, crying, withdrawing, "going along to get along"

Stress Threshold

Zone of Effective Processing

Looks like:

- Regulation
- Engagement in an appropriate task (e.g., at school or with friends)
- Any expectations or external triggers are managed

Baseline

Full relaxation without expectation: calm, cool, and collected

Looks like:

- Relaxation
- Calm body
- Good mood
- No tasks or expectations

Worksheet

Big Five Check-In Sheet

To help you stay focused on the Big Five areas, let's check in on them every time we meet. Take the check-in sheet home, complete it, and bring it with you to each session. You can even hang it in your room or on the bathroom mirror as a reminder. The more you practice new habits, the stronger they become. You can do this!

Date: ______________________________

Since our last session . . .

1. How would you describe your **sleep** most nights? Check all that apply:
   - ❒ Eight or more hours
   - ❒ Four to eight hours
   - ❒ Less than four hours
   - ❒ Restful
   - ❒ Tossing and turning
   - ❒ Hard to fall asleep
   - ❒ Woke up a lot
   - ❒ Nightmares

   Can you think of anything that kept you awake or woke you up? ______________________________

   ____

   Did you use sleep sounds or white noise? ______________________________

   Did you turn off screens at least one hour before bedtime? ______________________________

   Was your brain thinking of relaxing things or worrying things? ______________________________

   ____

2. How did you do with tracking your **technology use**?
   - ❒ Every day
   - ❒ Most days
   - ❒ Some days
   - ❒ Not at all

   Goal: Spend less than two hours a day on unstructured screen time

   Hours of structured tech each day: ______________________________

   Hours of unstructured tech each day: ______________________________

   Did you practice screen breaks or use blue light blockers? ______________________________

3. Tell me about your **movement**. Did you get up and move each day?
   - ❒ Every day
   - ❒ Most days
   - ❒ Some days
   - ❒ Not at all

   Goal: Get moving for at least one hour per day

   What did you do to get movement in your day? ______________________________

   ____

   What were your favorite movements to practice this week? ____________________

   ____

   What kinds of movement make you feel better/worse? ________________________

   ____

4. How was your **nutrition and hydration** this week?
   - ❒ Not great
   - ❒ Good
   - ❒ Excellent

   How often did you log your food and water?
   - ❒ Every day
   - ❒ Most days
   - ❒ Some days
   - ❒ Not at all

   How often did you eat the rainbow of foods?
   - ❒ Every day
   - ❒ Most days
   - ❒ Some days
   - ❒ Not at all

5. How often did you practice **self-regulation** each day?
   - ❒ Every day
   - ❒ Most days
   - ❒ Some days
   - ❒ Not at all

   Goal: Practice self-regulation five times a day

   What are a few of your favorite things to do to calm your brain and body? __________

   ____

   Can you think of any new things you'd like to try next week? ____________________

   ____

2

Anxiety

Anxiety is showing up in kids and teens like never before—hiding in bathrooms during class, refusing to go to school, avoiding extracurriculars, postponing milestones like getting jobs or their driver's licenses, and entrenching themselves in social media. All the while, they're relying heavily on their caregivers and other adults for everything from ordering at restaurants to negotiating grades and navigating social conflicts.

What is happening?

Anxiety is the same menace it has always been—fickle, impatient, and demanding. It wants to be addressed *now*, and its desire to escape or avoid is *always* stronger than its willingness to stay present and learn. With anxiety, everything feels like a crisis, and the only goal is to find relief as quickly as possible.

Combine this with unprecedented access to many forms of relief—social media, gaming, doomscrolling, texting rather than talking—and you have the perfect storm for the anxiety presentations you see in your clients and students today.

For years, most treatment interventions, though well-intentioned, have used a more reactive approach to anxiety and distress. Techniques to curb anxiety symptoms, like distraction, "as-needed" breaks from the classroom, homeschooling or virtual learning—often used at the first sign of discomfort (or worse, when anxiety is at an all-time high)—can inadvertently reinforce the idea that *avoiding distress is the solution to experiencing distress*. And while avoidance can (and often does) work well to feel better in the short term, it isn't a realistic long-term solution for living an engaged, healthy life.

The interventions in this chapter are diametrically opposed to a reactive approach. Instead of using tactics of avoidance, denial, and escape, these interventions aim to *approach and resolve* anxiety by drawing on neuroscience to help clients build self-awareness, acceptance, and agency, including:

- Providing psychoeducation on how avoidance compounds anxiety instead of reducing it
- Helping kids stay present in the current experience with the use of mindfulness techniques
- Regulating physiological escalation and psychological oversensitization with the use of graduated exposure techniques

- Creating individualized and immediately accessible coping strategies
- Impacting the self-regulation of a child's neurophysiological functioning

Key Concept

Reinforcement: In order to help a behavior grow into something different or change altogether, we need to remember how behaviors respond to input and reactions from the environment.

Case Example

Allie, 15, was referred to me by the Board of Education and Department of Juvenile Justice for treatment of generalized anxiety disorder (GAD). A high-performing student who was well-liked by her peers and never caused any trouble, Allie's behavior changed significantly when she started high school. It started with asking to stay home from school and quickly escalated to skipping classes; eventually, she refused to attend school altogether. The excessive absences landed her in the juvenile justice system for truancy. She was enrolled in a diversion program through the courts, with her primary goal being to "go to school." Allie's parents felt helpless. After all, they couldn't drag their child out of her bed, force her into a car, and escort her into school each morning. Desperate and scared, they brought their concerns to Allie's primary doctor, who diagnosed her with GAD and wrote a medical accommodation for the court to place her on "homebound" for her education. The court granted this request with the requirement, thankfully, that she also seek treatment. Relieved that Allie would not face legal consequences and tired of the daily power struggles with her, her parents agreed to this arrangement despite knowing she should "probably be at school."

As I got to know Allie, it was clear she had been struggling with anxiety for a long time—years, even—and that the added pressure and responsibilities of high school was what put her over the edge. She recalled a list of her "failures" that led to feigning illness and skipping classes: getting a C on a test she spent hours studying for, the popular girls making fun of her haircut (the one it took months for her to decide to get); pressure from her parents about her low pre-ACT scores and the likelihood she would not be accepted to her dream school "at the rate she's going"; a friend that had been distancing from her . . . the list went on, each example furthering her belief that she was not smart, capable, or good enough. For Allie, any perceived error, deviation from "the plan," discomfort, or minor mistake justified this negative self-appraisal, and she found herself "completely overwhelmed and getting depressed about it." She texted her mother to pick her up early from school one day to "get away from the stress," and before she knew it, she wasn't attending school at all anymore. She knew it was "not right to bail when things are hard" but lacked any belief that things could get better.

No one had taught Allie:

- Mistakes are an opportunity for change.
- Discomfort communicates that something needs to change.
- Practice is progress, not perfection.
- Perseverance grows grit (which is necessary for navigating adulthood).

Anxiety Key Concept

Reinforcement

To understand anxiety and how it functions, it's important to understand two concepts about behavior in general:

1. **Reinforcement *always* increases the likelihood that behavior will occur again.**

   Think about getting a reward; it feels good, so you do what you can to receive another one.

Behavior *You raise your hand in class.*	+	**Reinforcement** *You receive praise for raising your hand.*	=	**Stronger likelihood of repeating the behavior** *You raise your hand in class again next time.*

Sometimes the reward (reinforcement) means getting something unpleasant to end, like taking aspirin to make a headache go away—if it works, the behavior of taking aspirin has been reinforced, and the chances you'll do it again for the next headache have been strengthened.

You might see your own anxiety like that headache—an unpleasant experience that you want to go away—and the most common "aspirin" is to either escape it or avoid it altogether. Consider this example: You are feeling anxious about going to a party that you were invited to.

Behavior *You don't go to the party (avoidance).*	+	**Reinforcement** *Your anxiety goes away and you feel better.*	=	**Stronger likelihood of repeating the behavior** *You skip the next party (and the one after that).*

2. **Behaviors reinforced with *escape and avoidance* are the most resistant to change.**

Why? Because it works! The reward (relief from discomfort) is immediate and powerful, further reinforcing its efficacy and strengthening the chances it'll be used every time an anxious sensation comes up.

Crystallized Coping Skills *C, N*

Therapeutic Rationale:

Helping kids develop coping skills that work is more than providing a list of ideas and telling them to "try one when you feel anxious." Lists of coping skills are only ideas until actively practiced and encoded neurologically to become crystallized in the brain. For example, telling someone to get a drink of water is not as meaningful as helping them actively get up out of their seat to get the drink of water. The active nature of *doing* the skill, especially during times when the client is *not* anxious, aids in transitioning from a thought to a behavior, which improves the likelihood that they will tap into that skill later.

Goals:

- Develop crystallized coping skills
- Identify what types of coping skills work for a client and where/when they can use them
- Improve encoding of coping skills into long-term memory

Materials:

- *Active Coping Skills* handout
- *Passive Coping Skills* handout
- *Crystalized Coping Skills* worksheet
- Optional: A shoebox (or other container) and art supplies

Directions:

1. Explain to the client that gaining skills takes time and effort:

   "Our brains grow new connections by actively practicing a new skill, not just by talking about doing it. If I told you how to throw a baseball but never actually handed you a baseball to try it out, do you think you would learn how to actually throw a baseball? The same is true for coping skills. We could talk about all the ways you're going to cope the next time you feel anxious, but what would happen if you never actually tried any of them ahead of time? Today we're not only looking at and thinking about coping skills for anxiety, but we're also actually practicing them. This will train your brain to use those skills when you need them, instead of thinking about all the steps and getting lost in the thoughts."

2. Ask the client to think of a time when their anxiety felt overwhelming. Have them describe what happened, how they responded, and what they did or didn't do. Ask what would have helped them cope enough to stay in the moment. (Be sure this answer is not a way to avoid the anxiety!)

3. Provide the client with the *Active Coping Skills* and *Passive Coping Skills* lists. Discuss the difference between both types of skills—and why it is important to possess both:
   - **Active:** Can be done alone or with others; more of an "activity" that can be seen by others, like going for a walk, talking to a friend, or dancing
   - **Passive:** Usually done alone, in your mind; an activity others probably don't notice, like counting in your mind, doodling, or listening to music with earbuds
4. Have the client choose five skills from *each* list, then practice each of these skills in session. (If the skill involves another person, step in as that person in a role-play.)
5. Explore with the client whether each skill would have been helpful in the scenario they described earlier in step 2. Brainstorm other settings and circumstances where each one could be helpful.
6. Have the client transfer the coping skills they chose from the list onto the *Crystalized Coping Skills* worksheet.
7. Encourage the client to *actively practice* at least three of the coping skills each day as part of their routine. You can embed skills practice in future sessions too.

Variation: After choosing skills from the *Active Coping Skills* and *Passive Coping Skills* lists, have the client write each coping skill on a slip of paper and add it to a shoebox to use as a coping skills toolbox. Invite them to decorate the box if they'd like to.

Tier 1

School, Treatment, and Community Settings

Regular whole-classroom or group work around coping skills is helpful for normalizing anxiety, creating common ground, and validating shared experiences, and it doesn't need to be time-consuming. Consider posting a "coping skill of the day" or keeping an ongoing list in a shared space. Alternatively, students and group members can tape their individual lists to their desks as a reference.

Handout

Active Coping Skills

1. Vent with problem-solving to someone you trust.
2. Ask to step away from the environment for two minutes.
3. Engage in a conversation with a friend.
4. Go for a walk outside.
5. Sing or dance to your favorite song.
6. Do yoga poses (e.g., sun salutation, child's pose).
7. Step away from people who make you feel bad or have toxic negativity.
8. Ask for help with a frustrating or confusing task.
9. Do a chore (e.g., wash dishes, sweep the floor, pick up laundry).
10. Walk in place with your hands on your hips.
11. Play an instrument.
12. Take a warm shower or bath.
13. Talk to a trusted adult (e.g., caregiver, counselor).
14. Hug someone you trust for at least three seconds.
15. Help someone with a task.
16. Organize your desk, backpack, or room.
17. Wash your hands with warm water and put on good-smelling lotion.
18. Cook or bake something to give away.
19. Practice self-care (e.g., brush your teeth, wear your favorite outfit, brush your hair).
20. Write a letter to someone you love and deliver it.
21. Stand and stretch.
22. Blow bubbles.
23. Play a board or card game.
24. Let yourself cry for 10 minutes.
25. Stomp your feet on the ground for 20 paces.

Handout

Passive Coping Skills

1. Read a book or graphic novel.
2. Count to 10 with a slow breath after each number.
3. Think of your favorite animal, food, color, or song.
4. Take a nap or rest.
5. Stand in the sun or nature.
6. Ask yourself, "Where did this feeling come from?"
7. Color, draw, or doodle.
8. Journal your thoughts about just this moment.
9. Make a list of what is great about you (e.g., skill set, sense of style, good listener).
10. Make a gratitude list of all the things you are thankful for.
11. Write a short story or poem.
12. Use a small tactile fidget or stress squeezy.
13. Tell yourself, "This is just this moment and not forever."
14. Give yourself positive self-talk/affirmations (e.g., "I can survive this minute," "I am capable").
15. Eat a healthy snack or drink a warm or cold beverage.
16. Pay attention to your five senses in this moment.
17. Think of being a superhero with powers of calm and control.
18. Visualize your favorite place (e.g., beach, woods, comfy chair with a blanket).
19. Pet your dog, cat, guinea pig, bearded dragon, or other animal friend.
20. Focus all of your attention on an object across the room for 30 seconds.
21. Look at photos of things and people you love.
22. Visit a visual list of your favorite funny memes.
23. Close your eyes and listen to *everything* around you (e.g., air conditioning, birds chirping outside, traffic).
24. Smile in a mirror or at someone else.
25. Listen to a guided meditation or relaxation exercise.

Worksheet

Crystallized Coping Skills

Which coping skills have you practiced until they work for you? Write them down in the crystal, and mark *where* each skill works the best. Keep adding skills to this sheet as you discover and practice more.

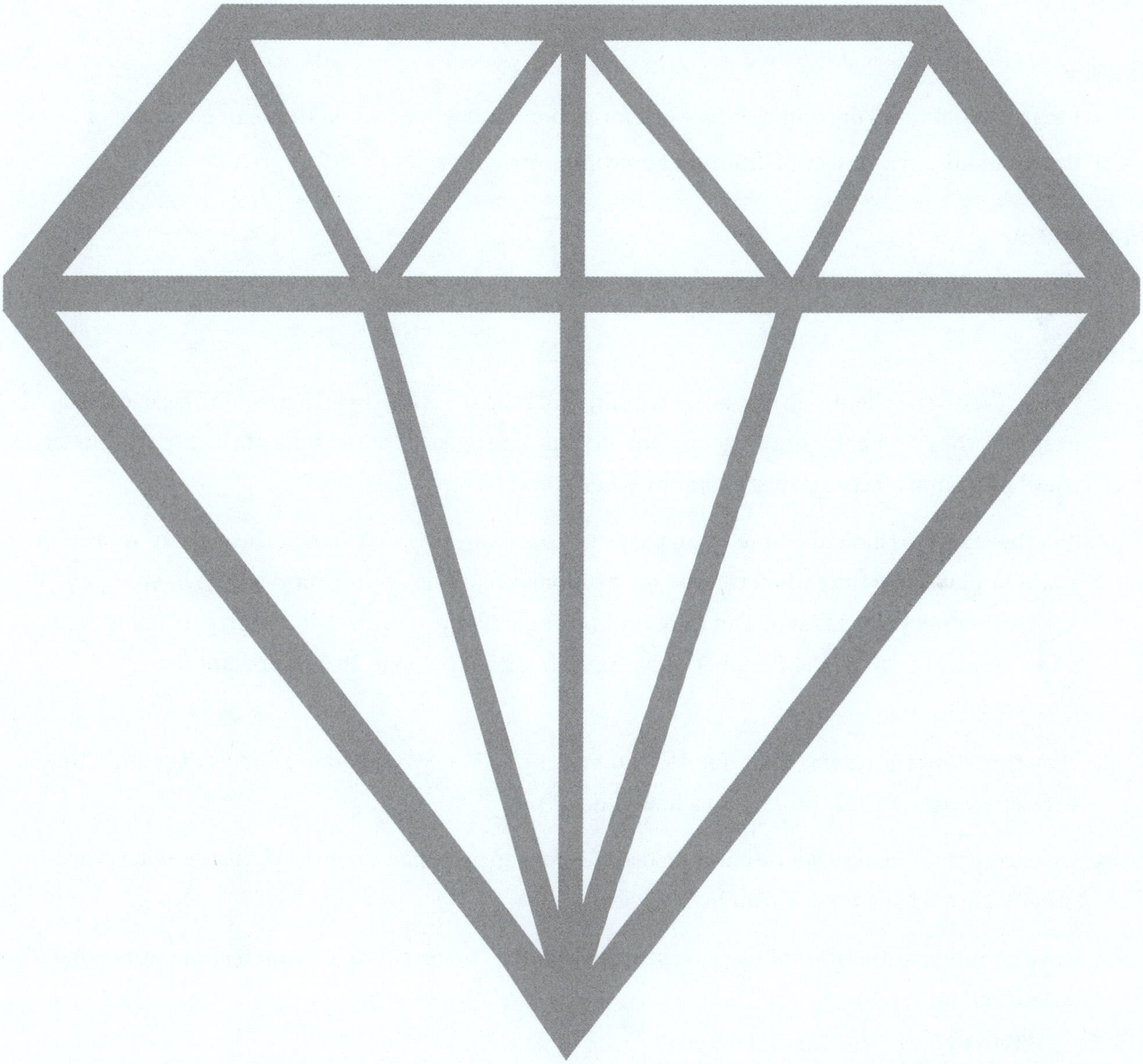

Coping in All Your Places and Spaces **C, N**

Therapeutic Rationale:

The type of coping skills a child is willing to explore and practice depends on their age, stage, and preferences—and not all coping skills are appropriate for every environment. Helping kids self-monitor and investigate where and when certain coping skills are best applied, and crystallizing those skill sets for long-term use, is the goal of this intervention.

Goals:

- Identify what types of coping skills work for a client and where/when they can use them
- Practice skills in a variety of different environments

Materials:

- *Coping in All Your Places and Spaces* worksheet

Directions:

1. Discuss with the client how not every coping skill is appropriate in all areas of their lives. For example, they probably cannot get up and do jumping jacks in the middle of the library, but they could pull out a piece of paper and draw when they feel anxious.
2. Ask the client to think of a time when they used a coping skill that wasn't the right fit for the space or place, or a time when they weren't prepared with an appropriate one. What happened? Were other people confused? Did they get in trouble? If needed, revisit the *Active Coping Skills* handout on page 37 or the *Passive Coping Skills* handout on page 38 as a prompt for discussion.
3. Give the client the *Coping Skills for All Your Places and Spaces* worksheet and assist with filling in each space and actively practicing a new skill.
4. Once complete, challenge the client to use the appropriate-place coping skills for at least two other locations and take note of how it goes.
5. Take a minute at the start of the next session to follow up on this and troubleshoot as needed. Ask the client:
    - What part of this worked for you?
    - What got in the way while you were trying to use it?
    - What were you thinking and feeling while you were practicing your skill?

Tier 1

School, Treatment, and Community Settings

Regular whole-classroom or group work around coping skills is helpful for normalizing anxiety, creating common ground, and validating shared experiences, and it doesn't need to be time-consuming. Consider posting a "coping skill of the day" or keeping an ongoing list in a shared space. Alternatively, students and group members can tape their *Coping in All Your Places and Spaces* worksheets to their desks as a reference. Be sure to reinforce healthy choices by acknowledging when someone uses a healthy skill with a high-five, head nod, or quick thank-you (in real time, whenever possible).

Worksheet

Coping in All Your Places and Spaces

Every experience is different—it all depends on the time, the place, the people who are there, and even how you are feeling! The coping skills you use in these places will likely need to be different too. Sometimes quiet or passive skills are needed, and other times, busy and active skills might work better.

Let's brainstorm two coping skills you could use in each of these different spaces:

Classroom	With Friends

Now think of three more places, adding two more coping skills you could use for each one. Choose from the following options or create your own: the playground, gym class, the classroom during silent reading, your bedroom, a sporting event, the lunchroom, the grocery store, the library, a wedding, a place of worship, or your grandparents' house.

The Stress and Worry Tree *C, Soc, M*

Therapeutic Rationale:

This intervention gives kids an external place to put their internal worries, allowing them to take a mental "break" from those thoughts. By identifying specific worries and emotions—and then creating some distance from them—children can experience relief from rumination and unhelpful thinking cycles. Placing the tree in a shared or community space where many people add their worries helps validate these experiences, fosters connection, and reduces feelings of shame.

Goals:

- Identify thematic worries and place them outside of the client
- Practice mindful focus for coping
- Validate worries and experiences as common
- Create a sense of community and peer helping
- Develop crystallized coping skills

Materials:

- *Stress and Worry Tree* template
- *Worry Leaf* template
- Poster board and paper
- Large wall space
- Optional: Sticky notes, cardboard

Directions:

1. In advance of the session, make several copies of the *Worry Leaf* handout on four colors of paper. Cut them out ahead of time or during the intervention.
2. Create a large tree using your method of choice to be displayed in your office or classroom. Be as creative as you'd like with the tree creation (I use cardboard and crumpled paper bags to create a 3-D version); just be sure to include a strong trunk and at least three to five strong branches. If you do not have room to create a large tree, use the *Stress and Worry Tree* template provided.
3. Explain to the client that the Stress and Worry Tree can hold on to their worries:

   "Sometimes worries can feel very heavy. Having a safe place to put them for a little while can help us feel lighter, and it lets our brain use that energy for other things. We can also put similar worries together on one branch, like one for family worries, one for school worries, and one for friend worries. This is helpful, because lots of times there is a certain kind of coping skill that can help release all *the leaves on one branch at the same time. The tree helps us see the worries, take them away from ourselves for a little while, and practice coping skills that work."*

4. Invite the client to write or draw one worry or stressful thought on a Worry Leaf or sticky note (one per leaf). Because their leaves will be displayed publicly, be sure to consider the Health Insurance Portability and Accountability Act and leave out identifying details.
5. Have the client place their worry leaves on the community tree branches. Have them cluster common topical worries on each branch, and don't be afraid to add extra branches.
6. As the tree is filled with leaves, it shows that everyone has worries in common, which normalizes and validates struggle. You can reflect here on how the tree is strong enough to hold everyone's worries, and that no one worry is going to bring it down.

Variation: Use the colors and shapes of leaves to delineate clients from specific classrooms, group days, and family treatment. Clients may be surprised to see others—even those they don't know—have similar worries too.

Depending on your setting and population, you can process further:

7. Once the tree is full of leaves, focus on one branch (area of worry) at a time, reinforcing a mindful approach to working on worries:

   "If you focus on all of the branches at the same time, you'll feel overwhelmed, but if you choose one at a time, it feels more manageable—just like worry."

8. As you look at common leaves, identify the worry and encourage the client to think of a coping skill that helps with it. As the coping skill is discussed or practiced, drop the leaf at the base of the tree to create a pile of "processed worries." In a group setting, this is a great opportunity for peer-to-peer teaching of skills (community).
9. The client's needs will determine what to do with the pile that remains. Some will want to keep them all as reminders of their work, others may want to destroy them (I've burned many worry tree leaves to ashes, especially for kids who resonate with the phoenix metaphor), or you can "compost" them to feed them back to the tree/self to show that "you are stronger when you learn to cope with stress." Creativity abounds here as well!
10. Keep the tree up in your environment, as worries can return or change and coping skills might need troubleshooting. Other therapeutic symbolisms you could incorporate could be weathering a storm, seasonality, and life cycles.

Tier 1

School, Treatment, and Community Settings

Place your Stress and Worry Tree in an accessible area like the lobby as a reminder of community and shared healing. Consider including "helper leaves," on which community members can write coping skills, helpful ideas, or encouragement and then attach it to a worry they see on the tree. Do be sure an adult is monitoring the content of the leaves regularly to screen for unhelpful or negative messages.

Template

Stress and Worry Tree

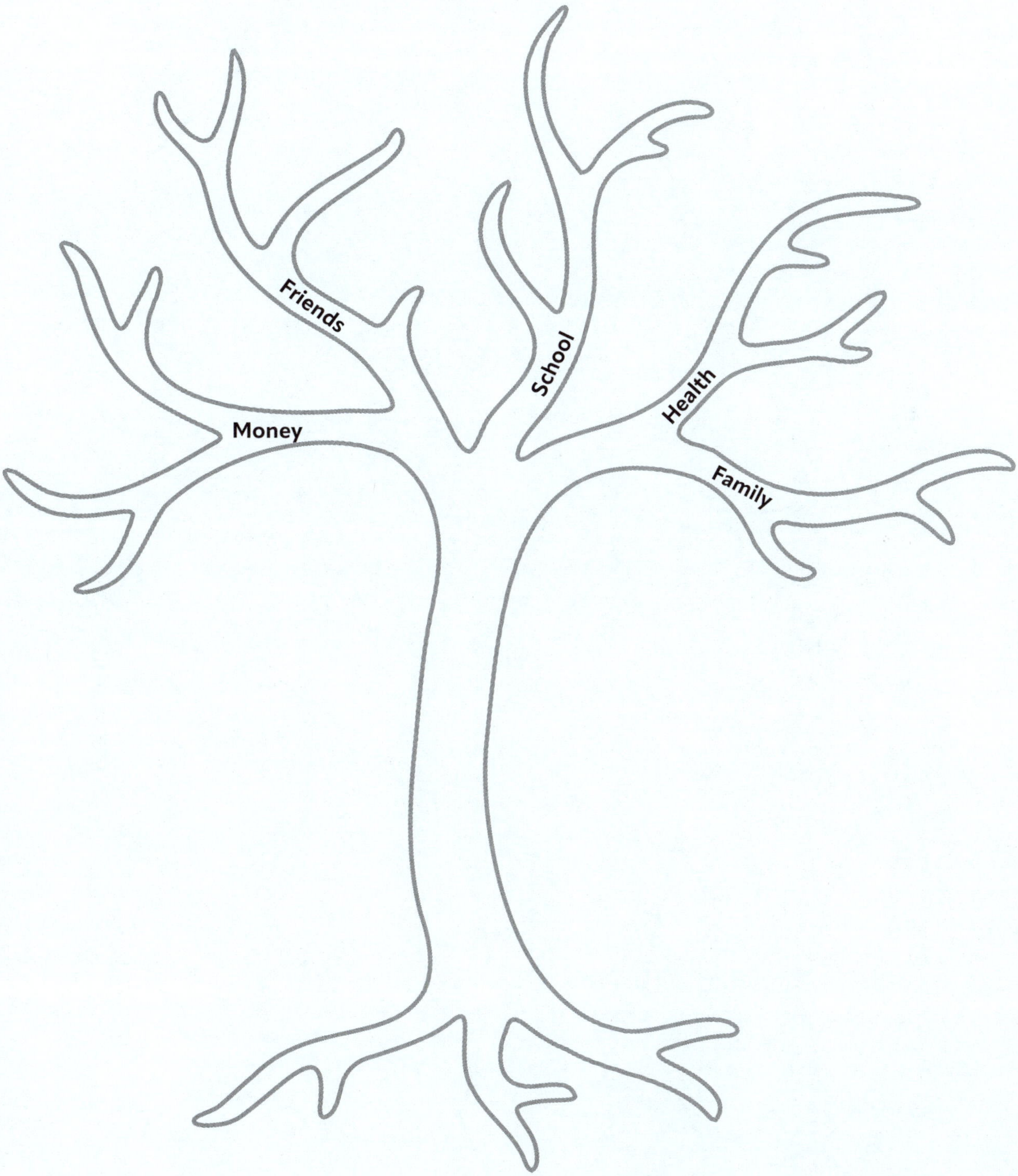

Template

Worry Leaf

Anxiety Appointments C, D

Therapeutic Rationale:

This distress tolerance intervention provides kids with a structured time each day to experience and focus on their worries. Through this scheduled worry time (anxiety appointment), kids learn that they are allowed to feel anxious or overwhelmed but they can stay focused on completing the task at hand and step away to manage their emotions *later*. Over time, the practice of allowing anxiety to temporarily exist—with a clear endpoint—teaches kids the skill of delayed gratification and the ability to tolerate discomfort. This puts them in control of their thoughts and emotions instead of their thoughts and emotions controlling them.

Goals:

- Experience worries in a structured way
- Promote delayed gratification of an anxiety expression
- Reduce the tendency to ruminate

Materials:

- A designated safe space, preferably *in* the environment
- A daily planner (paper or digital)
- Timer (preferably a sand timer for visual reinforcement)

Directions:

1. Introduce the client to the concept of anxiety appointments:

   "We can set aside a special time for our anxious thoughts and worries. When those pesky thoughts tell us to focus on them right now, *they now have to wait a little while and make an 'appointment' so we can spend the rest of the day focusing on the things we need to get done. These anxiety appointments will be scheduled at regular times each day so you can count on them being there for you."*

2. Find two times each day when the child has 5 to 30 minutes of free time (not overlapping with other activities) to focus on their anxiety. Times needed for specific types of anxiety might include the following:

   a. **Panic disorder:** Schedule 30-minute appointments to allow the child to fully recover after a panic attack (usually 10 to 14 minutes in duration).

   b. **GAD or adjustment disorder:** For those with ongoing anxiety or environmental triggers, set aside at least five minutes.

3. Use a daily planner or digital calendar to create scheduled anxiety appointments each day. This creates a visual reminder and helps keep the schedule consistent. For those concerned about privacy, consider using a symbol (like a visual cue or subtle physical gesture) to indicate when it's time for the anxiety appointment so it doesn't draw attention.

4. When it's time for the anxiety appointment, prompt the child to set a timer for the designated time. During this time, the child should fully focus on all of their anxieties or worries. It's a dedicated space to focus on whatever is bothering them. Reinforce to the child that it's okay to focus on their worries at this time: "It's okay to worry here."

5. Once the timer finishes, the child should reflect on how much of their scheduled time they actually spent worrying. Oftentimes, they'll find that much of the time was *not* spent worrying, which can help them process the concept that even though anxiety tells us it will last forever, it can only last for a little while before our bodies start to feel better.

6. Let the client know that anxious feelings will eventually end:

   "Anxiety and worry tell your brain that this will last forever, but sometimes it just needs a few minutes to feel better."

7. After about 7 to 10 days, most children's anxiety levels will begin to decrease. When the child gets more used to deciding when worries will get attention, gradually reduce the length of the anxiety appointment (e.g., 10 minutes instead of 15) or reduce the number of anxiety appointments per day. Continue making these adjustments as needed as the child's anxiety improves.

Tier 2 or 3

School, Treatment, and Community Settings

In classroom or therapeutic settings, a small rug can help establish a comfortable, clearly defined space, especially for younger children. Adding pillows or fidgets can further support regulation and engagement. Including a high-back chair that supports the head and reduces peripheral engagement can also be beneficial, particularly for children who are easily startled or have a history of trauma.

Advanced Anxiety Appointments **C, D, N, S**

Therapeutic Rationale:

To help kids cope with negative emotions, you want to permit anxiety to occur, but you *also* must continue to grow their distress tolerance through self-monitoring, active practice of crystallized coping, and self-regulation skill sets. This can also be expanded into a paradoxical intervention opportunity for long-term anxiety management.

> **Note:** As an advanced intervention, the following intervention should be practiced by clinical staff with appropriate training in behavioral health.

Goals:

- Increase personal self-control and awareness
- Develop skills for managing intense emotions and urges

Materials:

- *Your Thoughts and Your Body* worksheet
- A daily planner (paper or digital)
- Timer (preferably a sand timer for visual reinforcement)
- A designated safe space
- Notebook or journal
- Other items specific to the client's coping skill set

Directions:

1. Explain to the client that they will be learning to weaken their worry:

   "Let's teach our brains that the way we think about worry is bigger than the worry actually is. Sometimes we can challenge ourselves to try to make *anxiety happen. When we try to make our bodies and brains do what we spend a lot of energy pushing away, it can make the worry weaker and the body calmer more quickly. Everyone's anxiety appointments are different, just like all of us. Now that you know you have time for your worries, let's learn how to be in charge of your brain and body even more."*

2. Have the client participate in prescheduled anxiety appointments, as established in the previous *Anxiety Appointments* intervention, for at least 7 to 10 days.

3. At the end of this time period, direct the client to complete the *Your Thoughts and Your Body* worksheet.

4. After the client has a good handle on the structure and timing of anxiety appointments, begin to incorporate advanced processing and skill set practice.
5. For the next seven days, have the client practice any of the following exercises with blended incorporation and layered skills growth:
    a. Distract with wise mind. Engaging in action-oriented tasks can retrain cognition away from anxious thoughts. Some of these tasks might include the following:
        i. Heavy lifting: Sometimes children will be asked to do directed strenuous lifting tasks (e.g., stacking chairs, carrying books) to improve regulation of the reticular activating system.
        ii. Engaging in directed play or frontal cortex activities: For younger kids, this could be reading books, coloring, or imaginary play with a stuffed animal; for older children, offer more age-appropriate versions of these ideas if the client is interested (e.g., graphic novels, adult coloring books, anime).
    b. Use self-monitoring tools. These tools promote growth of self-awareness of anxiety antecedents and physiological responses. For instance, stemming from the *Your Thoughts and Your Body* worksheet, you may direct a client to do the following:
        i. Journal about the kinds of worries they have during the day and keep a tally of how often each specific worry returns.
        ii. Draw their worries and what they think about, showing what their body and brain are doing during that time.
    c. Incorporate the *Crystallized Coping Skills* intervention to the end of the *Anxiety Appointments* intervention. This can help the client actively practice the regulation of their thoughts and body before returning to regularly scheduled activities. This is self-reinforcing, and it is likely to increase healthy use of coping skills in generalized environments.
    d. Introduce a paradoxical intervention of "prescribing" the anxiety or worry to the client as they enter into the appointment. This engages a paradox (combating the fear of the fear response) because you are approaching the experience for which they are the most resistant to, which promotes rapid diffusing and recovery within 7 to 10 days. For example, you might prompt the following:
        i. "Worry as much as you can."
        ii. "Be as anxious as you can be."

Note: Caution should be taken for clients with a history of trauma or reactive attachment disorder, as the practice can be counterproductive due to the intensity of the sensory and physiological initiation.

Worksheet

Your Thoughts and Your Body

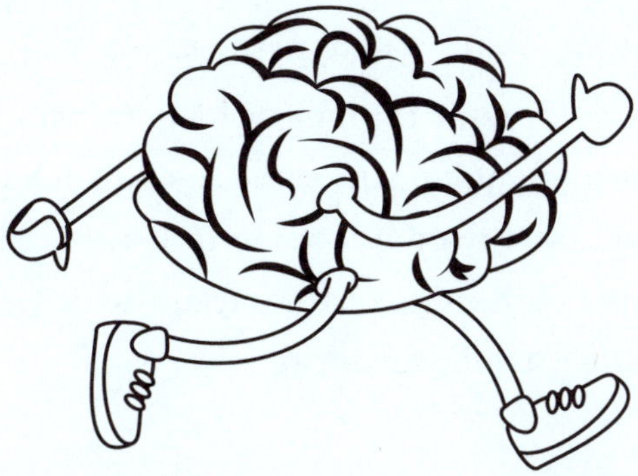

When you feel worried or anxious, your brain tells you things that might not be true—and your body reacts. Use this worksheet to look at what you are thinking and how your body acts. Then you can see what you can do differently!

Thought	Action	New Way to Do It

Anxiety Anchors

B

Therapeutic Rationale:

This technique utilizes classical conditioning (think Pavlov's dog, bell, meat powder) to pair a neutral stimulus with a practice of relaxation and calming, which transforms this item from neutral to conditioned. This newly conditioned stimulus now serves as an anchor for resolving anxiety in high-pressure situations in the moment, and without having to leave or escape the situation. This is an excellent tool for anxiety associated with court testimony, difficult visitations, permanency planning meetings, or performance-related/test-taking anxieties.

Goals:

- Create a calming conditioned stimulus
- Use an anchor for immediate self-regulation
- Improve self-control and awareness

Materials:

- *Anxiety Anchors* handout
- A neutral object (e.g., eraser, glasses case, hat) without an already connected perception of feeling or meaning
- A quiet place
- List of relaxation tools and techniques for the specific client you are working with

Directions:

1. Introduce the concept of an anxiety anchor:

   "Sometimes we can turn a very 'normal' thing into a calming object that helps us feel relaxed just by being near it, seeing it, or holding it."

2. Begin by being present with a neutral object. Direct the client to look at the object, sit with the object, touch the object, and hold the object.
3. Once the client is present with the item, begin pairing the neutral object with the active practice of relaxation, breathing, or calming thoughts.
4. Practice with the client in session and then direct them to do it on their own three to five times each day for three to five days.
5. With repetitive practice of pairing object with behavior, the neutral object (stimulus) will transform into a conditioned stimulus. With the conditioned stimulus in hand, kids can feel immediately relaxed and calm instead of needing to step away for calming time. As soon as they touch or are near their anxiety anchor, they will automatically transition into a state of calmness.

6. It is important to repeat the pairing process after using the item as an anxiety anchor for five days, as the item will lose its "battery charge" of relaxation after use. Guide the client to pair it the same way as it was initially paired in step 4.

Tier 3

School, Treatment, and Community Settings

This tool is highly effective for test- or performance-related anxieties. Typical accommodations for anxiety, such as extended time for test taking, are not as helpful as we'd like them to be (and may even be counterproductive). Using an anxiety anchor that has been paired one week ahead of time for performance-related anxiety can significantly decrease the use of extended time within three to five days.

Handout

Anxiety Anchors

1. Find an everyday object that is small enough for you to carry around with you to different places. This should *not* be an object that is special to you or that already has meaning (e.g., a gift from someone important, something with sentimental value). Instead, it should be a common and neutral item.
2. Hold and look at the item while actively practicing relaxation. Try any of the following exercises:
    a. Breathe deeply.
    b. Picture yourself holding this item while winning a game or getting an A on a test.
    c. Focus on the muscles used to hold the item and using your brain to help them relax.
    d. Think about only this thing in your hand and nothing else.
    e. Think of this item as an anchor to hold you in place when things get chaotic, difficult, or stormy around you.
    f. Say affirmations while you hold this item.
    g. Say a prayer for success while you hold this item.
3. Practice these things three to five times a day for five days, and you will find your item has become an easy tool to calm yourself down quickly.
4. Take this item with you to places you know you might feel worried or anxious.
5. Be sure to recharge your item with calmness after you have used it for a week, by repeating steps 2 and 3.
6. You can create several anxiety anchors in different places. Just be sure to take the time needed to charge them up.

Play Dough Magic **At, C, N, S, T**

Therapeutic Rationale:

Using art for emotional expression is well-grounded in research. This intervention utilizes a specific art medium, play dough, to help anxious kids process their emotions, express themselves, and self-regulate.

The closing step is imperative. Play dough is recognized as a "regressive" art medium: a material that lacks concrete boundaries and is highly engaging texturally. For some clients, using this medium is overwhelming to the limbic system and can lead to behavioral or emotional decompensation. For this reason, always close the activity with a structured or logic-based art medium. For play dough, this might be cutting the dough into pieces and putting it back into the container or washing hands and then drawing something specific afterward. A concrete tool and activity are the key here, so you can "close back up" what was opened during session.

> **Note:** Individual sensory experiences and abilities should be taken into consideration before engaging in this intervention.

Goals:

- Use structured and regressive art media to process emotions
- Label the limbic system with accurate emotions
- Increase opportunities for positive emotion through action and thought
- Promote recovery and emotional regulation

Materials:

- Play dough, possibly several colors (check for allergies)
- Flat surface
- Play dough tools (e.g., tongue depressors, paper clips, rolling pin)
- Structured art medium tools (e.g., pens, pencils, colored pencils, cookie cutters)
- Optional: *Play Dough Recipes* handout

Directions:

Activity 1: Inside/Outside Feelings Faces

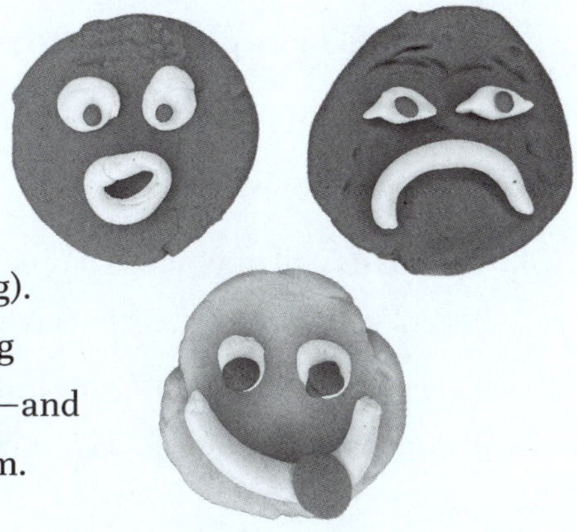

1. Direct the client to make a play dough face that shows the feeling they show most often *to the world* (i.e., outside feeling). For example, the client might show a smiling face, explaining that they try to smile for other people because it's expected—and others will then be less likely to ask questions or bother them.

2. Ask the client to hold their play dough face and think of a person, memory, or activity that connects them with that outside feeling. By making an internal reference point for feelings, they are better able to approach or avoid a certain emotion through engaging or circumventing that specific person, memory, or activity.

3. Next, direct the client to change the play dough face to show the feeling they feel the most on the *inside*, which may or may not be a different feeling than the first. For example, the client might show an overwhelmed face, explaining that they feel this a lot, as their body and brain are working hard on lots of things at once.

4. Ask the client to hold this play dough face and think of a person, memory, or activity that connects them with that inside feeling. Ask the client, "How are [*person, memory, activity, etc.*] and the feeling the same or different?"

5. Last, direct the client to change the play dough face to show the feeling they *would like to have* matching inside *and* outside (congruent emotion). For example, they might want a calm smile or a relaxed and peaceful feeling.

6. It is especially important to again have the client think of a person, memory, or activity that connects them with that matching feeling.

7. Let the client know that when they want to (or don't want to) feel a certain way, they now know the person, memory, or activity that puts them in control of their brain.

8. Validate that the client's feelings are their own feelings and all of them are okay to feel.

9. Complete the activity by putting away the play dough, closing the activity with a structured art medium (e.g., pencils, cookie cutters).

Activity 2: The Heart Surgeon

1. Direct the client to use play dough to visually represent their heart, making sure they show all the things about their heart that make it special or different from other people's.

2. Building onto what's already been created in step 1, have the client add more play dough to represent disease or injury.

3. Ask the client to consider how each of these things change the way the heart works or doesn't work.

4. The client will now act as a "heart surgeon," removing the disease or injury but making sure the heart keeps working. Then have them compare the "healed" heart to the original heart from step 1:

   "Let's look at your heart and see what's different. [Most individuals will see lines, fissures, lumps, and bumps.] *What do the markings on the heart mean to you?"*

5. If the markings look like scars, ask the client what having scars means about someone. They may answer that it means the person is healed, the person survived something difficult, or the person is even stronger than before.
6. Ask the client to tell you about a time when they thought they wouldn't heal, but they actually survived. Do they have scars left behind to remind them of how they actually survived?
7. Complete the activity by putting away the play dough, closing the activity with a structured art medium (e.g., pencils, cookie cutters).

Variation: Invite the client to create their own play dough at home using any of the recipes from the *Play Dough Recipes* handout.

Handout

Play Dough Recipes

If you are new to homemade play dough, welcome! There are so many ways to make the stuff. Here are three I recommend.

Just Like the *Real* Play Dough

1 cup flour

1 cup water

1 tbsp oil

1 tbsp powdered alum

½ cup salt

2 tbsp vanilla

A few drops of food coloring (keep adding until you get the color you want)

1. Mix all dry ingredients, then add oil and water.
2. Cook over medium heat, stirring constantly until reaching the consistency of mashed potatoes.
3. Remove from heat and add vanilla and food coloring.
4. Divide into balls and work in color by kneading.

Kool-Aid Play Dough

2½ to 3 cups flour

2 cups water

3 tbsp corn oil

1 tbsp powdered alum

½ cup salt

1 package Kool-Aid (any flavor)

1. Boil the water and add the Kool-Aid packet.
2. Mix all ingredients and knead with flour (may take up to 1 extra cup). Use more if the dough draws moisture in high humidity.

This play dough keeps well, has a nice fragrance, and is very colorful and flexible.

Nutty Butter Play Dough

1 cup peanut butter

1 cup powdered milk

1 cup honey

1 cup oatmeal

1. Mix together and play!
2. You can eat this play dough, but take caution in areas where you may have children with nut allergies.

This playdough recipe is often used in attachment treatment to get a child's hands working with an attachment figure to create a final product, and you can expand the intervention with feeding activities, which can promote positive attachment between caregiver and child.

Anxiety Sunglasses C, T

Therapeutic Rationale:

Allowing children to use mirrored sunglasses during anxiety-provoking interactions has been shown to decrease emotional escalation, increase task completion, and, regarding abuse disclosure and court testimony, increase the likelihood of the child providing accurate and complete information. For young children, this taps into their developmental stage (object permanence) that "if I cover my eyes, then no one can see me"; for older children and teens, it's more a matter of feeling more "protected" and "invisible" during emotionally charged situations or performances, allowing space between themselves and the audience. This intervention allows the client to stay in and participate in an anxiety-provoking environment rather than avoid it.

Goals:

- Decrease arousal states in high-anxiety situations
- Decrease the perception of trauma in graduated and flooded exposure states
- Decrease avoidance behaviors

Materials:

- *Anxiety Rating Scale* worksheet
- Inexpensive mirrored sunglasses
- Optional: *Big Daddy* (1999 film)

Directions:

When using this intervention, you likely already know what the anxiety-provoking situation is for the client. Feel free to adjust these directions based on the specific scenario.

1. Explain to the client how they can use anxiety sunglasses to feel calmer in difficult situations:

   "Sometimes, when we feel anxious or scared, we might cover our eyes to feel more protected and safe. These glasses are kind of like that. Wearing them can help us feel more comfortable and safe in situations that are tough or anxiety-provoking."

> **Optional:** Show the client the scene from *Big Daddy* where Julian wears the sunglasses in court. You can cue up the part of the movie beforehand or search for the specific scene on YouTube.

2. Introduce the *Anxiety Rating Scale* worksheet and work through each row with the client: For each level (row) on the anxiety rating scale, add a situation the client has gone through that corresponds to that rating.

3. Validate the client's anxiety or fear in unfamiliar, unpredictable, and high-pressure environments, discussing what they were thinking and feeling at this time. Then decide on appropriate coping skills / emotive-regulation tools that can be used at that level of the scale).

4. Have the client first practice wearing the sunglasses during neutral interactions, like talking about the weather, and reflect on feelings of security and safety. Rate these on the anxiety rating scale (these will likely be a 1 or 2) and create coping skills or tools for regulation if needed.

5. When the client is more comfortable, begin role-playing difficult situations—like disclosure events, court testimony (without leading language), book reports, and group activities—while they are still wearing the sunglasses. Rate these on the anxiety rating scale and use tools for regulation.

6. Finally, transition glasses use to real-life events, such as clinical sessions, court testimony, difficult classroom tasks, or group participation. Be sure the client has practiced their regulation skills thoroughly before entering the performance environment.

Tier 1, 2, or 3*

School, Treatment, and Community Settings

This intervention is an inexpensive and easily accessible tool for use in classrooms and therapeutic groups, especially for new students or members. Best practice is to use the glasses for everyone in the environment, but as comfort levels increase in the space, allowing the individual to remove the glasses can be representative of effective regulation in socially uncomfortable contexts.

* This intervention may be tier 1, tier 2, or tier 3 based on the number of children you are working with.

Worksheet

Anxiety Rating Scale

Your anxiety rating scale shows you how strong your anxiety or fear is. The bigger the number, the stronger your feelings and body reactions will be. Everyone feels things differently, so making your own scale helps you see when coping skills can be used to slow down. For each number, give an example of when you felt this way, discuss what you were thinking and feeling at that time, and write a skill you can use to calm down if you were in a similar situation again.

10
9
8
7
6
5
4
3
2
1

Tactile Grounders / Weighted Objects *S*

Therapeutic Rationale:

Weighted grounding objects can be used as a proactive tool for anxiety and emotional dysregulation because of their ability to decrease the physiological symptoms of anxiety, such as increased heart rate, labored breathing, and elevated body temperature. When used routinely, weighted grounding objects decrease activation of the ANS (fight or flight), allowing the client to develop distress tolerance. This intervention introduces kids to weighted grounding objects as a tool for managing anxiety and emotional dysregulation.

Guidelines:

- Weighted grounding objects are not meant for restraint or holding; the client should be able to easily move the object to different places on the body, and off the body completely, as needed.
- The object's weight should be less than 10 percent of the client's body weight to ensure safety, comfort, and portability.
- Weighted grounding objects are intended to be used for no more than ten minutes at a time to prevent overstimulation, desensitization, or further dysregulation.
- Pressure vests and weighted blankets are *not* appropriate weighted grounding objects for this intervention. These tools should be incorporated into sensory regulation through occupational therapy or neuropsychological treatment *only*, and they are intended to be regulated and individualized for appropriately titrated use. There are significant safety and legal risks associated with inappropriate use of these tools.

Note: Individual sensory experiences and abilities should be taken into consideration before engaging in this intervention.

Goals:

- Decrease likelihood of escape or avoidance; promote self-regulation
- Improve focus and stress tolerance
- Decrease excessive movement
- Develop skills for managing intense emotions and urges
- Improve access to prefrontal cortex function and neural growth

Materials:

- Weighted object
- *Weighted Grounding Objects: Examples, Ideas, and Tips* handout

Directions:

1. Introduce the weighted grounding object to the client (or make one with them!).
2. Explain the purpose of weighted grounding objects:

   "Sometimes when worrying starts to take over or we feel ourselves getting upset or anxious, this [object] *can help calm us before the feelings get too big. When we put it on our bodies, the weight we feel sends a message to our brains that it's okay to calm down. Isn't that cool?"*

3. Place the weighted object evenly across the client's lap, shoulders, or forearms, asking them if they can feel the weight there.
4. Guide them to focus their attention on the object and take three breaths.
5. Leave the object in place for up to 10 minutes while sitting quietly and breathing steadily. When the time is up, carefully remove the item and place it aside.
6. Tell the client that when they are worrying, feeling overwhelmed, or having a hard time paying attention, they can use the object again to calm down. Ask them if they can think of any places or situations where this might be helpful for them.
7. Remind the client that this item should only be used for 10 minutes. If they start to play with it like a toy, this should tell them that they are feeling better and can put it away until they need it again.

Tier 3

School, Treatment, and Community Settings

Consider turning weighted grounding object creation into a math, physics, geometry, or affiliated arts activity, if appropriate, or as part of a rapport-building activity.

Weighted Grounding Objects: Examples, Ideas, and Tips

There's no shortage of premade weighted objects on the internet if you'd like to purchase them. However, if you'd prefer to use what you have or make your own, here are my recommendations.

- **Weighted rubber nursing pillows:** These horseshoe-shaped pillows can be wrapped around a little one's torso or laid across the top of thighs when they are sitting in a crisscross-applesauce position. Most pillows like this also have covers that can be removed and sanitized as needed.
- **Rice-filled tube socks:** These are inexpensive, adjustable, and portable. I recommend sewing both ends of the sock closed rather than tying (unless you want the inevitable flinging of rice in your space). A sock is great as a weighted grounding object, as it's easy to evenly distribute the weight across it.
- **Stuffed animals:** Perform "surgery" on existing stuffed animals by opening them and filling them with rice, corn, beans, pebbles, marbles—whatever you have on hand! If allergies are a concern, substitute the filler material with nonfood items, such as sand, pebbles, or marbles.
- **Sensory components:** Get creative! Add sequins, buttons, Velcro strips, pockets, satin, or other textures for more tactile engagement. Warm them in the sun, cool them in a freezer, or even add essential oils (being mindful of allergies and sensitivities).

The Existential Oak Tree **C, D, N, S, T**

Therapeutic Rationale:

This intervention integrates sensory input with visual imagery to help clients ground themselves, stabilize their mood, tolerate environmental and internal stressors, and remain present in the moment without the need for escape or avoidance.

Children can then take this *experience* with them into difficult, high-anxiety provocation situations (e.g., conflict with peers, gatherings in large crowds, test taking) as a skill they can use independently and covertly among others.

This intervention utilizes touch therapeutically; however, because touch is not always appropriate for clients, I've provided an alternative of using a weighted grounding object. (See the *Weighted Grounding Objects: Examples, Ideas, and Tips* handout on page 65 for therapeutic guidelines.)

> **Note:** Individual sensory experiences and abilities should be taken into consideration before engaging in this intervention. If there is sensory sensitivity to grounding, you may need to start simply with the imagery and increase exposure to weighted objects over time.

Goals:

- Decrease likelihood of escape or avoidance; promote self-regulation
- Pair sensate memory with visual imagery
- Improve independent awareness of antecedents for escape
- Identify situations that require immediate protection versus situations of tolerable discomfort

Materials:

- *Existential Oak Tree Script* handout
- Weighted grounding object (client's preference)
- *Weighted Grounding Objects: Examples, Ideas, and Tips* handout
- Timer (preferably a sand timer for visual reinforcement)

Directions:

1. Begin with psychoeducation about distress tolerance, including how imagery and sensory pairing can improve the child's ability to "stay in the moment" by helping them stay rooted in the space.

2. Direct the child to journal about specific incidents of distress intolerance and different types of interactions that resulted in escape patterns:

   "Think about some of the times when you've felt so stressed, worried, or upset that you felt like you had to avoid or escape the situation. Where were you? Who were you with? What was happening that felt overwhelming?"

3. With the child, create a weighted object based on their body weight. (Review the *Weighted Grounding Objects: Examples, Ideas, and Tips* handout for best practice.)

4. Place the weighted object evenly across the child's lap, shoulders, or forearms, asking them if they can feel the weight there.

5. Guide the child in a grounding exercise:

   "I want you to pay attention to the feeling of the weight on your [body part] *and feel how it helps your feet stay flat on the ground . . . Feel your feet flat on the ground, holding you in place."*

   [You may need to increase the width of the client's stance to get a sense of feeling well-rooted.]

   "I'm going to tell you about the oak tree, and while I talk about the tree, I want you to feel your feet firmly on the floor and feel the weight helping you stay firmly in place.

   Only pay attention to the weight and your feet on the floor . . . If you notice or think anything else, that's okay, but you are focusing on yourself and being right here, *right* now."

6. Use the script in the *Existential Oak Tree Script* handout. If the child is comfortable doing so, ask them to close their eyes and focus their attention on being well-rooted.

7. Keep the sensory weight present quietly for 10 to 20 seconds for children under the age of eight, and as long as five minutes for adolescents and young adults, to encode the sensate memory.

8. After the time has elapsed, deepen the sensate experience by asking the client the following questions:

   a. "Can you feel the weighted object keeping you firmly in place?"

   b. "Can you feel how stable and strong you are?"

   c. "Can you feel yourself here right now?"

9. After the child answers the deepening questions, inform them that you intend to remove the weighted object from their shoulders or lap. Be very slow and intentional about releasing the weight, and if you have someone who wobbles with removal, slow your pace of lifting.

10. After it is removed, ask the child to stand, close their eyes, and try to return to the sensation of being rooted to the ground. When they are able to get back to being well-rooted, they can raise their hand into the air to confirm they have ingrained the sensory sensation.

11. Remind them that when things seem "crazy" or "dramatic," they do not have to get caught up in the storm and can get back to a sensation of being well-rooted and stable without ever having to leave the environment.

12. Assign this intervention as therapeutic homework to continue the pairing of sensate memory with existential imagery and ingrain distress tolerance into their daily practice. At home, the client can have an adult read the script, or you can make a recording of it.

Tier 2

School, Treatment, and Community Settings

In schools and treatment facilities, using this tool first thing in the morning can improve a child's ability to stay grounded throughout the day. Using it again at the end of the day can once again help to reset their nervous system, allowing them to participate in extracurricular activities with less dysregulation.

Handout

Existential Oak Tree Script

You are an oak tree.

Your roots grow deeply in the ground, wrapping around the stone and bedrock

. . . holding you firmly in place.

Your trunk is stable . . .

strong . . .

and healthy.

Your branches reach into the sunlight, filling you with energy and warmth.

You are strong . . .

healthy . . .

and stable.

Nothing can uproot you:

. . . no wind,

. . . no storm,

. . . no rain.

You are an oak tree.

You are strong and healthy.

You can endure and survive anything that comes along.

Note: You can add to this imagery as needed for increased levels of anxiety (e.g., *Your roots hold you in place, drinking the cool water from the ground, strengthening you . . . Your trunk is covered with bark, which protects you from nature and things that may brush against you . . .*).

Transitional Objects *At, S, T*

Therapeutic Rationale:

Transitional objects are an underrecognized resource in the treatment of anxiety (especially separation anxiety). More than just a "comfort item," a transitional object can be a specific item of sensory comfort (e.g., blanket, stuffed animal, pacifier), and it can also be a positive emotionally connected object that will represent safety and security (e.g., something that reminds the child of a loving caregiver or safe space). The goal is to develop the child's independence and autonomy.

> **Note:** Individual sensory experiences and abilities should be taken into consideration before engaging in this intervention.

Goals:

- Decrease anxiety around separations using transitional objects
- Decrease ruminative thoughts through the use of therapeutic distraction
- Practice skills in a variety of different environments

Materials:

- Transitional objects gathered from the client's environment
- *Transitional Objects* handout

Directions:

1. Introduce individually specific transitional objects to the child and any family members present:

   "Sometimes, when we are away from people that are really important to us, we can feel overwhelmed because they aren't right next to us. We can use a transitional object to help us still feel connected to them, and this can help us do our jobs and tasks until we are with them again."

2. Direct the caregiver to allow the child access to the transitional object when changing environments (e.g., when dropping them off at school or daycare).
3. The child should also have access to the transitional object throughout the day to relieve anxiety associated with separation from caregivers or transitional issues within instructional settings.

Tier 3

School, Treatment, and Community Settings

Transitional objects are accessible and discreet tools that kids can use during the many transitions of life depending on their needs: passing periods, school drop-offs and exchanges, foster-to-adoption changes, or admission and discharge from a treatment program. The sky's the limit here.

Handout

Transitional Objects

The following items are good examples of transitional objects you can provide to a child for help in reducing separation anxiety. These items can be used for a number of reasons, including children in foster care, children with deployed caregivers, children with deceased caregivers, children with caregivers who are incarcerated, children who feel anxiety when separated at school, and many more!

Transitional Object Examples

- An unwashed item of clothing from a caregiver, worn by the child at night to improve sleep
- A single piece of a large puzzle, distributed to each family member and assembled when all are together for visitation or at the end of the day (gestalt of the family system)
- Stuffed animals with voice recordings of bedtime books or stories recorded by a caregiver
- A licensed service/therapeutic animal or emotional support animal
- Turning a caregiver's sweatshirt or button-down shirt into a pillow or part of a patchwork blanket
- Spiritual or faith-based items, such as rosaries, text quotes, or incense
- A favorite book to read at home or school
- The photograph of a favorite family member or support staff individual
- An inexpensive watch, which can alert transition times or the expected return of caregivers
- Pipe cleaner bracelet:
    - Place one Cheerio or bead on the pipe cleaner for every hour the client will be away from their caregiver. For each hour that passes, the client removes (and can eat or place aside) one *O*, serving as a visual and tactile measure of time. Adjust the time intervals as needed based on the client's needs. I prefer using pipe cleaners rather than string, as they are sturdier for playgrounds and can be "reloaded" easily each night.

- Chronological albums or scrapbooks:
    - A flexible technique with many applications, this is a book filled with important people and memories, such as pictures of primary care providers and counselors, ticket stubs from movies, cards from support staff, letters written about the positive traits of the child, closure letters for terminated parental rights, or certificates denoting successes or movement between care facilities. Always leave more space available at the end of the scrapbook to add future experiences, relationships, and successes. This book should be taken with the child from one placement to the next to provide a sense of connection rather than an abrupt closure on each of their experiences through their childhood.

Items "Filled" with Love

Using any transitional object, have the client and caregiver "fill up" the object with love. The caregiver can say, "Here are all of my kisses and hugs for you for the whole day—let's make sure there are lots of them in there. By the time you come back to me, we will have to refill it." The child determines the number of hugs and kisses that should be added to the transitional object to fill it up. Have the caregiver add ten or more so it doesn't deplete throughout the day.

A great family systems activity related to this is to allow the adult to have their own piece of jewelry or transitional item that has been "charged with love" by the child. The caregiver can trade the item out for "recharging" by the child at the end of the day (not unlike anxiety anchors). As the item is normalized as part of the family routine, the likelihood that the child will use it increases.

Transition Hallways for Separation Anxiety *At, B, N*

Therapeutic Rationale:

Treating separation anxiety presents unique challenges compared to other clinical concerns, largely due to external factors that can significantly influence a child's progress—with school or daycare policies often being the most impactful. Diagnostic complexity is also a key consideration: The child's developmental stage, trauma history, and circumstances (e.g., domestic violence in the home, family member with a terminal illness, incarcerated caregiver) are all areas where a diagnosis of separation anxiety disorder would not be appropriate.

This intervention assumes that an accurate diagnosis has been made; that is, the presenting issue is an adjustment-related difficulty, and that the school or daycare environment is supportive of the therapeutic process. Also, while the focus here is on separation anxiety in educational or childcare settings, the core strategies can be adapted and applied to other separation contexts as well. The content has been intentionally written to support that flexibility.

Separation anxiety is normal and appropriate for all children. It would be more concerning if a two-year-old separated easily from their attachment figure without any reaction at all (but that's a different book). As a baseline, for children up to seven or eight years old, developmentally appropriate separation anxiety typically resolves within five to thirteen minutes after separation, and this adjustment period generally improves over the course of 7 to 10 days. For many kids, you would never even know it was happening.

When this process is interrupted, rushed, or otherwise impeded, especially for kids with an already anxious disposition, the risk of developing clinically significant symptoms increases significantly. Other things that are unhelpful for adults to do include:

- Labeling reactive behaviors such as crying, whining, clinging, running, and full-blown meltdowns as "disruptive" or "attention-seeking"
- Hastening the separation in general (not just unhelpful but counterproductive)
- Telling the child not to worry or that they should be over it by now
- Not regulating their own anxiety before attempting to help the child
- The caregiver being allowed to walk their child all the way into the school (three days of this is the absolute limit)

In the first two weeks of school, a child's job should be learning to self-regulate before focusing on tasks, socializing in a meaningful way, and processing new rules and structural expectations.

Goals:

- Resolve age-appropriate presentation of separation anxiety
- Improve recognition of more than one perceived attachment figure in each environment

- Create boundaries for safety in instructional settings
- Use a physical and visual cue to transition from one task to another*

Materials:

- Rolls of green and red duct tape or gymnasium tape
- Hallway (entrance to school, daycare, etc.)

Directions:

1. In the front hallway, just beyond the office, lay down a green line of duct tape from wall to wall (like a starting line for a race). At the other end of the hallway, entering into the instructional zone of the school, lay down a red line of duct tape (like a finish line). Be sure to communicate with custodial staff about this intervention before laying any tape down.
2. Allow caregivers or a positive peer to walk with the child into the transitional space while holding their hand.
3. At the red line, the care of the child is directly hand-to-hand transitioned to a school staff person (e.g., teacher, hall monitor, office staff, principal, vice principal).
4. The child can then have a ritual goodbye with the primary caregiver and proceed down the hallway with the staff person.
5. As they move down the hallway with the transitional caregiver, the child can share three great things, their favorite part of school, or even why they are important. If needed, the adult can prompt these questions. This practice helps the child initiate their day with a positive self-perception and engaging growth mindset, and promotes the age-appropriate timeline for resolution of social anxiety to occur naturally in the space and without need for specialized accommodation.
6. Caregivers may remain in the transition hallway until *they* have regulated and are able to leave.

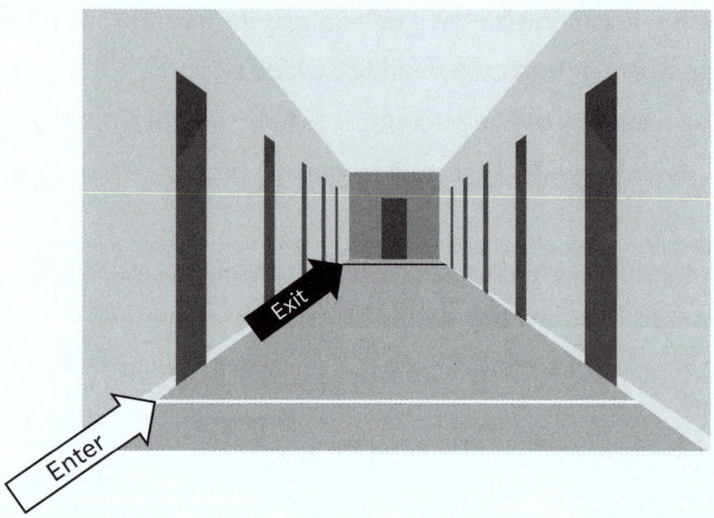

* This can also be a remarkably effective tool for children with symptoms of autism, who often require physical movement and visual engagement to improve transitioning in their world.

The Five Senses Scavenger Hunt / Sensory Soothing Box C, D, S

Therapeutic Rationale:

This intervention expands on the use of sensory input for anxiety management and regulation. By encouraging the child to explore and identify their sensory needs and preferences, this activity reinforces the notion that soothing anxiety can happen anywhere and anytime.

Note: Individual sensory experiences and abilities should be taken into consideration before engaging in this intervention.

Goals:

- Develop skills for managing intense emotions and urges
- Decrease likelihood of escape or avoidance; promote self-regulation
- Create a sensory soothing item

Materials:

- *The Five Senses Scavenger Hunt* worksheet
- Sensory soothing container (e.g., shoebox for younger kids, drawstring backpack for adolescents)
- Plastic sealable baggies
- A number of small sensory items
- Phone or camera

Directions:

1. Ahead of session, place sensory items around your office or space. At least three items should appeal to each of the five senses, such as fabric swatches of differing textures, scented tea light candles, sugar-free candy, lotion, or toys that make noise.
2. Explain to the child that sensory items can help them self-soothe:

   "All around us are things that cue our five senses. [Introduce the five primary sensory areas with examples.] *How we experience those cues are unique to each person, and we can use the ones that are soothing to us to help our brains worry less and our bodies remain calm. Today we're going to explore which sensory experiences help you with this."*

3. Introduce *The Five Senses Scavenger Hunt* activity sheet, a container, and a few plastic baggies. The easier these bags are to open, the better—those with large, external zippers work well. Invite the child to explore the space to find at least one item for each sense that they experience as pleasing, soothing, calming, or helping them "chill."

4. Ask the child to find several items in each sensory area and add them to their sensory soothing container.
    a. Do not offer or allow clients to use items that could be utilized for self-harm, such as paperclips, rubber bands, or acetone-based chemicals.
    b. To avoid combining scented items, you can provide a plastic baggie for that item and then place it in the bigger container.
    c. For items too big to fit in the container, consider taking a photo of the item or placing small pieces of the soothing object into the bag.
5. After items are gathered, review the contents of the soothing box with the child. Have them show you each item and explain or show you how it is soothing or calming for them. Once this is completed, the item can be placed back in the container for future use. If they are unable to do this, do not include the item in the container.
    a. Children with trauma history often identify or collect items that are *familiar* but not necessarily *soothing* to their senses (e.g., a scent connected to a location where abuse occurred, a song that was playing at the time of a car accident). Clinical judgment is crucial here, and these types of trigger items should *not* remain in the soothing container.
    b. Children with anxiety/trauma histories are often good at soothing others but not themselves. If the child repeatedly demonstrates how the item might be soothing for you but struggles with using it themselves, gently redirect them to "show me how you use this."
6. Discuss ways the child can use their items covertly in their life to help prevent or cope with anxiety (e.g., rubbing a piece of fabric while at the grocery store, during a visitation hearing, or in a high-conflict family session).
7. Encourage the child to use their items as needed and to feel free to add or remove items as needed.

Note: The core of this intervention is the creation of the sensory soothing box—most importantly, the reviewing of the items added to it. The scavenger hunt is there to add a playful component; feel free to adjust as needed!

Tier 2 or 3*

School, Treatment, and Community Settings

Sensory boxes are good for performance-based anxiety, such as taking a test or speaking in front of the class. Have the child spend 10 minutes with their box ahead of the "performance" (outside of the environment when possible), engage in the task for 20 minutes, and then spend 10 minutes of free-range movement or with the box again.

* This intervention may be tier 2 or tier 3 based on the number of children you are working with.

Worksheet

The Five Senses Scavenger Hunt

Your mission is to find at least one item in each area of your five senses that helps you feel calm, relaxed, happy, mellow, chilled out, or content. Some things can be used for more than one sense.

Sight 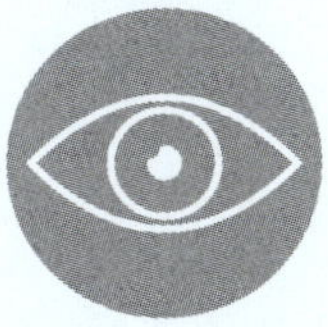	
Touch 	
Taste 	
Smell 	
Sound 	

If the things you find can fit in your container, place them there. If the item won't fit, take a picture or draw or write about it on this worksheet. You can even make a song or dance! When you're done, everything will go in your box so you can use it again later.

Quiet Time (QT) C, S, N

Therapeutic Rationale:

Taking quiet time is a proactive, front-end strategy that allows a child to intentionally self-regulate before moving into scheduled activities. Asking someone to immediately engage in something after leaving a busy or sensory-intense environment is often counterproductive to academic or therapeutic success. By inserting a brief three- to five-minute pause—kept intentionally short to prevent it from becoming an avoidance opportunity—children can support self-regulation before engaging in another task.

Goals:

- Decrease anxiety by injecting a pause for self-regulation
- Decrease baseline ANS activity before engaging in higher-order cognitive/processing tasks
- Practice skills in a variety of different environments

Materials:

- Chair (e.g., bean bag chair for younger children, hammock chair for adolescents)
- Sand timer
- Soothing items (e.g., a stuffie, simple art supplies, calming music)

> **Note:** Individual sensory experiences and abilities should be taken into consideration before engaging in this intervention. Soothing items can also be individualized if you are working with a single child (tier 3 application). For instance, you might use the prepared sensory soothing box created during *The Five Senses Scavenger Hunt / Sensory Soothing Box* intervention.

Directions:

1. Explain to the child the importance of the pause:

   "Sometimes when our day starts busy and stressful, all we can think about is our worries. This makes it hard for our brains to work on anything else and to focus. If we take a few minutes first *to help our body and brain calm down, called quiet time, then we are better able to get other things done well."*

2. Before taking some quiet time, have the child identify a soothing item they want to bring with them, either from their sensory soothing box (see *The Five Senses Scavenger Hunt / Sensory Soothing Box* intervention on page 75) or others you've made available.

3. Have the child go to the quiet time space immediately upon entering a therapeutic or academic environment. The space should include a comfortable place to sit.

4. Explain to the child that they are going to take some quiet time before they start their day/task. Show them the timer so they can track how much time they have left, if needed. Allow the child to start the sand timer for an increased sense of control.
5. When the timer is up, let the child know it is time to get started on their day/task. Give them recognition for the quiet time they've taken.

Tier 1 or 3

School, Treatment, and Community Settings

Quiet time is an excellent whole-group practice to use at transition times for improved processing, attention, and emotional regulation.

Say What You Mean and Mean What You Say C

Therapeutic Rationale:

Anxiety often fuels catastrophic thinking and negative predictions about social interactions, leading children to become overly agreeable or helpful. Kids may find it "easier" to give in to these anxious thoughts, even to their own detriment, and inadvertently create patterns where they are taken advantage of into adulthood. Proactively teaching tactful assertiveness—such as using "I" statements—helps children recognize their comfort levels, set healthy boundaries, and avoid overextending themselves.

Goals:

- Practice assertiveness with tact
- Use "I" statements in communication
- Practice preemptive boundary setting paired with confident eye contact and body posture

Materials:

- *The Four Steps of "I" Statements* handout
- *"I" Statements Practice Scenarios* worksheet
- *Anxiety Rating Scale* worksheet
- Mirror or video recording device

Directions:

1. Explain to the client the importance of boundaries:

   "Sometimes anxiety feels worse when we lack confidence in saying no or setting boundaries. There are times when it's appropriate to set limits—such as when someone is taking advantage of us or encouraging harmful behavior—and times when saying no is inappropriate, like avoiding classwork or chores. We need to learn how to assert ourselves in healthy ways. Today we'll discuss how to tell the difference and practice communicating assertively."

2. Ask the client to think of a time when they had difficulty communicating their opinion to someone or felt taken advantage of by another person.
3. Have the client use the *Anxiety Rating Scale* worksheet (see page 62) to decide where on the scale they would rate having a conversation with this individual about what happened. Then decide together whether this conversation is a real possibility or not.
4. Encourage the client to reflect on the potential motive of the other individual (e.g., gain power or control, manipulate a situation, get out of a responsibility).
5. Discuss the best possible outcome: How would it feel to have this conversation? How would they know it was successful? What do they want out of it?

6. Introduce *The Four Steps of "I" Statements* handout and then practice scenarios using the *"I" Statements Practice Scenarios* worksheet, using as many of them as needed to get a good idea of the concept.
7. Role-play "I" statements with the client to communicate thoughts and feelings regarding the interaction, including nonverbal communication like body posture and eye contact.
8. Depending on the scenario, play the "devil's advocate" to help prepare the client for legitimate pushback.
9. Return to the *Anxiety Rating Scale* worksheet so the client can reassess their level of anxiety after role-playing.
10. Encourage the client to continue practicing in front of a mirror or recording themselves and watching it back. This self-monitoring will help reinforce the skills, particularly the nonverbal communication.

Tier 1

School, Treatment, and Community Settings

Assertiveness is beneficial for everyone and doesn't need to be time-consuming. Post *The Four Steps of "I" Statements* handout in a shared space or at individual desks, or send copies home to caregivers.

Handout

The Four Steps of "I" Statements

Step 1
"I feel . . . "

Step 2
"When . . . "

Effective "I" Statements

Step 3
"Because . . . "

Step 4
"This is what I need . . . "

Worksheet

"I" Statement Practice Scenarios

1. Your teacher seems to call on other people, but not you.

   I feel: ____________________

   When: ____________________

   Because: ____________________

   This is what I need: ____________________

2. Your friend always tells you they get to go first when you are playing games.

   I feel: ____________________

   When: ____________________

   Because: ____________________

   This is what I need: ____________________

3. You feel like you do more housework than your sibling.

   I feel: ____________________

   When: ____________________

   Because: ____________________

   This is what I need: ____________________

4. Your neighbor always asks you to help them with their yard.

   I feel: ____________________

   When: ____________________

   Because: ____________________

   This is what I need: ____________________

5. A kid at your lunch table keeps asking you if they can have some of your food.

   I feel: ______________________________

   When: ______________________________

   Because: ______________________________

   This is what I need: ______________________________

6. The same kid in class always asks to look at your work before they finish theirs.

   I feel: ______________________________

   When: ______________________________

   Because: ______________________________

   This is what I need: ______________________________

7. Your grandparent talks a lot about your weight or clothes.

   I feel: ______________________________

   When: ______________________________

   Because: ______________________________

   This is what I need: ______________________________

Your Support Net   *C, Soc, T*

Therapeutic Rationale:

Even with constant digital "connection," many young people struggle to form genuine, supportive relationships. Fear of rejection, limited social skills, and existing anxiety often contribute to this challenge (and the isolation from the COVID-19 pandemic didn't help on this front). More than simply making a list of people they know, this intervention helps clients assess the quality of their relationships, set realistic expectations within them, and recognize which people are best suited to help with specific problems. Having reliable, supportive people across settings and situations strengthens the ability to manage discomfort and navigate unexpected changes more effectively. It also reduces overreliance on specific individuals, such as therapists and school counselors.

Remember, just because a person is *in* a child's life, it doesn't mean they are a healthy or appropriate support. For example, in homes where there is significant substance use, chronic incarceration, limited adult supervision, or poverty, the likelihood that the child can rely on the adults at home is minimal. For some kids, this exercise may bring up difficult realizations about family—the people who *should* be there for them (which is all the more reason to create the net). Take the time to also explore neighbors, extended family members, coaches, siblings, and community members as possible "net people."

Note: My use of support "net" is intentional to convey the concept of people who will "catch" the client on their hard, medium, and good days. I recommend against using the phrase *support system*, as it may carry a negative connotation for kids involved in, or familiar with, external systems such as juvenile justice, child protective services, or other social services (i.e., the "system").

Goals:

- Expand social support
- Explore trustworthiness in others
- Validate the phrase "I am not alone"
- Develop prefrontal connections with cause and effect for behaviors
- Improve the ability to stay present in an environment with healthy support

Materials:

- Invitations (paper or electronic)
- *Who Will Be in Your Support Net?* worksheet
- *Your Support Net Calendar* template

Directions:

1. Explain to the client the importance of support people:

   "When we are struggling with anxiety on an especially hard day, being alone with this feeling only makes things worse. It's important to find people who can support us during those hard moments! We also need support on the days in the middle where we just need a little help, as well as on good days when we want to share good news. As you can imagine, this usually isn't just one person doing it all! We want to create a 'net' of people we can reach out to for different things at different times."

2. Help the client begin a list of "net people" in their lives. Have them use the *Who Will Be in Your Support Net?* worksheet if they need some help coming up with people. Start with identifying one person who is available during business/school hours.
   a. If they have trouble thinking of someone, you can be the first to volunteer. Make it clear that you are available to them during specific times with expectations clearly stated (e.g., You will return their call within two hours anytime between 7 a.m. and 6 p.m.). Be sure to stick to the plan yourself to avoid blurring boundaries or reinforcing negative behaviors, as kids will test limits!
   b. After they have accessed you appropriately three times, it's time to brainstorm people who are available when you are not, so you can add more "weave" to the net (especially during times outside of the hours you are available).
   c. If you have a kid that already has some great support net people, don't hesitate to move beyond this step!

3. Have the client invite each person to be a part of their net using a text message, note, or electronic invitation. The key is for the client to clearly define what it means to be available for support and ask for confirmation:
   a. "I would like to ask you to be in my support net."
   b. "I would like you to be available to me on Monday, Wednesday, and Friday between 6 p.m. and 9 p.m."
   c. "I will not just reach out to you with the tough times, but also when I have something great I want to share with you, because I trust you."
   d. "Please RSVP and let me know if you agree to be a support person for me."

4. As the client receives RSVPs, add them to the *Your Support Net Calendar* template for visual reference by writing their name, drawing a picture, or cutting out a photo of the person. Place the reference on the corresponding day/time they agreed to. The client may also color in boxes for different locations or other identifiers.

5. The client should continue to expand their support net to cover all times in the day and all days of the week (adding weave to the net in a healthy way).

6. Prepare the client that some people may say no. They may not be capable of participating because of their schedule or their own responsibilities. But encourage the client not to give up on the person after an initial no. A good response for this is, "They're just saying no for now, but later they might be able to help you. The good news is that we have a clear answer and you know where things stand."

Tier 1 or 3

School, Treatment, and Community Settings

The support net intervention is especially useful during discharge planning from treatment or when a child is transitioning back to school. Identifying supportive people *before* discharge helps ease the transition, reduces dependence on support staff, and lessens the likelihood of repeat hospitalizations or further unplanned breaks from school.

Worksheet

Who Will Be in Your Support Net?

It's important to develop a support net with the *right* people. Use this guide to help you brainstorm some people who might be available for you to contact in the good and the difficult times.

1. Who is always there for you, even when you feel frustrated?

    ____

2. Who cares about how you're feeling when you get upset?

    ____

3. Who makes you feel good about yourself, even when you don't?

    ____

4. Who helps you calm down the quickest?

    ____

5. Who explains things to you in a way you can understand?

    ____

6. Who is someone who is friendly and kind to others?

    ____

7. Who is someone who likes to help others?

    ____

8. Who is someone who is good at solving problems?

    ____

9. What time of the day is the hardest for you to pay attention or work hard? Who is available during those times?

    ____

10. Where do you go when you want to calm down and feel happy? Who is usually there?

    ____

Template

Your Support Net Calendar

	Early Morning	Middle of the Day	Afternoon	Evening
Monday				
Tuesday				
Wednesday				
Thursday				
Friday				
Saturday				
Sunday				

Passcode Word (Younger Ages and Stages) *C, N, T*

Therapeutic Rationale:

Kids with anxiety who are younger, either chronologically or developmentally, often seek constant reassurance that they are okay, healthy, or safe, particularly during transitions. This can be taxing for caregivers and support staff, who may end up responding with exasperation through tone of voice, nonverbal communication, or invalidating comments, which increases a child's anxiety and decreases the likelihood they will ask for help in the future. Using a code word between adult and child is a quick and concise intervention to communicate safety without having to use repetitive reassurance. It serves as a "stamp of approval" from a trusted caregiver that can be used in a variety of person-to-person transitions.

Keeping this passcode protected and private within the child's family is crucial to the effectiveness of this tool. If the word is openly shared, the protective veil is lifted: The word loses its meaning and anxiety will increase. However, you should avoid referring to the word as a "secret," as this is a common phrase adults use as a means for grooming. Relatedly, refer to gifts and parties as "surprises," and teach kids to inform a safe adult if anyone encourages them to keep a secret.

Goals:

- Create a quick communication tool that conveys safety and reassurance
- Reduce anxiety during transitions in different environments

Materials:

- *Making a Passcode Word* worksheet

Directions:

1. Explain to the client why a passcode is important:

   "Sometimes we need to be told lots of times that something, someone, or someplace is okay. That can take a bunch of time, and it keeps us from starting what we need to because we are worrying. We are going to create one word with your caregivers that will be a signal that all *of your worry questions can be answered. When you hear that word, you'll know right away that the person, place, or activity is okay."*

2. Using the *Making a Passcode Word* worksheet, direct the client and their family to agree on one passcode word that will remain *private* between only them and other trusted adults.

3. Role-play the use of the word in typical anxiety-inducing situations. For example:

   a. Someone unexpected picks the client up from school or an activity.

   b. The client meets a new teacher or counselor.

c. Someone rings the doorbell and asks the client if they can come inside.

d. The client starts a new therapeutic group or extracurricular activity.

4. Encourage the client and their caregivers to use their passcode whenever needed.

Tier 3

School, Treatment, and Community Settings

This technique is quick and effective for young children struggling with increased anxiety with transitions, especially when changing educators and support staff or moving between settings. If you are working with youth who are easily influenced or manipulated by their peers, this tool is also for you. By being a source of protection in appropriate safety situations, you have bonded yourself as a trusted attachment figure, which also decreases children's anxiety.

Worksheet

Making a Passcode Word

Like a passcode unlocks a safe, a passcode word unlocks *safety*. This kind of passcode is a special word that will only be shared with and used by adults you really trust, like your caregivers. When they say the passcode word, it means that the activity, place, situation, or person you're worried about is okay and safe for you to be around. This worksheet will help you create your passcode word.

What are some questions you would ask to know whether a situation or person is safe?
Example: Do my caregivers trust this person?

1. ______________________________
2. ______________________________
3. ______________________________
4. ______________________________
5. ______________________________

Now pick a word that will stand for "Yes, it's safe!" (answering all of your worry questions at once). Write this word in the box below. The word you and your family pick should be:

1. Uncommon (not used a lot), so it stands out when you hear it
2. A little funny, as it can help you feel better in your brain
3. Easy to remember
4. Agreed upon by every member of the family

Passcode Word (Older Ages and Stages) *C, At, T*

Therapeutic Rationale

Older children and teens—either chronologically or developmentally—often experience anxiety that makes it difficult to assert themselves with peers, especially those they see as more powerful, popular, or admirable. Even when a situation feels uncomfortable or risky, many default to "going with the flow," increasing the likelihood that they will make poor decisions, such as substance use or other risky behaviors. While avoidance isn't always negative, and can be a form of self-protection, these youth often lack the confidence to voice their discomfort. For this age group, the passcode word serves as a tool to discreetly activate a supportive adult who can "be the bad guy" and provide a safe exit from challenging social situations, which reduces the risk of peer rejection.

Keeping this word protected and private within the family is crucial to the effectiveness of this tool. If the word is openly shared, the protective veil is lifted: The word loses meaning and anxiety will increase. However, avoid referring to the word as a "secret," as this is a common phrase adults use as a means for grooming. Relatedly, refer to gifts and parties as "surprises," and teach kids to inform a safe adult if anyone encourages them to keep a secret.

Goals

- Provide quick communication that means "I need help"
- Decrease anxiety in potentially dangerous social situations where appropriate avoidance should be practiced
- Promote improved collaborative caregiver-child relations

Materials:

- *Communication Contract* worksheet
- Optional: *Making a Passcode Word* worksheet

Directions:

1. Explain to the client why a passcode word is important:

   "When we are out with friends who want to make poor choices, it can be hard to assert ourselves and say no, because worries about being left out or rejected can get in the way of positive choices. We are going to use a passcode word as a way for you to call for help from an adult when your anxiety gets in the way of protecting you."

2. Have the client work with their family to agree on one passcode word that will remain *private* between only them. You may use the *Making a Passcode Word* worksheet on page 92 or create the word by brainstorming on a separate sheet of paper.

3. The client and their caregivers should sign the *Communication Contract* worksheet to establish safe caregiver protection plans.
4. Role-play the use of the word in typical anxiety-inducing situations. For example, a client's friends might try to convince them to:
    a. Drink or use drugs
    b. Trespass on private property
    c. Fight with someone
    d. Break curfew
    e. Bully someone on social media
5. Encourage the client and their family to use their passcode word whenever needed. The client should also be sure to educate their support net about the phrase: When the support person hears this word, they should follow through with support *immediately*.

Worksheet

Communication Contract

I know that going out with my friends is a privilege I have worked hard to earn, and I get to keep this privilege by agreeing to the following:

1. When I am out with my friends, I **agree to call my caregivers** at ______________________ p.m. and ______________________ p.m. If I do not call at these times, I expect them to attempt to contact me.
2. I will let my caregivers know my plans with friends. If these plans change in any way, I will call my caregivers and **ask permission** before I do anything different.
3. I will let my caregivers know who I am with and provide them with the contact information for the adults who will be there. My caregivers will **meet my friends and their families** before I am allowed to go somewhere without supervision.
4. I will follow curfew unless I have **obtained permission** otherwise. I will call immediately if I know I will not be home on time.
5. I will use the passcode word any time I **do not feel safe** or I am uncomfortable with something my friends want me to do. My caregivers will help me *immediately* if I use the passcode word.

______________________________ ______________________
Signature (child/teen) Date

______________________________ ______________________
Signature (caregiver) Date

3

Depression

Depression among children and adolescents continues to rise, alongside increases in suicidal thoughts and self-harm. Chronic sleep deprivation, mounting academic pressure, and a lack of meaningful connection—often replaced by superficial engagement on social media—are leaving young people feeling hopeless, unworthy, and unsure of who they are or where they belong at a time when forming identity is already difficult.

While depression is often associated with "low-gas-in-the-tank" symptoms, such as lethargy, low mood, indecision, and fatigue, it can also present in less recognized, more *active* ways—through agitation, irritability, anger, and stubbornness. Because this presentation is frequently misinterpreted as a behavioral problem rather than a mood disturbance or depressive episode, traditional consequences may exacerbate symptoms by invalidating the individual's emotional experience and increasing dysregulation, furthering risk of self-harm or suicidal ideation.

In other words, depression is more complex and delicate than many of us realize. Depression is more than a mood.

This chapter draws on evidence-based interventions from well-supported therapeutic approaches, such as DBT, social rhythm theory, mindfulness, and CBT. The crux of this work is *validation*, which I define as the experience of being truly heard, believed, and affirmed.

Remember, a depressed mind bombards an individual with messages of *I'm not good enough*, *It doesn't matter anyway*, and *No one cares*, so when a young person who is depressed asks for help, it's a huge, risky step for them that must be handled with care.

The interventions in this chapter will focus on shifting mindset for learning skills, including:

- Validating clients to grow hope, worth, and social engagement
- Improving self-esteem and self-concept
- Reversing lethargy and low motivation
- Preventing suicidal ideation and self-injury

Note: While there are certainly comorbidities among depression and other disorders (especially ADHD and anxiety), the interventions in this chapter aim to address depression (and its full spectrum of symptom presentation) specifically. I recommend blending these interventions with those from other chapters too.

Key Concept

Validation: Consistent validation of a child leads to regulation, confidence, emotional stability, and hope for the future.

Case Example

Billy, 12, was referred to me for assessment and treatment of "clear oppositional and defiant behaviors." When he arrives, his movement is sloth-like, sidling to the chair and almost folding in half with collapsed posture. Initially, his only response to questions during intake is a slight shrug of his shoulders. When he does eventually speak, his vocal tone is low and mumbled. He asks more than once when the appointment will be over and has limited affective expression outside of occasional breakthrough anger and agitation, including cursing toward his mother when he thinks her responses are incorrect.

Billy is failing most of his classes at school and receives detentions and suspensions regularly for being argumentative or defiant. His mother indicates, "He is a real problem at home and school, and has been like this since he was 8." She lists multiple failures in socialization, academic performance, and behavioral compliance. She says, "The school has seen that he was a behavior problem for a very long time, and he might end up getting expelled. I'm exhausted." Billy has a limited group of peers that he interacts with beyond online gaming, rarely leaves his room, no longer goes to meetings for the Dungeons and Dragons Club (once his favorite), and eats nothing his mother makes for dinner.

Billy's mom seems surprised when I inquire about a family history of mood issues, any sleep and eating routines in the home, and whether Billy has ever made threats of harm to himself. She says, "Well, yes. He said he wanted to kill himself a few months ago, but that was just to get attention."

At this point in the interview, Billy sits up in his chair and answers some questions independently and with thoughtful reflection. When he leaves the intake—and out of earshot of his mother—he pauses and says to me, "Everyone thinks I'm just a bad kid, but I really feel empty all the time and just don't care."

No one has taught Billy:

- All thoughts and feelings are valid.
- Everyone is worthy and has value.
- Everyone is capable of success.
- We are more than what people see on the outside.

Depression Key Concept

Validation

Validation is the active practice of acknowledging, recognizing, and nonjudgmentally engaging with another individual's thoughts, feelings, and behaviors. Validation allows the other person to feel heard, connected, and worthy. Validation says *Your experiences matter.*

Consistent validation → ***Regulation, confidence, emotional stability, hope for the future***

Conversely, *invalidation* is communicating to someone through words or actions that what they are thinking, doing, or feeling is not legitimate, true, or meaningful, leading them to feel unseen, ashamed, isolated, and full of self-doubt. Invalidation says *Your experiences are wrong.*

Consistent invalidation → ***Low self-concept, worthlessness, hopelessness, persistent dysregulation***

Let's say a student in class is clearly frustrated by the current assignment she's supposed to be doing independently. Her head is down on the desk, her laptop is pushed away, and she's muttering, "I can't do this, and no one cares anyway." Consider the two different paths the educator in the class might take.

Invalidating Responses

"You can do this—just stop telling yourself you can't."

"Just go find someone to help you!"

Validating Responses

"I agree, this is something new and a bit confusing. Let's work to figure it out together."

"I'm sorry you are frustrated right now. Give me two minutes and I'll come back to help."

Note that both sets of responses are attempts to be helpful. However, the invalidating responses jump immediately to solutions, and the use of "just" suggests those solutions should be easy to do. The validating side, on the other hand, tries to connect with the student's experience first and conveys that support is available when she's ready. The shift is subtle and crucial.

Depression Beast

C

Therapeutic Rationale:

This intervention aims to improve the client's awareness of their depressive symptoms and the conditions that contribute to making it better or worse. It uses a depression "beast" to help clients conceptualize their experience of depression and start to identify what "feeds" it (i.e., makes it worse) while also externalizing it as something outside of who they are, which can help to transform it into something they can change.

Goals:

- Increase awareness of symptoms of depression
- Identify thoughts, feelings, and behaviors that occur during depressive episodes
- Externalize symptoms and experience of depression

Materials:

- *Depression Beast* worksheet
- Variety of art supplies (e.g., colored pencils, crayons)

Directions:

1. Explain to the client the concept of a depression beast:

   "Depression is more than just feeling sad. Sometimes it's when we feel down, tired, or grumpy for a long time—weeks or even months—and it starts getting in the way of school, friendships, or fun. When we're depressed, it feels like there's a heavy beast on our back, weighing us down and affecting how we think, feel, and behave. Everyone's depression beast looks different. Today we're going to explore yours."

2. Walk through the *Depression Beast* worksheet with the client, encouraging as much information as possible. Younger children may need additional prompting.

3. Consider asking the client to give the beast a name—this helps externalize symptoms, separates the depression from who the client is as a person, and can serve as a quick verbal cue for awareness (e.g., "Is Beasty nearby?").

4. After the activity, offer some reflection prompts. For example:
   a. "How large is your depression beast? Does its size change?"
   b. "What color is it?"
   c. "If it had a motto, what would it be?"
   d. "How close is it to you right now?"

e. "Can you ask it to step away so you can [*get homework done, be with friends, etc.*]?"

f. "What 'feeds' your beast, making depression worse?"

5. Encourage the client to share their beast with a trusted adult or friend to help others understand what they are going through and how they can help.

Tier 3

School, Treatment, and Community Settings

Helping a kid identify and describe their depression beast, including how it shows itself in the setting in which you work, improves your ability to provide support. For example, noticing a student's hygiene has declined or that they have been withdrawing from classmates may be clues that improve your awareness of situational contributors to the depression presentation. This allows you to address triggers for depression you may not have recognized, as well as realistically adapt the environment to functionally meet the needs of that individual. For example, certain phrases used in group feedback, such as "That's not right," may be perceived as failure, increasing a child's task and social withdrawal. With this knowledge, you can be more aware of your words when addressing students.

Worksheet

Depression Beast

Depression can feel like a heavy beast on your back, affecting how you feel, think, and behave. Use this worksheet to explain with words or images what it's like when you feel depressed.

Your depression beast's name: ______________________

How You Feel (e.g., sad, irritated)

Thoughts You Have (e.g., "Things won't get better," "There's no point in trying")

What You Do (e.g., sleep a lot, snap back at people)

Is Your Depression Beast Nearby? C

Therapeutic Rationale:

This intervention further expands on the *Depression Beast* intervention by helping the client identify signs or "pink flags" (i.e., prodromal symptoms) that indicate they may be at risk for increased severity of depressive symptoms. By identifying both internal and external signs, the client can use this awareness to proactively intervene and rein in the beast to gain control over their symptoms.

Goals:

- Increase awareness of internal and external signals of depression onset

Materials:

- *Is Your Depression Beast Nearby?* worksheet
- Variety of art supplies (e.g., colored pencils, crayons)

Directions:

1. Explain to the client the signs of incoming depression:

   "Even though it feels like our depression beast comes out of nowhere, there are usually ways to tell when it's sneaking closer. We call these 'pink flags'—not quite full-blown red flags that the beast has taken over, but signals that it may be approaching. When we are more aware, we can do something to help protect ourselves before *it comes and takes us over. Today we're going to identify your pink flags."*

2. Introduce the client to the *Is Your Depression Beast Nearby?* worksheet to help them discover their "pink flags." If they are having difficulty coming up with signs that their beast is near, encourage them to consider what other people might notice (or even have them ask people). For example, are they lying in bed for several hours at a time, eating less than normal, or skipping basic hygiene tasks?

3. Discuss with the client that the proximity of the beast should be checked on regularly, and help use that information to empower them to make healthy choices. For example, a client's pink flag might be that they don't brush their teeth regularly; when this happens, they will make an effort to do so as well as call to make an appointment with you.

Tier 3

School, Treatment, and Community Settings

This intervention is customizable to any setting. In schools, pink flags may look like a child engaging less in class discussions or frequently arriving late. In therapeutic groups, the flags may look like decreased participation, shrugging off responses, or passing on their turn to contribute to discussion. Knowing this information can help you provide more meaningful support.

Worksheet

Is Your Depression Beast Nearby?

Even though it feels like your depression beast comes out of nowhere, there are usually ways to tell when it's sneaking closer. Use the spaces below to write or draw "pink flags" that your depression beast is approaching.

What are three steps you can take to stop the beast from getting closer?

1. ____

____

2. ____

____

3. ____

____

Flip the Switch (Opposite Action) *C, D, N*

Therapeutic Rationale:

This intervention targets depression-reinforcing behaviors (e.g., laying around, procrastinating, failing to eat for several hours, skipping hygiene tasks) that have become habituated over time to create a baseline of lethargy, fatigue, and low motivation. A core skill from DBT, opposite action (OA) activities replace habitual behaviors with more adaptive ones to create a new emotional state, which can improve self-awareness, motivation, and mood. (Levels of feel-good neurotransmitters like dopamine and norepinephrine increase with OA activities.) Using the metaphor of a switch is a concrete way to conceptualize OA for young clients—with one small action, the situation can completely change.

> **Note:** If you've completed the *Depression Beast* and *Is Your Depression Beast Nearby?* interventions, it will be helpful to continue the metaphor in this intervention and beyond, adding OA options as they are explored.

Goals:

- Increase motivation and decrease lethargy
- Expand social support
- Redirect depressive thoughts and behaviors

Materials:

- *What Is Opposite Action?* handout
- *Flip the Switch* worksheet

Directions:

1. Explain opposite action to the client:

    "When we feel depressed (or when the depression beast is around), it's easy to fall into unhealthy habits like laying around a lot, scrolling too much, skipping hygiene tasks, or withdrawing from our friends. And even though we know these things are not helping us to feel better, it's hard to find motivation to change them. Opposite action, or doing the opposite, is a helpful tool for this."

2. Provide psychoeducation by reviewing the *What is Opposite Action?* handout with the client.
3. Complete the *Flip the Switch* worksheet with the client to help them practice changing their actions.

Tier 3

School, Treatment, and Community Settings

OA is a useful tool for academic and treatment settings, particularly with children who become dysregulated easily during transitions between classes or groups. Consider creating an "OA container" with simple and safe OA activities to be drawn from to help support children during these times.

Handout

What Is Opposite Action?

Opposite action (OA) is an emotional regulation skill where you intentionally do the *opposite* of what your feelings are telling you to do. It's like a little trick for your brain that works because how you behave changes how you feel (not the other way around). Depression often tells you *not* to do something helpful (e.g., laying around, isolating yourself from friends and family, skipping meals), which can make your mood worse. With OA, you learn to *behave* differently so you can *feel* differently.

Six Tips for Getting the Most Benefit from Opposite Action

1. **OA activities should last five minutes:** Activities of at *least* five minutes are most effective in making long-term changes to your brain chemistry.
2. **Time your OA activity:** Set a timer, or better yet, do the activity with another person so you know you are finishing the full five minutes.
3. **Use your support net:** At first, it might be hard to see exactly *when* to use your OA activities, so finding someone from your support net to help you see more clearly can be helpful to start.
4. **Brainstorm a variety of OA activities:** It's best to have ideas for many activities so you can cover many places and circumstances (e.g., jumping on the trampoline, talking to a friend/family member on the phone, playing with your pet, doing a craft, dancing to music). Your brain will make excuses like "Oh, I can't do [*that activity*] right now because the situation isn't perfect."
5. **Keep an open mind and a positive (or at least neutral) mindset:** Affirmations like "I can do this," "It's only for five minutes," or "I want to feel better, so I'll try this" can be helpful.
6. **OA works quickly!** If you do these activities consistently, you can expect to start feeling better in three to seven days.

Worksheet

Flip the Switch

A helpful way to think of opposite action (OA) is like flipping a switch—one small action turns everything around. Brainstorm some OA activities that you can do when your depressed brain tells you not to do anything at all. Two examples have been provided to get you started.

What You Are Doing Now	How You Can Flip the Switch
I feel tired, so I'm going to lay in bed all day today.	Take a five-minute walk around the block. Then I can get back in bed if I want to.
I don't feel like talking to people, so I'm going to ghost everyone on texts and social media.	I can write back to at least three people, even if it's just with something simple, like an emoji.

OAs for All the Days and All the Ways **C, D, N**

Therapeutic Rationale:

This intervention builds on the *Flip Your Switch (Opposite Action)* intervention by helping clients create a ready-made list of opposite actions to use across settings and circumstances, increasing the likelihood they will use them during a depressive episode. A core skill from DBT, OA activities replace habitual behavior with more adaptive ones to create a new emotional state, which can improve self-awareness, motivation, and mood. (Levels of feel-good neurotransmitters like dopamine and norepinephrine increase with OA activities.)

Goals:

- Increase motivation and decrease lethargy
- Expand social support
- Redirect depressive thoughts and behaviors

Materials:

- *What Is Opposite Action?* handout
- *Flip the Switch* worksheet
- *OAs for all the Days and all the Ways* worksheet
- Variety of art supplies (e.g., colored pencils, crayons)
- Optional: Mason jar or other clear container

Directions:

1. Review the *What Is Opposite Action?* handout (page 109) and the *Flip the Switch* worksheet (page 110) with the client.
2. Explain to the client the importance of OAs:

   "When we feel depressed (or when our depression beast is around), we tend to rationalize not making healthier choices because the circumstances aren't just right. For example, if my OA is to go for a walk outside, but it's raining and cold, I might think, 'I guess I'll just lay here instead.' Sound familiar? The goal of this exercise is to create a list of OAs you can tap into even when the conditions might be less than perfect. Remember, OAs are literally *the opposite of what we feel like doing in that moment, so let's be prepared for all the justifications not to do them."*

3. Complete *OAs for All the Days and All the Ways* with the client.
4. Encourage the client to use this list when they are feeling unmotivated or lethargic.

Variation: Have the client decorate a mason jar or another container, cut out each OA from the worksheet (or make a separate list to be cut), and place them in the jar.

Tier 3

School, Treatment, and Community Settings

OA is a useful tool for academic and treatment settings, where children who often disengage from peers in group and classroom settings could benefit from being challenged to replace these behaviors with action and engagement. Create containers with OA activities that are appropriate for each area of the facility, and support children in selecting an item and completing the five-minute activity. You can also pair them with a peer or staff person if needed. Regular practice will result in rapid improvement in energy, focus, and participation.

Worksheet

OAs for All the Days and All the Ways

Opposite actions are *literally* the opposite of what you feel like doing when you are depressed, so it's important that you're prepared with more ideas than justifications. For each setting in the following table, write down some OAs or other activities to create a ready-made list for when your depression beast comes around.

Setting	OAs or Other Activities
Indoors	
Outdoors	
When it's sunny	
When it's raining	
When you're alone	

Setting	OAs or Other Activities
When you're with others	
At school	
In your room	
With your pet	
During the day	
During the evening/night	

The Reality Journal A, C, M

Therapeutic Rationale:

The reality journal helps clients with depression focus on smaller, bite-sized pieces of time rather than trying to tackle the past, present, and future all at once. Grounded in acceptance and commitment therapy, this intervention encourages acceptance of the reality of the moment and committing to creating a *life worth living* to decrease suffering.

Goals:

- Decrease suffering through mindful focus on the present moment
- Move past negative life events and prevent negative fortune telling

Materials:

- *What Is Suffering?* handout
- *Reality Journal Comic Book* worksheet
- Notebook
- Variety of art supplies (e.g., colored pencils, crayons)

Directions:

1. Explain to the client that they will learn to be present and focused on what is happening "right now," which we sometimes call *mindfulness*.

   "When we focus our thoughts and feelings on our memories from the past or our worries about the future, we lose sight of the reality of the here and now. This can cause us to feel weighed down, unsure of ourselves, undeserving of happiness, and hopeless that it will always be like this. This activity helps you let the unchangeable past wash away, prevent negative thoughts about a future that hasn't happened yet, and start living in the present."

2. Introduce the client to the *What Is Suffering?* handout. Remind them that thoughts of the past and the future are where depression and anxiety lie. The present moment is the one place they do have control.

3. Discuss the privacy of a journal: What the client writes does not have to be shared, though let them know that sharing may help relieve the weight of depression and daily burdens. For clients who are younger or who may like to express themselves differently, offer them the *Reality Journal Comic Book* worksheet, which lets them share their thoughts more visually.

4. **Journal Entry 1:** Ask the client to write about (or draw) one thing that happened today that resulted in them feeling sad, hurt, or worthless. Be sure that they mark the time this occurred.

5. **Journal Entry 2:** Ask the client to then write about (or draw) the first time they felt even slightly better after the problem from journal entry 1 occurred. Be sure that they mark the time this occurred.
6. Discuss with the client how the initial problem (journal entry 1) might make them feel like the bad thoughts and feelings would last forever. However, when they look at the second journal entry, they can see it only lasted [*amount of time*], and "that is a time bite you can manage, instead of all of it at once."
7. Ask the client to continue journaling throughout the day, repeating steps 4 and 5. This helps them to reflect on *smaller* pieces of time rather than chewing on the whole day, month, or multiple years (i.e., suffering).
8. Help the client recognize that problems are in fact temporary, and what makes them persist are the feelings and thoughts that hold on.
9. Have the client dispose of the list at the end of the day (saying goodbye to the past) and start fresh the next day (an active challenge of mindful moments). Explain that carrying experiences from the past (that are already done and gone) can keep them in a negative mindset that tries to influence fortune telling, contributes to feelings of hopelessness, and keeps them from being present.

Tier 2 or 3

School, Treatment, and Community Settings

This technique can be used as a whole class activity or an activity done in groups. You can adjust this slightly by using visual cues for past, present, and future, and ask kids to point to where their focus is in this moment. Perhaps they failed a test last week and cannot move past a sense of failure to successfully focus on learning new material. Help them recognize that when their brains are in the past, they cannot attend to the current lessons. In therapeutic groups, similar techniques can assist in directing kids toward what they are able to control, which is only what is in front of them.

Handout

What Is Suffering?

Painful thoughts, feelings, and experiences are an inevitable part of being human. Pain turns to *suffering* when you attempt to control, change, deny, avoid, or fight against those experiences. There are many ways we do this, but two of the most common ways are (1) *ruminating on the past* (depression) and (2) *worrying about or attempting to predict the future* (anxiety), thereby denying us the ability to be in the present moment (the one place we do have control!). In this way, suffering is a *choice* we make in response to pain.

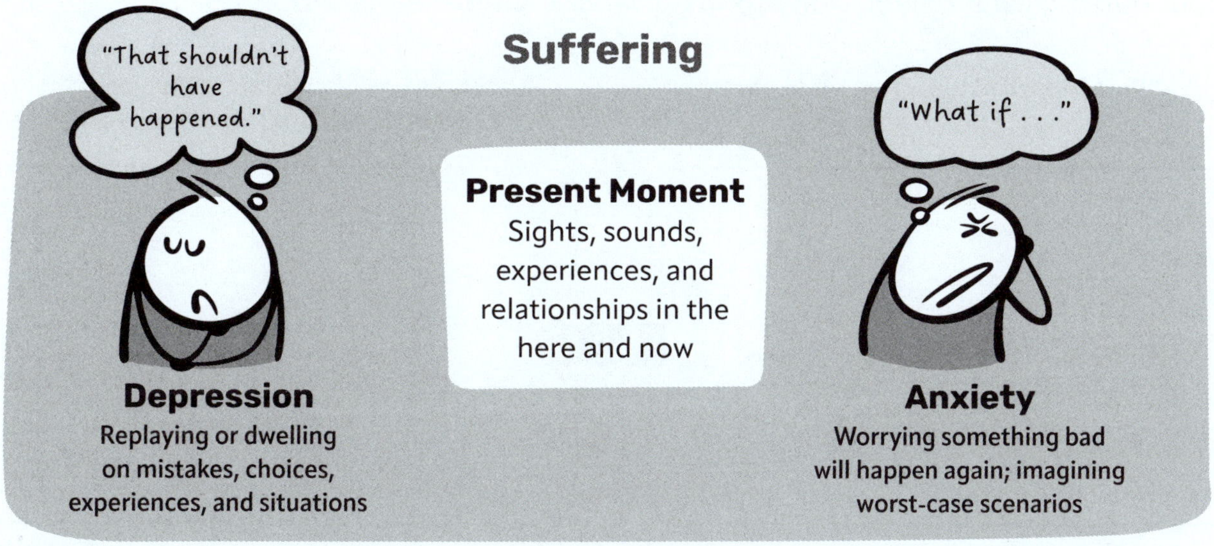

Acceptance, on the other hand, is when you acknowledge the pain without allowing it to dominate your current experience. With acceptance, you choose to focus on what you can control: the here and now.

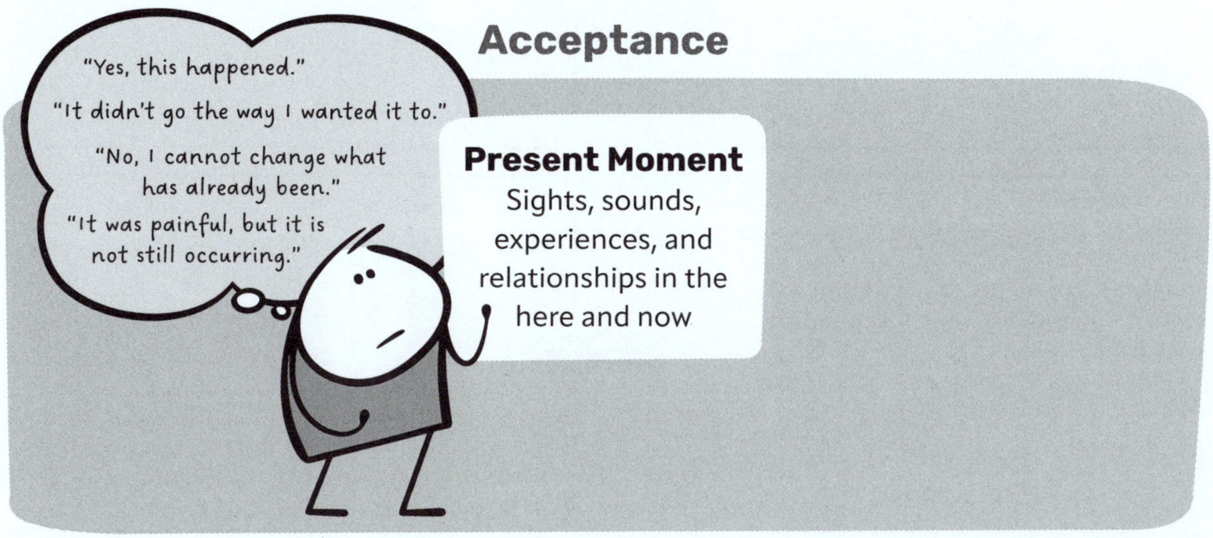

Worksheet

Reality Journal Comic Book

Continuously thinking about experiences from the past and worrying about possible events in the future can keep you in a negative mindset. This worksheet can help you learn to stay more in the here and now.

In the left box, write about (or draw) one thing that happened today that made you feel sad, hurt, or worthless. Be sure to mark the time this occurred somewhere in the box. Then, in the right box, write about (or draw) the moment that you felt even slightly better about the original problem. Don't forget to write the time in this box as well!

What happened today that made you feel sad, hurt, or worthless?		When did you feel slightly better about the event in the left box? What happened?
	→	
	→	
	→	

Self-Esteem Gift Box **C, D**

Therapeutic Rationale:

Low self-esteem and confidence are precursors to feelings of depression, hopelessness, and worthlessness, which, left unaddressed, are shown to increase suicidal ideation and self-injurious behaviors. Helping clients see through the fog of negative self-assessment to accurately recognize their strengths and abilities is the first step toward improving positive self-appraisal (and increases resilience to others' unhelpful opinions about them).

Goals:

- Identify positive self-characteristics
- Counteract feelings of hopelessness and poor self-esteem
- Create a reference point for growth and change

Materials:

- *Something Great About You* template
- Shoebox or other container
- Variety of art supplies (e.g., colored pencils, crayons)
- Variety of craft supplies (e.g., ribbons, buttons, yarn)
- Colored paper
- Photos or clippings from magazines
- Slips of paper or notecards

Directions:

1. Explain to the client the importance of positive self-image:

   "Sometimes when we feel depressed, it can be hard to see the good things about ourselves. A depressed brain tends to focus on the negative, so sometimes we have to go out of our way to bring positive things to light, especially when we don't feel good about ourselves. That's what we will do with this activity."

2. Guide the client in creating a "Self-Esteem Gift Box"—a personalized and decorated shoebox (or other container) with a notch cut out of the top (like a comment box) to insert slips of paper.

3. Complete the *Something Great About Me* worksheet alongside the client, and then have them cut out each slip and add it to their decorated box.

4. As the client works on their box (or ahead of the session), jot down positive comments from you to the client, such as progress they've made in treatment or meaningful statements they have made in session. Add them to the box as well.

5. If possible, gather positive comments about the client from educators, family members, group leaders, and others, and place them in the box as well. Sarcasm or backhanded compliments (e.g., "You are very nice when you're not talking back to me") should never be added to the box, even if the client "gets" it.

6. The client can take the box home or keep it in your office (depending on the setting).
   a. If any boxes are kept in the office, make sure that clients only have access to their own box.
   b. If the client takes their box home, tell them that the only "rule" is that they may not destroy or otherwise disregard any of the comments. (They're all true!)

7. Remind the client that when they have a difficult day or week, they can return to the box over and over again to remember how meaningful they are.

8. To expand strength building further, teach the client to recognize when the box has helped them cope at a difficult time. They might write something like "Today I had a hard day, but I opened my box instead of [*contemplating suicide, self-mutilating, hiding in the bathroom at school, etc.*]."

9. Moving forward, the client should continually add more positive statements to their box. Encourage the client's support net to do the same. At minimum, it's helpful to refer to it when something positive happens (e.g., "Wow, you got a B on that test you were sure you'd fail. Be sure to write that one down and put it in your box!").

Variation: Have the client hold a "box-opening party" with a small group of supportive people (who have also contributed comments to the box). At the party, the client can read and share each comment, providing their perspective on how it feels to read them.

Tier 1

School, Treatment, and Community Settings

This intervention can be used as a transitional tool for all settings. In schools, it can be used when students graduate or move to a new internal team. In treatment settings, it can be helpful when a patient finishes their program or moves to a less restrictive setting. Hearing from peers instead of adults can be extremely rewarding and supportive during a change.

Template

Something Great About You

Fill out the following cards with positive things about yourself. Then cut out each one and place them in your self-esteem gift box.

Something Great About You	Something Unique About You
Something You Are Good at Doing	Something You Like About Yourself
Something That Makes You Special	Something You Contribute To

Automatic Negative Thoughts C

Therapeutic Rationale:

A core feature of depression is negative thinking about the self, others, or the world, which exacerbates feelings of sadness and hopelessness. This intervention taps into classic CBT by teaching kids about automatic negative thoughts, including how to identify them and—more importantly—how to reframe them.

Goals:

- Recognize automatic thoughts
- Reframe thoughts for accuracy
- Create a reference for what is fact and what is fiction

Materials:

- *Automatic Thoughts* worksheet

Directions:

1. Introduce the client to the concept of automatic negative thoughts:

   "Did you know we have thousands and thousands of thoughts every day? When we feel depressed, many of those thoughts are negative—things we don't like about ourselves, others, or the world; things that aren't fair; replaying bad things we did or said. Because how we think impacts how we feel, it's important that we look at our thoughts. That's what this activity is all about."

2. Complete the *Automatic Thoughts* worksheet with the client.

3. Challenge the client to continue to practice replacing a negative automatic thought with a positive one, and then reflecting on how emotions can change.

Tier 1

School, Treatment, and Community Settings

This intervention can be used ahead of an especially difficult concept, unit, or standardized testing cycle to help students prepare their mindset for the challenge. It can also be used after a challenging test, when a mistake is made, or when a student perceives they have "failed" at something. Daily check-ins on overall mindset as a group are also recommended. CBT is widely used in treatment programs; this intervention may be a good introductory exercise for identifying thoughts and how to reframe them.

Worksheet

Automatic Thoughts

The way you *think* changes the way you *feel*. If you think negative thoughts, you are more likely to feel down, sad, or bad about yourself. If you think positive or even neutral thoughts, you are more likely to feel happy, calm, and relaxed. This is why when you feel depressed, it's important to look at your thoughts (because they are probably making you feel worse).

Like the name suggests, automatic thoughts happen *very fast*, making it hard to notice when they're happening. And these thoughts also tend to be untrue—in fact, they usually don't even make sense! This is why it's important that you recognize when they're happening and reframe them into something more helpful.

Here's an example:

What Happened	Automatic Thought	Reframed Thought
I got an F on my test.	I'm stupid and will never learn! I'm such a failure.	This was a tough test, and the only one I've ever failed. Maybe next time I could study more or ask for help.

If you failed a test, which thought would help you feel better—the automatic one or the reframed one?

Your turn. Use the following table to write about times that something negative happened—what was your initial automatic thought? Then consider how you can reframe that negative automatic thought into something more positive and realistic.

What Happened	Automatic Thought	Reframed Thought

Personal Love Letters **C, N**

Therapeutic Rationale:

Building on the *Automatic Negative Thoughts* intervention, this intervention aims to "rewrite" negative self-narratives to build a more positive mindset. This intervention goes beyond simple affirmations by pairing the client's self-appraisal with their appraisal of others, which can also improve mood. Starting with positive appraisal of others and then transitioning into self-reflection allows the brain to navigate around the negative neural habituation.

Goals:

- Improve positive self-appraisal
- Create a brain change to grow a genuine sense of happiness (limbic system) and positive self-esteem (cortex)

Materials:

- *How to Write a Personal Love Letter* handout
- *Your Personal Love Letter* template
- *Automatic Thoughts* worksheet
- Stationery, blank paper, or blank greeting cards

Directions:

1. Explain to the client how negative thoughts can ruminate:

   "The more we think a certain thought, the more automatic it will become in our brains. Sometimes when we're depressed, our brains get stuck thinking only negative things about ourselves. Today we're going to work on changing that and allowing positive thoughts to come into the brain."

2. If needed, the client can review their *Automatic Thoughts* worksheet (on page 123) and discuss what kinds of internal feelings are connected to those types of thoughts, such as embarrassment, discomfort, or shame.

3. Ask the client to write (or dictate) a short letter to at least two family members or loved ones, telling them why they love them and why they are so important to the client. The client can write these messages on stationery, cards, or plain paper .

4. Then ask the client to use the *Your Personal Love Letter* template to write a letter to themselves with the same message: why they love themselves and what is meaningful about them. (This is easier said than done. I once had a client spend three sessions trying to complete this.)

5. The client should then review the letter to themselves, looking for automatic thoughts and self-appraisal. Guide them to remove the negative thoughts and leave behind only the appraisal. Help them reflect on how feelings can improve with a new way of thinking and have them rewrite as necessary.

6. Invite them to keep a copy of the letter and read it when they are feeling doubt or when negative automatic thoughts try to take over.

Tier 1

School, Treatment, and Community Settings

This technique is useful when applied as a whole-group activity, which can incorporate academic coursework into the task itself (e.g., reading, writing, grammar, following directions). You can also pair kids up with a peer, first writing about their peer and then about themselves. Allow children to take the final products with them to serve as direct positive self-appraisal.

Handout

How to Write a Personal Love Letter

1. Write to yourself as if you were addressing your favorite person in the world.
2. Take time to apologize for being so hard on yourself.
3. Start with addressing negative self-assessments. For example:
   - I know you struggle with feeling confident about your body . . .
   - I know you sometimes feel powerless . . .
   - I know you compare yourself to others every day . . .
4. Combat the negative self-assessment:
   - You are beautiful.
   - You are strong.
   - You are enough.
5. Identify the things that are amazing about you, inside and out:
   - You are loving, kind, and helpful.
   - You are genuine and real.
   - You are intelligent and capable.
   - You are good to the people you love.
   - You are creative.
6. Remind yourself that these positive things are true:
   - Even when you feel tired, you are still all these good things.
   - Even when you feel like you are failing, you can still overcome this obstacle.
7. Close with a loving expression:
   - Warmly
   - With love
   - Hugs and kisses
   - XOXO

Template

Your Personal Love Letter

Dear ______________________________,

The Cathartic Letter C, A

Therapeutic Rationale:

Cathartic letter writing is a tool for emotional expression that can be quite valuable for clients who are depressed, particularly those who tend to internalize their thoughts and feelings. The goal of this intervention is to allow the client to openly and fully express themselves to another person (or themselves) in an emotionally safe, therapeutically contained environment. It is particularly helpful for clients who ruminate, who were not given a chance to express themselves to someone, or who struggle with closure from past events. Be aware that this process can be incredibly overwhelming or activating for some clients (e.g., writing to a perpetrator), so it is imperative to build in time to self-soothe or co-regulate. Sending the letter to the person is *not* advised; I find this exercise to be most beneficial when the client knows they will destroy it at the end of the session.

Goals:

- Release negative emotion in a therapeutic environment
- Gain closure regarding an experience that might otherwise be unresolvable

Materials:

- Stationery or blank paper

Directions:

1. Explain to the client the importance of letting go of certain thoughts:

   "Sometimes we have an experience that is so impactful that we cannot turn our minds away from it. We stay stuck in the thoughts and memories of that time and have a hard time accepting it, so we cannot move forward. One way we can let go of those thoughts and feelings is by writing a letter to someone who was involved, to the situation itself, or to ourselves."

2. Have the client identify an experience that they are having a difficult time letting go of. Invite them to reflect on the emotions connected to the experience and how these feelings impact their thoughts about themselves, others, and the world (revisit the *Automatic Thoughts* intervention on page 123 if needed).

3. Ask the client to write (or dictate) a "no holds barred" letter to the person, the situation, or themselves, being as descriptive as possible (tapping into all five senses if possible).

4. Invite the client to read the letter aloud in session.

5. Process the client's emotions before and after the letter, noting any changes. Be sure to engage in a grounding exercise before ending the session.

6. Give the child the option to keep the letter or destroy it together in session.

Tier 3

School, Treatment, and Community Settings

Students can use cathartic letter writing to address peer conflicts, relational aggressors (bullies), or staff issues, particularly when the issue interferes with academic performance. Clients in treatment centers or foster care benefit from writing letters to parents whose rights have been terminated, perpetrators, social workers, court personnel, kinship providers, and the like.

Magic Mirror

C

Therapeutic Rationale:

This tool works well for depression because it encourages children to find positive attributes about themselves using a "magical mirror" that can see their inner qualities. Suspending reality to "look deeper" is a fun and engaging way for clients to explore their positive traits (and receive positive feedback from others).

Goals:

- Identify and practice positive affirmations
- Decrease depressive symptoms

Materials:

- *Magic Mirror* worksheet
- Variety of art supplies (e.g., colored pencils, crayons)
- Variety of craft supplies (e.g., ribbons, buttons, yarn)
- Optional: A small mirror

Directions:

1. Explain to the client what the magic mirror can do:

   "Sometimes we need support to see the good things about ourselves. That's what this magical mirror does—it sees all *of you—not just the outside, but also what is special* inside *of you, even if you don't see it right now."*

2. Provide the client with the *Magic Mirror* worksheet (or an actual handheld mirror) and ask them what they "see" about themselves. Invite them to draw or write their answers on the worksheet.

Note: Many individuals are uncomfortable looking into a mirror. Use clinical judgment to determine whether this is an appropriate intervention for your client.

3. Then, emphasizing the "magic" of the mirror, ask the client process questions like:
   - "The mirror sees you one year from now. What is different about you?"
   - "Now it's picking up on your special powers. What are they?"
   - "Now it sees what a kind friend you are. What does it see you doing?"
   - "It sees the greatest day of your life. What is happening?"
   - "The mirror sees you helping others. How are you helping them?"

4. Have the client add these responses on the magic mirror as you go, creating a collage of positive attributes and images.
5. If the client chooses to draw, consider adding color or craft supplies, like yarn for hair.
6. Encourage the client to take their mirror home as a reminder of their positive traits, perhaps placing it next to a mirror at home. Encourage them to recite the positive attributes to themselves every morning or night.

Variation: Get the client's adults involved: Have their caregivers, educators, or staff members draw or list positive attributes about the child. Then add them to the mirror with glue or tape.

Tier 1

School, Treatment, and Community Settings

This intervention is an effective whole-classroom activity in elementary schools (and maybe middle school, depending on developmental stage) for recognition of positive attributes and relationship-building among students.

Worksheet

Magic Mirror

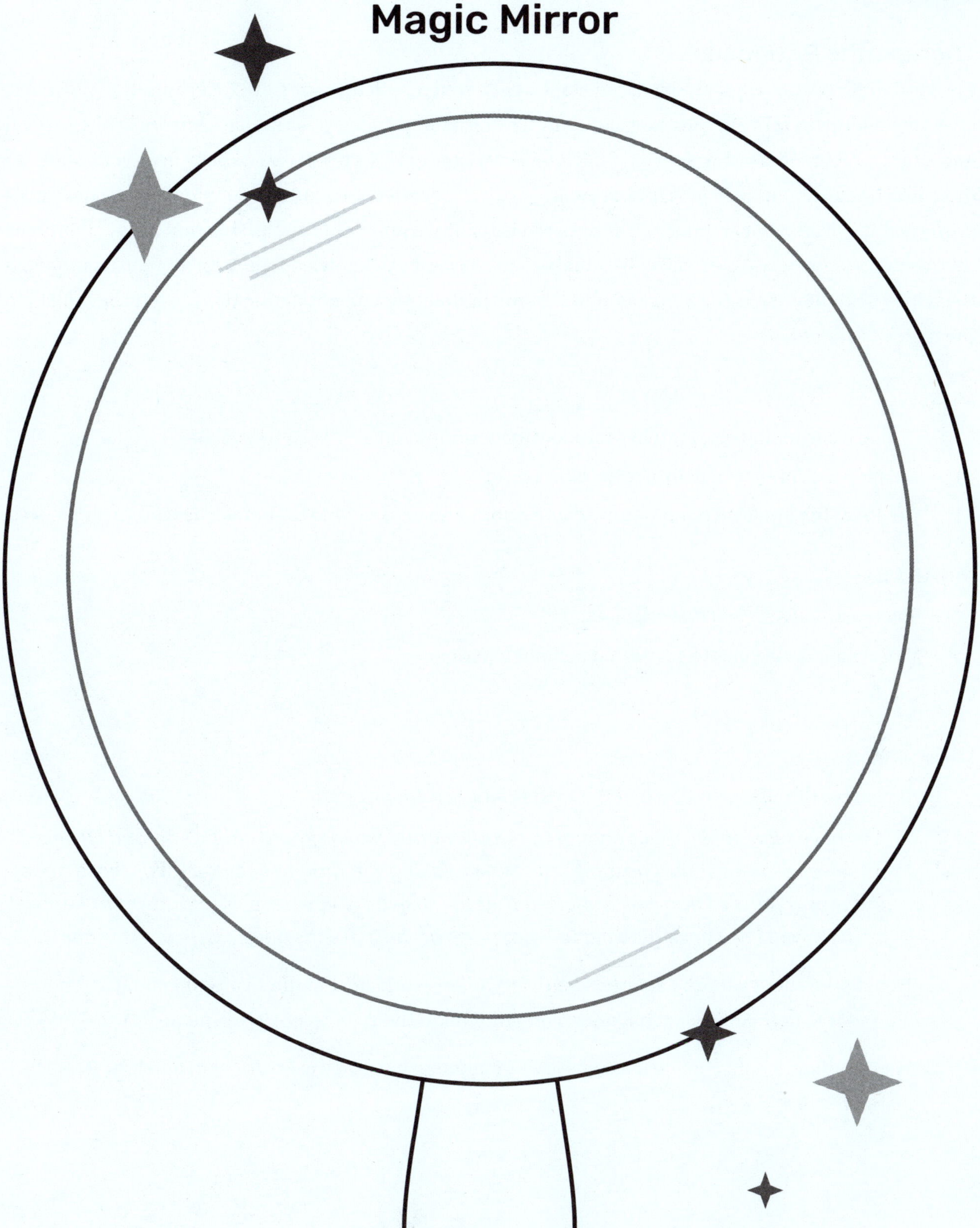

Personal Art Gallery *At, C, N*

Therapeutic Rationale:

Up until now, we have scaffolded multiple skills that challenge kids to focus on the positives, investing energy in affirmations to grow confidence and improving positive self-esteem. These are all important precursors to this activity, which will start to teach kids how *all* experiences contribute to their individuality and self-perception, be it positive, negative, or neutral. Seeing these experiences presented in chronological order can serve as a visual illustration of growth. This tool helps clients see that each of their past experiences is valuable and deserves acknowledgment for how it has molded them into who they are in the here and now: Events in their past do not define them—but they *can* help them grow stronger.

Goals:

- Create a chronological reference for identity development
- Develop acceptance of painful experiences
- Create a "life book" to reference life connections and experiences that make us who we are

Materials:

- *Your Personal Art Gallery* worksheet
- Variety of art supplies (e.g., colored pencils, crayons)
- Binder

Directions:

1. Explain to the client that each of their experiences is important:

   "We have learned all about changing our thoughts, feeling more confident, and letting ourselves grow past our most difficult times. Taking the time to see that all *of those good and messy parts of our lives work together to make us who we are, is important to help us see how much we have grown and what parts of those things have made us stronger."*

2. Provide the client with the *Your Personal Art Gallery* worksheet to draw or write about experiences in their life that have been meaningful to them (both positive and negative).

3. Ask the client to talk about each experience, including how they were affected and how it changed them.

4. Invite the client to display their life stories in a "gallery," placing the artwork on their walls at home. The most important or transformative experiences should be featured most prominently.
    a. The client may share the story of each experience with family members or friends.
    b. If an experience is private or too emotionally sensitive to display, the client can put this story in a safe place instead of hanging it up. Alternatively, they may cover it with a drape or another piece of paper. This is a good opportunity for a "special museum showing," where they reveal them to attendees only after being screened for trustworthiness.
5. The client should return to the gallery to "visit" their memories briefly, eventually returning to the present. Seeing these memories can be a reminder of all the things they've overcome and how the past has shaped them.
6. The client should continue to add pictures to the gallery as time goes on. As new pictures go up, they can place the others in a binder (in chronological order) to reference when needed.

School, Treatment, and Community Settings

If privacy and risk of oversharing is a concern, personal art galleries can be extrapolated to include *group* milestones, posted on a bulletin board in the classroom or hallway as a way to create cohesion among the group. Create a timeline of events as the year progresses, allowing children to reflect as a class or group: "Remember when this difficult time happened? What did we learn from it?"

Worksheet

Your Personal Art Gallery

Wise Mind **D, C, M, N**

Therapeutic Rationale:

Wise mind is an emotion regulation skill from DBT that's especially helpful for managing depression. It's based on the idea that we all operate from three different states of mind: (1) emotional mind, (2) rational mind (also called reasonable or logical mind), and (3) wise mind. This intervention helps depressed clients recognize which state they're in and guides them toward making balanced, thoughtful choices from their wise mind, which in turn develops a stronger sense of self-efficacy, hopefulness, and confidence.

Goals:

- Promote wise-mind approaches for problem-solving and emotional regulation
- Promote mindful management of stressors

Materials:

- *Wise Mind* handout

Directions:

1. Explain to the client the concept of the three states of mind:

   "Imagine you have two parts of your brain that help you understand the world and make decisions. One part is your emotional mind: Here you find all your big feelings like sadness, anger, and jealousy. Your emotional mind wants to react right away to everything instead of thinking things through! The other part is your rational mind: It's like a robot that thinks through everything with logic, rules, and facts, and it forgets about feelings. Now imagine there's a third part—your wise mind. This mind is the smartest one of them all! It listens to both the emotions and the reason to help you make good choices. Let's look at some examples."

2. Introduce the *Wise Mind* handout, reiterating each mind's purpose. Consider personifying each one with characters from pop culture:
   - **Harry Potter:** Hermione is rational mind, Ron is emotional mind, Harry (or Dumbledore) is wise mind.
   - **Star Wars:** C-3PO is rational, Anakin Skywalker is emotional, and Yoda is wise.
   - **Super Mario Brothers:** Luigi is rational, Bowser is emotional, and Mario is wise.
   - **Marvel:** Iron Man is rational, Hulk is emotional, and Captain America is wise.
   - **X-Men:** Cyclops is rational, Wolverine is emotional, and Professor X is wise.
   - **Frozen:** Elsa in *Frozen* is rational, Anna is emotional, and Elsa in *Frozen 2* is wise.

3. Ask the following process questions to apply the concept to the client's life:
   - "What would happen if we let our emotional mind make all our decisions?"
   - "What if our rational mind made all our decisions?"
   - "Can you think of a time you made 'emotional' choices? Rational? Wise?"
   - "What did each one feel like?"
   - "Do you tend to use emotional, rational, or wise mind the most?"
   - "Does [*person in their life*] tend to use emotional, rational, or wise mind the most?"
   - "Can you think of a situation where you wish you would've used wise mind?"
4. Apply the concept to depression specifically with the following process questions:
   - "What might the emotional mind say when we feel depressed?" (e.g., "Nothing matters; it won't get better," "I'm overwhelmed by sadness," "Isolate and avoid everything," "Engage in self-harm behavior")
   - "Rational mind?" (e.g., "There's no reason to feel this bad—what is wrong with me?" "I need to get over this," "Ignore feelings and engage in numbing," "I feel stuck")
   - "Wise mind?" (e.g., "The pain I feel is real, but it doesn't mean I can't take small healthy steps forward—validate feelings *and* choose helpful action")

Tier 1

School, Treatment, and Community Settings

This tool is extremely effective in all settings. I recommend incorporating this into curricula and displaying a visual reference to it in multiple places to help kids respond, process, and learn more effectively. Be sure to provide acknowledgment and praise when you see them make wise-minded decisions so you can further reinforce the skill.

Handout

Wise Mind

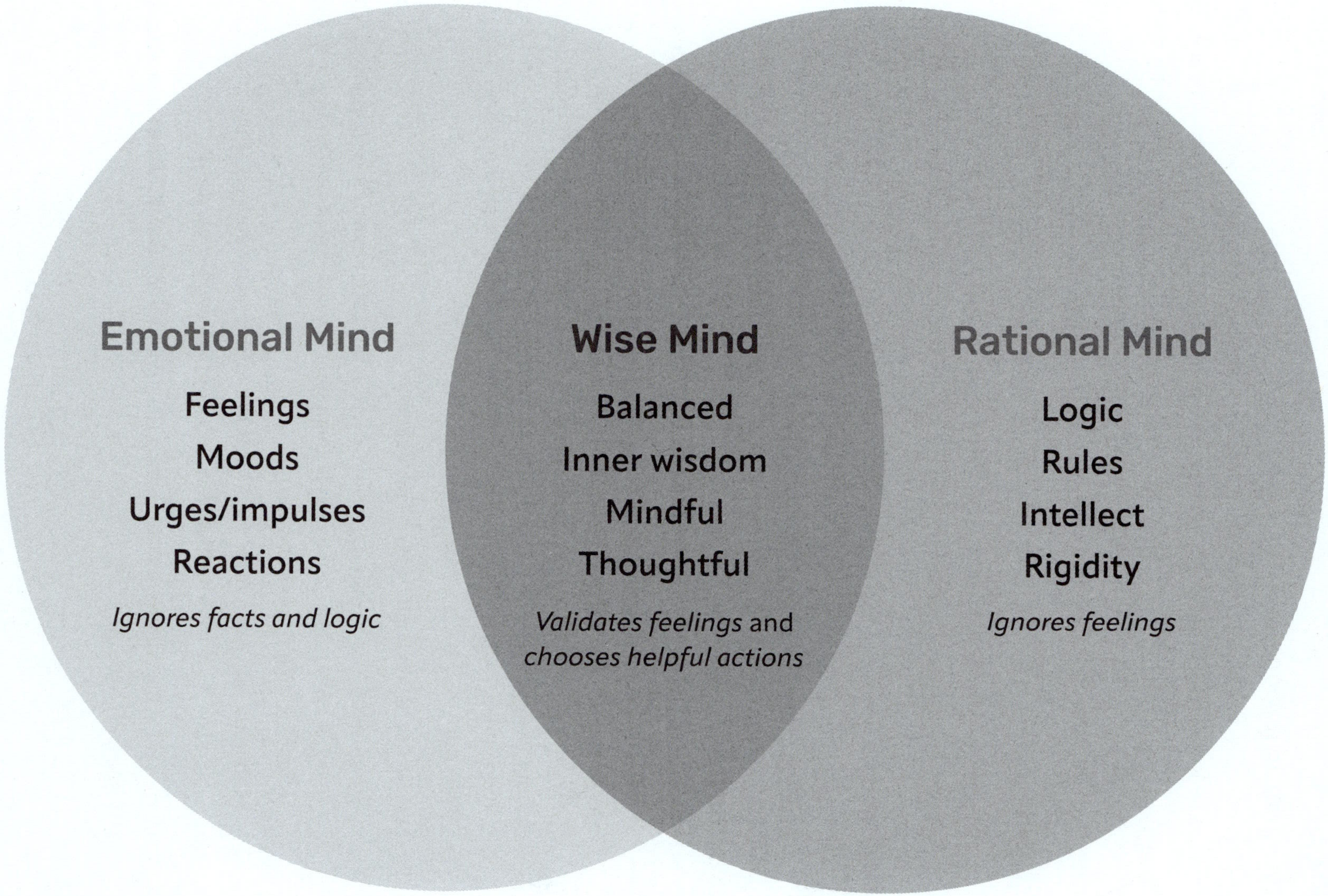

Wise Mind Detective **C, D**

Therapeutic Rationale:

This intervention scaffolds on the *Wise Mind* intervention by increasing awareness of when the client has used or is using emotional, rational, or wise mind—and what the consequences of that choice were (positive and negative). By acting as "detectives" in their own lives, it helps clients to further reinforce problem-solving abilities and a sense of agency, both of which are markedly impaired during depressive episodes.

Goals:

- Provide psychoeducation on the emotional, rational, and wise minds
- Create wise-mind options to exchange for habituated emotional/logical responses

Materials:

- *Wise Mind Detective* worksheet
- Optional: *How to Get to Wise Mind* handout

Directions:

1. Explain to the client how the different "minds" show up in thoughts and feelings:

   "Remember, our emotional mind *is all about big feelings and fast actions—like a knee-jerk reaction. Our* rational mind, *on the other hand, uses only thinking and logic and can disconnect us from our feelings. Both minds give us important information, but neither should be in charge all the time—because that can lead to problems. That's where wise mind comes in. Our* wise mind *helps us slow down and combine our feelings and thinking before we act."*

2. Introduce the *Wise Mind Detective* worksheet:

   a. Reflect on how being a detective can help the client identify which mindset is taking control earlier on, and how this can help them plan for wise-mind approaches (e.g., perspective-taking, weighing pros and cons).

   b. Help the client complete the worksheet, practicing awareness of the more dominant mindset, and make several plans of action to achieve wise mind.

3. If the client is having a hard time helping their wise mind grow, provide them with the *How to Get to Wise Mind* handout.

Tier 1

School, Treatment, and Community Settings

Having visual cues for wise-mind balance can help promote the notion of metacognition in your classroom space. This tool is essentially teaching awareness (metacognitive knowledge) and control of mental processing (metacognitive regulation), which helps adjust the entire classroom's approach to problem-solving and planning, whether it be for class content or peer interactions.

Worksheet

Wise Mind Detective

Knowing which mind—emotional, rational, or wise—is in charge during a situation is one of the ways you can start making better, wiser choices. Think about two recent situations where your depression may have caused you to miss out or feel bad about yourself. Then answer the following questions to help you discover which mind you were in—and how you could have responded differently.

Example:

- **What happened?** *On Saturday, my friends wanted to go out, but I felt depressed.*
- **What choice did you make?** *I ignored their texts, laid around, and scrolled on my phone.*
- **Which mind was in charge?** *Emotional mind: My sadness felt so big that I didn't want to talk to anyone.*
- **What were the consequences?** *I felt worse and lonely, and I beat myself up for not being a better friend.*
- **What would have been a wise-minded action step?** *I could've at least replied to them, or I could have gone out for just an hour or something. I know it does help my depression to get out of the house.*

Scenario 1:

1. What happened? ______________________________

   ____

2. What choice did you make? ______________________________

   ____

3. Which mind was in charge? ______________________________

   ____

4. What were the consequences? ______________________________

____

5. What would have been a wise-minded action step? ______________________________

____

Scenario 2:

1. What happened? ______________________________

____

2. What choice did you make? ______________________________

____

3. Which mind was in charge? ______________________________

____

4. What were the consequences? ______________________________

____

5. What would have been a wise-minded action step? ______________________________

____

Handout

How to Get to Wise Mind

Wise mind often shows up as a calm thought, a gut sense, a clear next step, or a feeling of steadiness. While you can't force yourself into it, you can create the conditions for it to come forward by exercising mindfulness and nonjudgment.

Mindfulness + Nonjudgment = The Path to Wise Mind

Sit still and take four to six deep, cleansing breaths. Go inward:

- **Observe:** Notice your thoughts, feelings, and sensations.
- **Describe:** Put words to your observations, sticking to the facts and using neutral language: "My thoughts are racing. I feel anxious. My breathing is shallow." Avoid judgments. Label what is happening, not whether it is "good" or "bad."
- **Participate:** Bring your full attention to one thing you can sense (e.g., your breath, a sound, the feeling of your feet on the floor). Stay focused in the here and now. If your thoughts jump to the past or the future, simply bring them back to the moment.

Then, access your wise mind:

- **Ask:** What is a wise way to handle this situation? What does my wise mind know?
- **Name and act:** "My wise mind says to pause." Take one small step to do it.

ACCEPTS: Coping in a Crisis **C, D**

Therapeutic Rationale:

This intervention uses the ACCEPTS distress tolerance skill from DBT. The purpose of ACCEPTS is to help clients get through intense emotions *without making the situation worse*—namely, engaging in self-injury, substance use, or other risky behaviors. The purpose of this intervention is to create a pause between a difficult emotion and an impulsive or risky act, thereby increasing safety and decreasing the need for crisis services or psychiatric hospitalization.

Goals:

- Develop skills for managing intense emotions and urges

Materials:

- *Your ACCEPTS Skills* worksheet

Directions:

1. Explain ACCEPTS skills to the client:

   "When something happens that feels like a crisis—such as an argument, a breakup, or a betrayal—our emotional mind often takes over. The feelings can become so intense that they feel unbearable, as if they will never end. In these moments, people may feel strong urges to cope in unsafe ways, such as self-injury, substance use, or even thoughts of ending their life. Although we may know in our wise mind that crises do pass, the intensity of the moment makes it hard to access that understanding.

   During these times, we need tools that help us get through the experience without making the situation worse. This is where ACCEPTS skills come in. ACCEPTS skills are ways to cope with intense emotions and urges by calming the nervous system until we are able to make more wise-minded choices. By using ACCEPTS, we create space between what we are feeling and how we act, reducing the risk of doing something unsafe or harmful. ACCEPTS is not about solving the problem—it's about surviving the moment so we can address the problem later from wise mind.

   Today we're going to review what these skills are and identify ones that are a good fit for you."

2. Provide the client with the *Your ACCEPTS Skills* worksheet, and help them fill it out if needed. Some useful questions you can ask can be:
    a. "What are your favorite positive distractions to practice?"
    b. "What are your least favorite distractions, and how can you transform them into something that works for you?"
    c. "What are some areas of ACCEPTS you need to try for the first time? Are there any you've tried but could practice more regularly?"
3. Invite the client to take their *Your ACCEPTS Skills* worksheet home so they have a list of skills for when they need it. Remind them to practice using their skills, and let them know they can add or subtract items from their list after trying them out with fidelity.

Tier 1

School, Treatment, and Community Settings

In classrooms, having a visual reference (which is even better with pictures) for positive distractions to replace escalated emotional responses allows for a quick point-and-go reference without having to engage verbally. Remember, when children are above their threshold, verbal interactions can be counterproductive. Instead, using a visual item can engage different processing areas of the brain and improve encoding of new ways of being.

Worksheet

Your ACCEPTS Skills

This worksheet will have you brainstorm ideas for exactly what to do when you need an ACCEPTS distraction. With this list, you will be likely to use them when the time comes! You can also complete this activity right when things seem crazy and overwhelming. Some examples are included for each area, or you can come up with your own ideas.

Activities: What is something you can do to keep busy? (Hobbies, going for a walk, reading, watching a movie, listening to music)

____

____

Contributing: How can you help someone else or do something kind? (Volunteering, donating items/money, doing something thoughtful)

____

____

Comparisons: What is another experience you can compare with this one? What was different, harder, or easier? (How did you get through a hard time in the past? What is a past memory that made you feel happy, empowered, or calm?)

____

____

Emotions (opposite): How can you interrupt this emotion with another emotion? (Watch something funny, listen to music that changes your mood, play with a pet, talk to a friend)

____

____

Push it away: How can you take a short break from the problem? (Build an imaginary wall between you and the problem, put the problem in an imaginary box on a shelf)

____

____

Thoughts: How can you preoccupy your brain to think about something else? (Count backward, name the colors of things you see around you, do math problems or logic puzzles)

____

____

Sensations: Which of your senses would be most effective for you to evoke? How can you feel these? (Hold an ice cube, put a cold washcloth on your forehead, eat something spicy or sour, squeeze a stress ball)

____

____

4

ADHD

Our understanding of ADHD has significantly evolved over the years. Once considered a childhood behavior problem that is best controlled by stimulant medication, we now recognize that inattention, hyperactivity, and impulsiveness are not simply behavioral issues, but signs of a neurodivergent brain—one that is fundamentally wired differently—not just in childhood but across the lifespan. And while medication remains an important tool, environment, skill-building, and approach matter too.

Individuals with ADHD show differences in the frontal and prefrontal cortices, the brain regions responsible for executive functioning. When these areas are still developing, challenges with attention, planning, emotional regulation, and impulse control are common. Because the prefrontal cortex continues to mature until around age 25—well beyond the years children are in our care—this highlights the need to adjust our expectations and to provide early, supportive interventions that can positively influence brain development over time.

With better knowledge of brain function comes the need for greater patience, empathy, and support. Many individuals with ADHD also experience co-occurring anxiety and depression, and this is hardly surprising. After years of struggling with academic performance, social rejection, frequent correction by adults, and feeling "different" or "difficult," many develop a negative self-concept shaped by repeated experiences of failure or criticism. As a result, the mental health risks for this population are significantly higher: Individuals with ADHD are three times more likely to experience suicidal ideation and five times more likely to develop a substance use disorder (Di Salvo et al., 2024; Srichawla et al., 2022).

ADHD is not just about focus or behavior—it's a whole-person issue that requires understanding, support, and proactive care from educators, clinicians, and families. Because of this, this chapter differs from the previous ones in that it includes interventions for the individual and brain-based structural environmental changes for educational settings. You'll also note threads of occupational therapy woven throughout to aid in improving movement control, supporting emotional regulation, and decreasing impulsivity.

The interventions in this chapter will focus on:

- Improving impulse and emotive control
- Thinking with more flexibility
- Planning and prioritizing
- Self-monitoring
- Initiating and completing tasks
- Improving personal organization and working memory

Key Concept

Dual-hemisphere processing: As the brain has two distinct sides, activities are most effective for children with ADHD when they are both *verbal* and *hands-on*, promoting neural connections and growth.

Case Example

Marie, 8, was referred for assessment for "impulsivity" and "defiance." Her teacher shared that Marie has trouble with listening, waiting her turn, interrupting, interjecting her unsolicited opinion, bothering other students during class instruction, failing to turn in homework, making mouth noises, breaking pencils, rocking in her chair, and running out of the room regularly.

Marie's parents describe her as bright, precocious, and creative, and also "very loud and disorganized." They express concerns about her daring acts and risky play behaviors, saying, "She never seems to think before she talks or acts." This has been a problem since she was in pre-K, where she was kicked out of three centers due to her behavior. Her mom says, "I just want her to follow the rules and do what we ask of her. She's grounded 90 percent of the time at home." Last week, they found her in the barn with a jump rope tied around her neck, but her dad says, "She just said she was playing around." Marie does not have any history of self-harm or suicidal ideation.

When I meet Marie, she tells me, "I try really hard to listen, but my teacher is *soooo* boring, and I already know all the answers for the test, so why do I have to do the homework? My aide gets mad at me and just does most of my work for me anyway. No one wants to play with me at recess, and I feel like no one likes me at all. I like to climb high, run fast, and jump because it makes me feel good. I feel like I want to give up on everything because I can't do anything right and I make too many mistakes."

Marie has a 504 plan at school for behavioral intervention, but she has never been prescribed medication for ADHD or received outpatient counseling support.

No one has taught Marie:

- A thought does *not* have to be a behavior.
- Mistakes are an opportunity for change.
- If we persist, we can achieve.
- We are more than our behaviors.
- Our brains can learn new ways of doing things.

ADHD Key Concept

Dual-Hemisphere Processing (Part 1)

A common myth about ADHD is that something is "wrong" with the brain. That isn't true. The ADHD brain simply processes information *differently*, and understanding this helps us support kids with ADHD more effectively. Here's how:

The brain has two hemispheres that work together, each with different responsibilities:

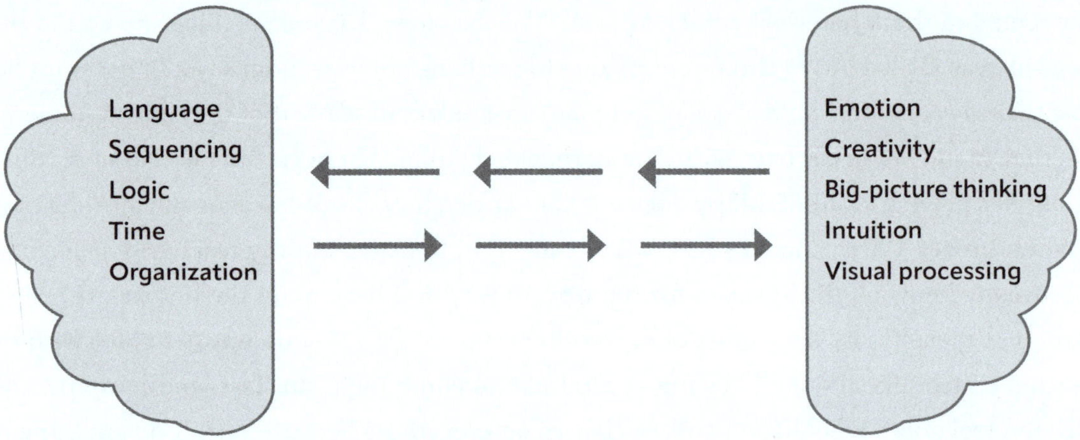

In a neurotypical brain, the two hemispheres communicate smoothly with each other for most tasks. In an ADHD brain, that communication is less consistent and regulated, and people with ADHD tend to be more right-hemisphere dominant:

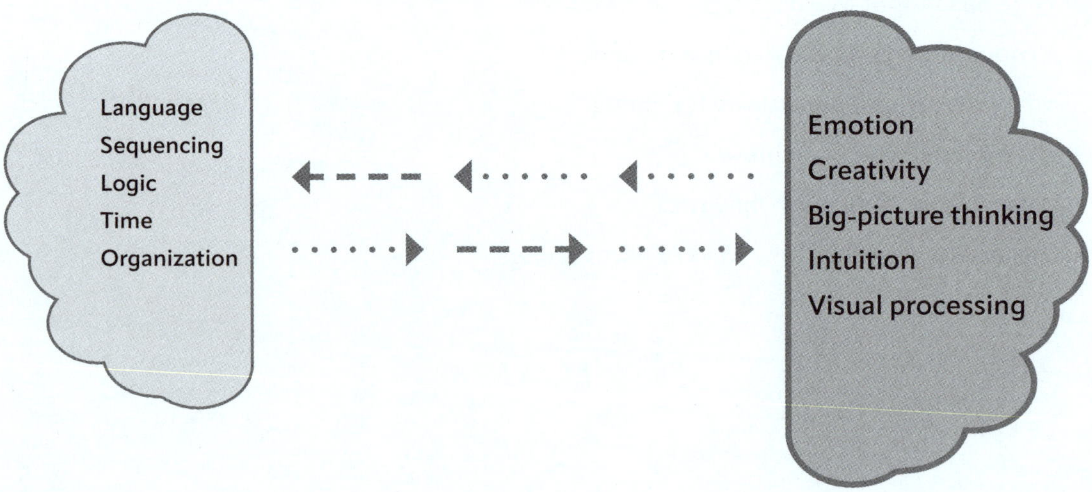

This discrepancy in brain function is why people with ADHD often say to themselves things like:

- I have great ideas . . . but I have difficulty executing those ideas.
- I know exactly what to do . . . but I never do it.
- I understand concepts . . . but I can't meet deadlines.
- I seem easygoing . . . but I sometimes overreact, or "blow up" when I'm upset.
- I excel at hands-on learning . . . but I don't follow verbal or written instructions well.

This also helps explain why kids with ADHD often struggle in a world where most instruction, therapy, and parenting rely heavily on verbal directions with many steps.

ADHD Key Concept

Dual-Hemisphere Processing (Part 2)

Kids with ADHD learn best when verbal instructions are paired with movement or hands-on activities, helping *both* sides of the brain work together and promote neural connections and growth.

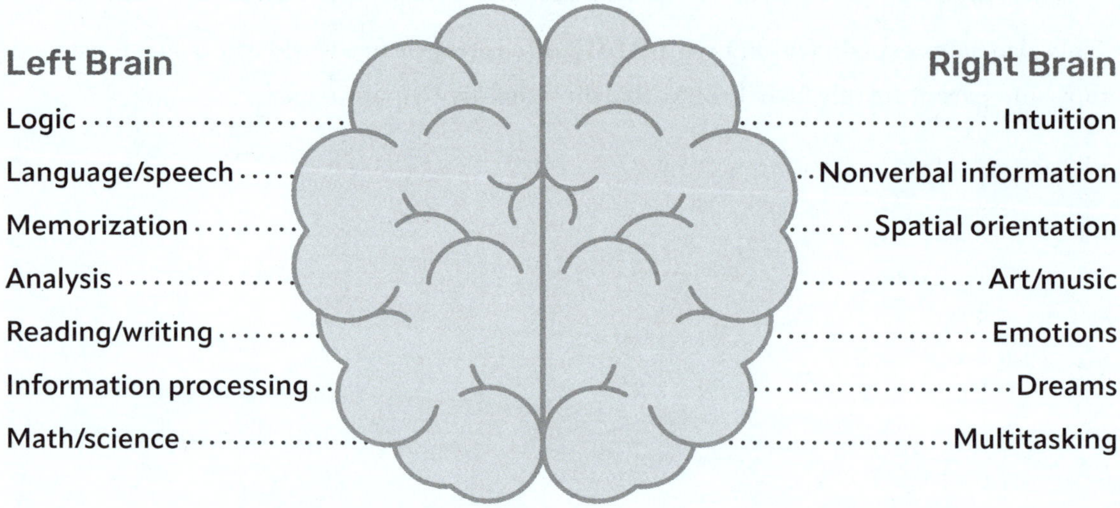

Activities that use both sides of the brain might look like:

- Standing while spelling words
- Making checklists and using color-coding
- Drawing while talking
- Turning chores into games or races
- Tossing a ball while talking through a problem
- Doing the first step of a task together
- Movement or stretching between tasks
- Saying "put on your shoes" while handing them their shoes
- Using a fidget while listening

With consistency, these types of interventions improve the brain's function in these areas:

- Encoding
- Working memory
- Long-term memory
- Processing speed
- Cognitive flexibility

Understanding Executive Function

People with ADHD have brains that work a bit differently—especially in a part called the *prefrontal cortex*. The prefrontal cortex is like the command center of the brain, and it's located at the front of the head behind the eyes. This is where we find executive function (EF), a set of cognitive skills that help in controlling thoughts, emotions, and actions. This serves as the foundation for critical thinking, problem-solving, planning, decision-making, and completing tasks. There are eleven skills in all, but they fall into three core areas: (1) working memory, (2) cognitive flexibility, and (3) self-control.

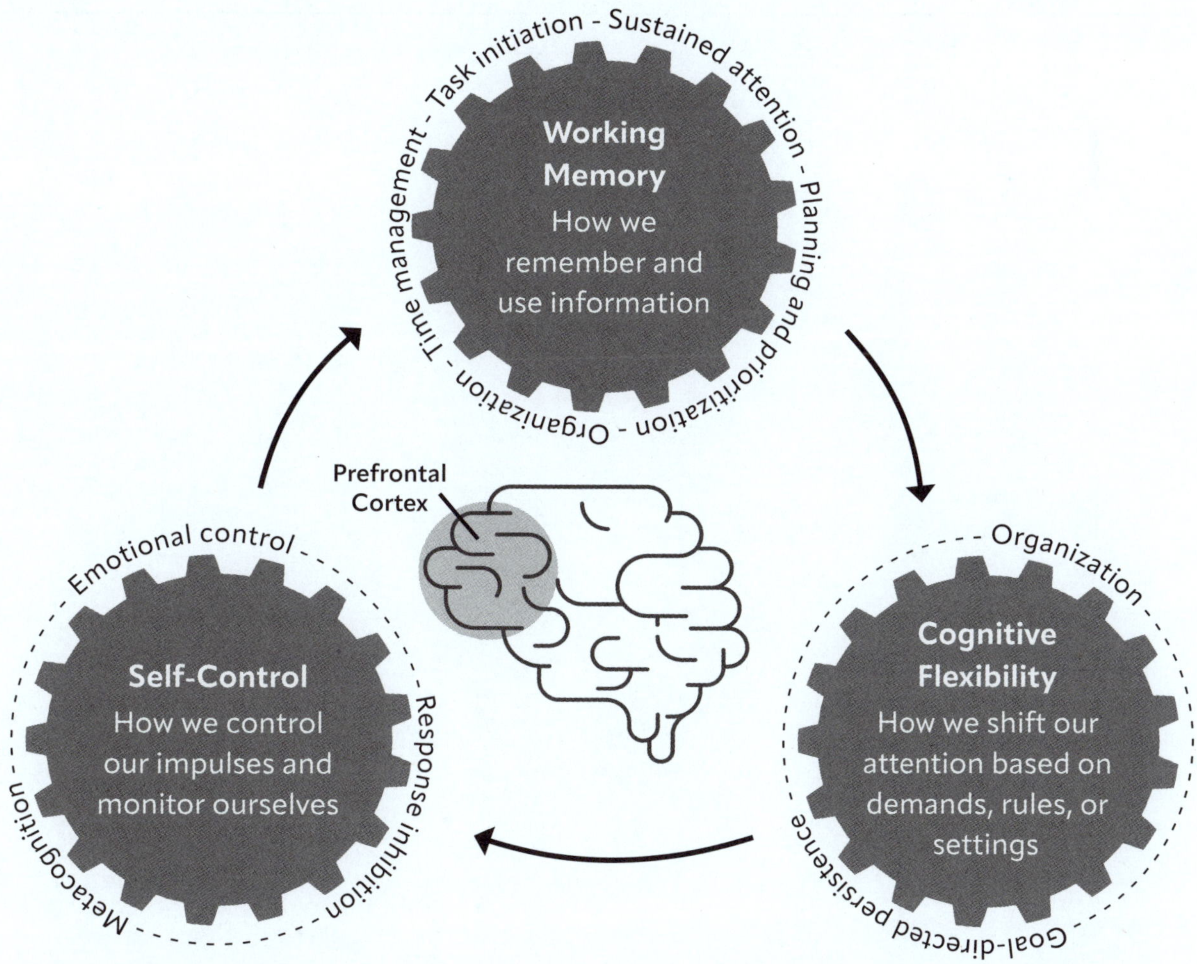

The three core areas of EF are part of the prefrontal cortical functioning and are influenced and altered by neurotransmitters, such as dopamine, acetylcholine, serotonin, and norepinephrine. The following table breaks down what these neurotransmitters do.

Dopamine	Acetylcholine	Serotonin	Norepinephrine
The "reward" chemical, which increases with pleasure Plays a role in movement, memory, learning, mood, and arousal	The "movement" chemical; responsible for controlling skeletal and smooth muscles, digestion, breathing, and heart rate Plays a role in memory, learning, attention, and cognitive flexibility	The "mood" chemical; responsible for mood stability, sleep, digestion, movement, and pain Plays a role in learning, memory, sleep-wake cycles, and sexual desire	The "arousal and attention" chemical; responsible for sleep cycles, memory, mood, and fight or flight Plays a role in maintaining sleep-wake cycles, focusing to perform tasks, and encoding of information

Fidget or Distractor? *B, N, S*

Therapeutic Rationale:

Excessive movement—shifting in seats, fidgeting, foot-tapping, frequently getting out of seats—is a hallmark symptom of ADHD. This hyperactivity isn't merely restlessness, but rather the brain's way of triggering important chemicals to help with regulation and focus, and it may be a sign of underdeveloped core strength or vestibular awareness. The use of a fidget item is a common practice in classrooms and therapy offices as a generally low-cost, widely available means for helping kids focus. The challenge is that many items marketed as fidgets end up being distractions that don't support attention—instead competing for it. This intervention aims to differentiate between a fidget and a distraction and, more importantly, to empower kids to choose the fidgets that are the most helpful for them.

> **Note:** Individual sensory experiences and abilities should be taken into consideration before engaging in this intervention.

Goals:

- Improve task focus, working memory, and impulse control

Materials:

- *Fidgets* handout
- Variety of fidgets

Directions:

1. Introduce the client to fidgets:

   "Using a fidget is a great way to keep our hands busy so we can concentrate, but sometimes they can be more distracting than helpful. Today we're going to learn how fidgets help us and the best ways to use them so we don't get in trouble with them or bother the people around us."

2. Provide the client with several different types of fidgets; allow them to explore the fidgets, identify ones that are appealing, and decide which ones will be helpful.

3. Have the client practice using the fidget as you do a structured activity (e.g., read a short passage, group discussion).

4. Discuss the difference between a fidget and a distraction: Tell the client that if the fidget can be seen by a lot of people, touches other people around them, or makes noise, it has become a distractor and will be taken away. Be sure the client understands the difference between a fidget and a distraction and clarify as needed.

5. Playfully challenge the client to show how many ways they can be distracting with the fidget. Then hold your hand out and request that they give it to you, reiterating that distractors will be taken away. This step is important in training the brain through practice of removing and reflecting on the fidget/distractor in a *non-overstimulated* state; then, when the client is *overstimulated*, the removal is less likely to cause a meltdown.

6. Continue to "try on" various fidgets to help the client determine which ones are best for them.

7. Encourage them to proactively bring their fidget to mealtimes, homework time, therapy sessions, classrooms, the library, or tests.

Tier 1

School, Treatment, and Community Settings

Provide a designated container with a variety of fidgets (e.g., different textures, abilities, weights) for your classroom and groups. Safety is paramount, so make sure the items you provide cannot be used as a weapon or tool for self-injury (particularly in self-contained settings).

Handout

Fidgets

Fidgets can stay; distractors go away!

Fidgets are . . .	Distractors are . . .
Quiet	Noisy
Mostly hidden	Touching others
Helpful	Drawing attention

- Beaded bracelets or zipper bracelets
- Stress balls (e.g., foam, gel, mesh)
- Lava lamps or glitter jars
- Sandpaper strips
- Spinners with slow, visual patterns
- Tangle toys
- Pop-it toys
- Chewelry (chewable jewelry made from safe silicone)
- Oral motor tools (e.g., chewy tubes or z-vibes)
- Fidget cubes (silent) or fidget pads
- Slime with glitter or color-changing features
- Sugar-free gum or mints
- Reusable straws or chewy pencil toppers
- Soft fabric swatches (e.g., velvet, fleece)
- Textured putty or therapy dough

Fabric Sticks for Focus *N, S*

Therapeutic Rationale:

Tactile engagement—particularly through the use of sensory tables—has shown that specific textures can enhance the brain's ability to maintain focus and stay task-oriented. This effect is linked to activity in the cuneate nucleus, a part of the brainstem that helps modulate and filter sensory input. Certain tactile experiences can help the brain prioritize relevant information, supporting attention during classroom instruction, therapeutic activities, homework, and daily tasks at home. Four key textures are especially effective: the rough (hook) side of Velcro, the soft (loop) side of Velcro, smooth satin or silk, and corduroy fabric. This intervention is designed to help clients understand how tactile input can support focus. As part of the process, they create a personalized, portable tactile tool that includes these textures, giving them a self-regulation strategy they can use across settings.

Note: Individual sensory experiences and abilities should be taken into consideration before engaging in this intervention.

Goals:

- Improve task focus, task persistence, and impulse control
- Decrease universal sensitivity to sensory input in the cuneate nucleus

Materials:

- Swatches of Velcro (both sides), satin/silk, and corduroy
- Scissors
- Double-sided tape
- Six-inch plastic rulers or wide wooden craft sticks

Directions:

1. Introduce the swatches of fabric to the client. Have them feel each one, and explain that touching textures like these can help them focus on a task.
2. With the client (or in advance), cut one-inch by three-inch strips of each of the four swatches/textures. To minimize risk, it is not recommended to create strips longer than six inches, especially with populations that are high-risk for self-injury or harm to others (such as choking).
3. Using double-sided tape, securely wrap each fabric strip around the ruler or craft stick.
4. Encourage clients to take their fabric sticks with them to use during class, transitions, tests, therapy, and more. Remind them to self-monitor how well each texture works for them!

Variation: Instead of (or in addition to) the fabric sticks, have children attach the strips of fabric to the underside of their workspaces to serve as a built-in sensory station.

Tier 1

School, Treatment, and Community Settings

This intervention is beneficial for all kids, not just those with ADHD. Having textured fabric, either on the sticks or adhered to desks and tables, available in your classroom, office, or group therapy room is an inexpensive, nondisruptive tool for improving engagement and focus.

Resistance Bands *N, S*

Therapeutic Rationale:

This strategy is deeply rooted in occupational therapy and neurodevelopmental models of intervention for ADHD. The use of resistance bands—originally popularized in occupational therapy settings—has become increasingly accepted in schools and treatment facilities and is now also being successfully used in homes, such as at the dinner table or in study areas. Resistance bands provide a tool that children may press their feet down against, bounce their calves against, or hook their legs behind and stretch forward. It's a common misconception that the movement itself is what reduces restlessness; in fact, the key therapeutic element is the *resistance*. That's what activates the brain's prefrontal cortex, helping improve focus, sensory processing, and motor planning—all of which are essential components of executive functioning, particularly working memory. Over time, this kind of sensory-motor engagement can support the development of higher-level thinking skills, such as problem-solving, reasoning, and multitasking. This intervention walks through how to use them therapeutically.

Note: Individual sensory experiences and abilities should be taken into consideration before engaging in this intervention.

Goals:

- Regulate the brain's need for movement
- Improve working memory, regulation, and problem-solving

Materials:

- Resistance bands, nonlatex torniquets, or industrial-sized rubber bands

Directions:

1. Explain to the client how resistance helps them focus:

   "This band wraps around the legs of your chair. When you push, pull, or stretch it with your feet and legs, it helps your brain stay focused and calm. It's here for you to press your feet or legs against to help the parts of your brain that tell you to move to stay busy and focus better on what's going on around you."

2. Guide the client to place a resistance band around the front two legs of any chair. Be sure the size of the band allows for enough resistance—no slack or drooping.

3. Invite them to sit down and bounce their calves against the band, step on and push down on it with their feet, or put their shins behind it and push forward.

4. Encourage the client to use a band like this during instructions, tests, dinner, or homework time to help their brain stay focused.

Tier 1

School, Treatment, and Community Settings

Like fidget tools, this intervention is one I recommend for *all* students and group participants regardless of diagnosis or age. Keep resistance bands available in your space, either as optional or as part of your standard setup, or encourage kids to take them to classes or activities if possible.

Pacing Runways B, N, S

Therapeutic Rationale:

In contrast to historical approaches to treating ADHD that emphasized restricting movement, this intervention offers permission for *appropriate* movement. Movement improves task maintenance, directed action, sustained effort, and persistence on tasks, all of which fall in the EF areas of cognitive flexibility and working memory. Pacing runways are designed to be an accessible, but contained, permissive movement area.

Goals:

- Improve task initiation, task persistence, and task completion
- Accommodate vestibular and proprioception movement needs
- Improve bilateral self-regulation and impulse control

Materials:

- Duct tape/gaffer tape
- Space on the floor of your area

Directions:

1. Using a roll of duct/gaffer tape, run a line of tape from one wall to the other (or as long as you can fit) in the back of your instructional/group space. Then, about two feet away, run a second line of tape parallel to the first, creating a runway. At minimum, the pacing runway should be eight feet long.

2. Explain to the students or group about movement preferences:

   "Some people are sitters for learning, but some people like to stay busy. We all have our own way of doing things. Sometimes our need to move wants to take us away from where we are supposed to be. It would be much better if we had a place to go in *the room, so we can move and learn at the same time."*

3. Introduce the pacing runway, which is a place that *anyone* in the space can go to when they feel the need to move. Show everyone where they can go, and model walking back and forth from one end of the runway to the other.

4. Review the rules for the runway (and consider posting them on the wall near it as well): *We keep our bodies and words to ourselves. We stay in the runway as long as we need it and return to our seats when we're ready.* (Many of the rules from the *Fidget or Distractor* intervention will overlap with the runway rules, so review this if necessary.)

5. Invite kids to practice walking in the runway, and direct anyone who isn't following the rules back to their seats (always with the invitation to "try again").

Note: The pacing runway should be *in* the room and not out in the hallway. It should also be accessible to everyone that needs it, to prevent inadvertent reinforcement of escape and avoidance behaviors.

Tier 1 or 2*

School, Treatment, and Community Settings

Most educators are (understandably) wary of allowing students to get up and move freely about the room as they choose, perhaps as a tier 3 accommodation—I would be too. Instead, this intervention creates a compartmentalized space that is identified as a tool for movement. The paradoxical effect of this intervention is fascinating: When *all* students are allowed to use the pacing runway (tier 1), interruptions, distractions, and off-task behavior decrease significantly. The initial adjustment to the added movement subsides within 7 to 10 days. In treatment settings, the pacing runway can be placed inside a communal area or group room, depending on setup and safety considerations.

* This intervention is a tier 1 application if used as a group instructional task, and generally results in tier 2 if only a few students in your room use it regularly.

Visual Movement Boxes **B, S**

Therapeutic Rationale:

Like pacing runways, visual movement boxes are an intervention that embraces—rather than challenges—the need for movement by providing a clearly defined space marked with visual boundaries. This allows movement in a way that minimizes distraction to others while improving focus, and it significantly decreases the frequency of verbal reminders.

Goals:

- Improve task initiation, task persistence, and task completion
- Accommodate vestibular and proprioception movement needs
- Improve bilateral self-regulation and impulse control

Materials:

- Duct tape/gaffer tape (optional: in different colors and patterns)
- Space on the floor of your area

Directions:

1. Using a roll of duct/gaffer tape, create a square on the floor around the client's desk, with approximately one foot of space on both sides, at the front, and behind the chair. I recommend against using portable items, such as carpet squares, to create the box. Not only are they too tempting to play with, but they're often left behind in settings where the child transitions.
2. If the client is in the instructional seat less than 70 percent of the day, it is entirely appropriate to remove the chair altogether, giving them more movement space (as long as they have ready access to the chair as needed).
3. Review the rules for the movement box with the client:

   "Sometimes you like to move away from your seat, and it's okay to get up and stretch, but leaving this space can be distracting for other kids. This area is where you are allowed to move. Anywhere inside of this space is yours, as long as you don't stand on the chair or desk."

4. Have the client show you how they can move around the desk comfortably. Remind them that they don't have to ask for permission to move in this space, but if they move outside of the space you will remind them to "Go find your space." (Please do not say "go to your box.")

Variation: Use a variety of colored and patterned rolls of tape, assigning a different one to each child. Use this tape to create a movement box in their various places (e.g., cubby, centers, "pie piece" during circle time). This promotes organization and independence while also supporting movement needs.

Tier 1 or 2*

School, Treatment, and Community Settings

Visual movement boxes can (and should) be universally applied in classrooms and therapeutic groups and residential settings, not only to support movement needs but also to reinforce boundaries and personal space (particularly when there is trauma history).

A common concern among professionals is that allowing movement will distract peers. In practice, I have found the opposite to be true. Within 7 to 10 days, peers typically become desensitized to the additional movement and are less distracted overall—especially compared to the frequent verbal interruptions and redirections that occurred before the intervention.

* This intervention is a tier 1 application, but if space prohibits universal application, a tier 2 application is appropriate.

Line-Up Lists B, S

Therapeutic Rationale:

Waiting in line is a persistent challenge for most kids with ADHD because it taps into several skill-deficit areas at one time—standing still, appropriate proximity to others, keeping their hands to themselves, not blurting out, boredom, and delayed gratification. A typical practice for neurotypical kids is *exhausting* for kids with ADHD because of the energy spent on self-control alone. This can lead to irritability, fatigue, and low or no response to verbal redirection from educators and staff. Line-up lists are a simple and effective intervention that builds impulse control, social awareness, and delayed gratification skills.

Note: This intervention is written for a classroom setting and works only in cases where the students will line up in a predetermined order.

Goals:

- Improve impulse control, social awareness, and patience
- Promote independence and agency
- Promote bilateral processing of visual spatial experiences

Materials:

- Numbered list of students (to match order of line)

Directions:

1. Explain to the class how they will learn to line up:

   "Sometimes it's hard to stand and wait in line, and even harder if we are going to do something really interesting or exciting. I know we've always just told you where to go before, but now we are going to teach you how to be a visual detective, so we can help your brain figure out where you're supposed to be."

2. Ask the students to find their name and location on the list *before* forming the line.

3. Once lined up, prompt the students to be a "detective" by paying attention to who is standing in front of them and behind them. Remind them that these are the people to look for to know if they are in the right spot in line.

4. If a student migrates away from their place, rather than giving a verbal redirection of where to go, use the list as a visual reminder and say, "*Show* me where you are supposed to be." If needed, remind them to tap into their detective skills—who is in front of them and who is behind them—as a visual engagement.

5. Positively reinforce the student's ability to independently find their own location and be aware of their social surroundings. You can give them a nod of the head, a smile, or (if they can tolerate it) a verbal "nicely done."

Tier 1

School, Treatment, and Community Settings

An adaptation to this intervention for community use (e.g., libraries, grocery stores, anywhere you wait in line) would be having the caregiver give prompts like "Use your eyes, and find where we are we in line" or "How many people are in front of us? How many are behind us? How long do you think it might take until it's our turn?"

Stripping the Environment **B, S**

Therapeutic Rationale:

Children with ADHD struggle not only with attention, concentration, and organization, but also with being easily distracted by unnecessary visual and auditory stimuli. Many classrooms, therapy offices, and treatment settings overwhelm kids with excessive information—wall posters, colorful pathways, decorative mobiles, motivational signs, and other items that clutter every visual plane—and they usually have little relevance to the task at hand. The most effective learning environments use minimal but purposeful cues. As a general rule, the front half of a classroom or clinical space should include only what is essential, such as:

1. Daily classroom or communication/treatment rules
2. The current homework or task assignment
3. Approved behavioral charts
4. Three visual "priming" boxes (see the *Priming the Cognitive Pump* intervention on page 184 for details)

Limiting extraneous stimuli doesn't mean the space must feel cold or sterile. Warm, neutral-colored signage can keep the environment simple yet welcoming.

The back half of the room is the best place for creative, visually engaging materials that reflect personality and support social connection. In early elementary classrooms that use centers, a neutral-colored sheet or curtain can help cover unused areas and reduce distraction. When working with families, encourage them to consider the home environment as well. Many children are expected to complete homework at cluttered kitchen tables full of mail, crafts, food, and other distractions. Help caregivers identify a specific, clutter-free workspace that minimizes visual overload.

Goals:

- Decrease visual extraneous stimuli
- Improve opportunity for task-orientation
- Assist with task closure and transitioning
- Improve classroom and therapeutic focus and encoding of novel information

Materials:

- Demarcated areas for placement of instructionally necessary information
- Flat white sheets or shower curtains

Directions:

1. Explain that some environments are busy, and it can make it hard to focus:

   "Our job is to help you to learn and stay focused on new information, but sometimes things around us can be very distracting. We are going to look for things in this room that you notice."

2. Ask your class or group participants to take five minutes to observe their environment and write down anything that they notice in each of their five sensory areas. Create a scale of distractibility from 1–10, and ask each child to rank their placement on the scale (where 1 is "no distraction" and 10 is "cannot focus"). Make sure they are observing only the front and side walls within the instructional or therapeutic space, as the rear is set aside for unstructured time.

3. The children should review the responses and mark down the frequency of each distracting item in the space. Of the items with the highest scores, decide which are necessary for instruction or group participation, and begin stripping unnecessary extraneous stimuli. If items cannot be removed, you may consider covering them with a sheet or curtains.

4. It can be helpful for children to assist in removing and replacing the items they find distracting, as they can help decide if the item needs to be disposed of or if a replacement will decrease distractibility.

5. Clearly introduce and define compartmentalized visual areas for the four things that must remain: classroom rules, assignments, behavioral charts, and priming boxes.

6. After a week of instruction, return to the original task of five minutes of observation to determine whether removal of unnecessary stimuli has improved task focus and encoding of information. Have the participants rank items again on the 1–10 scale, and individually address rankings of 6–10 to determine whether more stripping of the environment should occur.

Tier 1

School, Treatment, and Community Settings

Not only can this environmental change in a classroom setting improve focus and concentration for students with ADHD symptoms, but it can also be beneficial for students that experience anxiety or overstimulation. Make this a standard practice for any space where you are providing instruction or therapeutic intervention.

Effective Classroom Seating *B*

Therapeutic Rationale:

A traditional classroom management technique is to place children with attentional issues in the front of the classroom to minimize distractions. This has proven to be problematic because the front of the room is an open space with a lot of activity—students are approaching the teacher's desk to ask questions, leaving the room, and grabbing tissues, among other things. The lack of visual boundaries makes it *harder* to focus, not easier. Kids with ADHD seated in the back of the classroom don't fare much better—there, they experience too much auditory and visual stimuli (see the previous *Stripping the Environment* intervention). Rather, the best location for a student with ADHD is in the *center* of the classroom. Here, they have visual boundaries from their neighbors' desks around them, minimal movement, and limited cues in the visual planes. This improves the EF skills of self-control and working memory.

Goals:

- Improve self-awareness of boundaries
- Create a space conducive to learning
- Improve encoding of novel information

Materials:

- A new seat for the child in the center of the classroom

Directions:

1. Explain to the child why they are getting a new seat:

   "Sometimes sitting in the front of the room can be confusing. It's hard to understand why some kids can move while other kids cannot. Sometimes when they move around, talk, or leave the room, it tells our brains that we can do that too. We are going to try a different seat so you can look to your neighbors to get more information about moving, and keep all those other things from drawing your attention."

2. Place the child in the center of the room and ask them to visually identify the students around them. Let them know that they will know they are in the correct seat if they see these students. (See also the *Line-Up Lists* intervention on page 168).

3. Discuss and visually cue the rules for movement, including letting the child know how to ask for help as needed during class or group tasks.

4. After a few days, ask the child to identify any further extraneous sensory inputs, and make accommodation as necessary.

Tier 2 or 3

School, Treatment, and Community Settings

This location for seating can be adjusted in all classes and often results in significantly improved task-orientation and encoding of information. Students also show improved awareness of movement and non-movement times as they use the support of their peers around them. This also decreases the likelihood that students will wander about the space during times that are not set aside for unstructured activities. You layer with this tool by using visual cues to identify when structured time is occurring and when the transition to unstructured activities is occurring.

Visual Checklist

B, N

Therapeutic Rationale:

Kids with ADHD often struggle to follow multistep directions due to difficulties with working memory and encoding. They may remember the first part of an expectation but lose track of later steps, and then become frustrated and give up. As a result, educators and caregivers may say things like "They aren't listening," or "They know what to do, they just aren't doing it," framing the difficulty as a behavior problem rather than a skill deficit that needs support. Visual checklists help bridge this gap by providing multistep directions in a way that supports dual-hemisphere processing. By pairing verbal instructions with visual cues, they reduce cognitive load and create a greater opportunity for success.

Goals:

- Increase successful completion of multistep directives
- Promote bilateral processing of linear tasks
- Improve effort and motivation to engage in tasks

Materials:

- *Visual Checklist: Examples and Guidelines* handout
- Paper or laminated copy of the *Visual Checklist* template
- Dry-erase markers and eraser
- Variety of art supplies (e.g., colored pencils, crayons)
- Photos or clippings from magazines
- Scissors
- Tape

Directions:

1. Explain how a checklist can help with multistep directions:

   "Sometimes when a task feels really big or overwhelming, it helps to break it into smaller steps using a checklist. Let's think of a job you have with lots of steps—maybe one where you forget what comes next, get frustrated halfway through, or lose track of what you're supposed to be doing."

2. Review the *Visual Checklists: Examples and Guidelines* handout with caregivers or educators. Conceptualize the activity with the adult, noting that they must set expectations before the child chooses their tasks within those parameters.

3. Introduce the child to the *Visual Checklist* template. Together, create a list of steps to complete a task. Next to each step, the child should draw or add in a visual cue with photos or other images. If they are using a laminated version of the template, have them use dry-erase markers. (Laminated sheets are great for tasks the child will do over and over again.)
4. Invite the child to complete the task using their checklist, marking each step complete as they progress. They can either cover it or check it off to increase internal organization and persistence.
5. For each new task the child works on, use a new copy of the *Visual Checklist* template. If they are using a laminated version of the template, have them erase the list (and remove any images) before starting a new one.

Note: While you can use a digital format for checklists, I recommend using physical mediums. Physically checking something off a list can create a sense of closure and an internal boost of self-efficacy and self-esteem (a dopamine hit!).

Tier 3

School, Treatment, and Community Settings

Cueing for multistep directives is a common special education accommodation in IEPs; however, in practice, it is often a paraprofessional delivering each step verbally, which decreases the chances the steps will be encoded independently. Using a visual checklist is a great solution here. Create laminated versions for any repetitive tasks the student engages in throughout the day, and check each step off the list as they go. If the student gets off-task or regresses, erase the checks back to the nearest step as opposed to starting all over—this will decrease overwhelm and keep the student engaged. It also decreases all-or-nothing thinking in students who tend to be more rigid, such as those with obsessive-compulsive disorder.

Handout

Visual Checklist: Examples and Guidelines

Guidelines:

- **Consider your child's age and development.** Kids ages 3 to 8 should have no more than two or three responsibilities; youth ages 9 to 15 can have five to seven on their list.
- **Keep it simple.** "Clean the bathroom" isn't one task—it's more like 52.
- **Feel free to mix up your child's responsibilities.** With a good drawing or icon as a visual cue, there is little confusion on what needs to be done, but be ready to answer any questions if needed.
- **Let the child choose their first option.** You may have multiple responsibilities for the child, but they should choose which they want to complete *first*; this gives them a sense of agency while still meeting expectations.
- **Return to the list when the tasks are done.** Provide a check-in to look over the quality of their work (e.g., "Did you do the best job that you can?").
- **Check off tasks only when the child has put forth age-appropriate effort.** If not, ask them to try it again (but do not do it for them).
- **When the list is done, erase it completely or throw it away.** You can also keep copies in a folder or binder to show their history of success.

Examples:

Chores

1. Put your clothes in the laundry basket.

2. Put your books back on the shelf.

3. Put your dishes in the sink.

Math: Simple Addition

1. Start with the bigger number.

2. Count up using the smaller number.

3. Use your fingers to help.

4. What number did you end on?

Template

Visual Checklist

How to: ________________________________	
	Step 1:
	Step 2:
	Step 3:
	Step 4:
	Step 5:

The 20/10 Rule **N, S**

Therapeutic Rationale:

Most individuals can sustain focused, task-oriented work for about 20 minutes before benefiting from 10 minutes of free movement. For individuals with ADHD, focused attention tends to peak closer to 17 minutes before performance begins to decline. Beyond this point, work quality often degrades as their focus shifts from doing the task well to simply finishing it, which can lead to frustration, power struggles, and reduced quality of work.

The 20/10 rule aligns with what neuroscience tells us about the ADHD brain and provides a practical framework for putting this understanding into action.

Goals:

- Improve task initiation, task persistence, and task completion
- Improve self-esteem and self-efficacy

Materials:

- Timer (preferably a sand timer for visual reinforcement)

Directions:

1. Explain to the child the 20/10 rule:

   "We're going to work on [task] *for 20 minutes, then take a 10-minute break to move our bodies. After the break, we'll come back and work on* [task] *for another 20 minutes, and we'll keep repeating this until the task is done. We're going to try our best to focus and work hard during the 20 minutes. Taking movement breaks helps our brains rest, so when we come back, we can think better than if we tried to power through without a break."*

2. Set the timer for 20 minutes and let the child begin the task. Allow the child to stand or shift their weight during the task if needed.
3. When 20 minutes is up, provide the child with options for movement (no screens). They might stand, stretch, pace, go for a walk, or get the mail.
4. After 10 minutes, have the child return to the task for 20 minutes or until it is complete.

> **Note:** Ensure that the environment is prepared ahead of time (e.g., good lighting, prepared materials, limited distractions) and that basic needs (e.g., hunger, bathroom) are met. This allows the child to solely focus on the task for the entire 20-minute period.

Tier 1 or 3*

School, Treatment, and Community Settings

Incorporating movement into lesson plans or therapeutic programming is a great way to follow the principles of 20/10 without needing to follow it exactly. For example, if you are working on spelling words in a classroom, a social activity such as a spelling bee incorporates free-range movement within the task itself.

* This intervention is a tier 1 application, but if specific adjustments are needed for kids with a shorter degradation time, this would be a tier 3 application.

Altering Verbal Antecedents **B, C**

Therapeutic Rationale:

All behaviors are a result of an antecedent (trigger) and the internal response (either thought or feeling) to that trigger. Most people attempt to step in *after* the internal response has occurred to resolve the "escalation." The problem with this approach is that it's too late: Once a trigger-response cycle has started and the internal response has taken over, the behavior is likely to progress. A common trigger for kids is an adult's use of language. This is either due in part to difficulty processing what is being said, tone/volume interpretation, or shutting down of higher-order verbal processing due to increased escalation.

Altering verbal antecedents focuses on changing the way adults give instructions or redirection to young people—preventing the cycle from occurring in the first place—which decreases the chances the child will lose focus on the task at hand or become escalated and engage in challenging behaviors. This intervention addresses EF skills of self-control and cognitive flexibility.

Goals:

- Proactively approach behavioral and task expectations
- Decrease the likelihood of emotional impulsivity
- Promote healthy communication between individuals
- Improve transitions and shifting
- Increase effort and engagement in tasks
- Alter counterproductive verbal antecedents

Materials:

- *Antecedent-Response Cycle* handout
- *Altering Verbal Antecedents* handout

Directions:

1. Provide the caregiver or educator with the *Antecedent-Response Cycle* handout to review the trigger-response cycle.
2. Guide them to create a list of examples when a child in their care appeared to have an incongruent emotional response to their request. Then have them choose one of the examples and review it using the following questions:
    a. What was the antecedent (i.e., what seemed to trigger the child)?
    b. What thought or feeling did you expect?
    c. What thought or feeling did the child actually have?
    d. How did that translate into a behavioral response?

3. Have the client reflect on what thematic verbal triggers are present, such as:
    a. "You need to . . ."
    b. "No, you can't . . ."
    c. "Why are you . . ."
    d. "What are you doing . . ."
4. Provide the caregiver or educator with the *Altering Verbal Antecedents* handout and have them consider how they could alter this interaction. Use the three rules:
    a. Don't ask a question you already know the answer to.
    b. Don't make requests for behaviors when a child is obviously irritable, agitated, or otherwise involved in an activity.
    c. Don't make long verbal lists or expectations for children. (See the *Visual Checklist* intervention on page 174 for a review on giving task lists to kids.)
5. Have the client practice the rules on the *Altering Verbal Antecedents* handout consistently for 7 to 10 days, and then return to a previously identified interaction to determine whether altering the verbal antecedent prevented the development of emotional impulsivity or improved the relational interaction.

Tier 1

School, Treatment, and Community Settings

Schools and treatment facilities often use functional behavioral assessments (FBAs) to disrupt the antecedent-response before it begins. These assessments examine the antecedent, internal response, and behavioral pattern of a student or client, which then informs how the professionals involved will approach and interact with the child.

Altering verbal antecedents can become second nature with practice in the classroom, and it is a well-modeled skill for other peers in that environment. This is also a useful practice for group processing in therapeutic settings and will likely result in keeping youth present for group activities instead of experiencing shutdown due to unnecessary negative antecedents.

Handout

Antecedent-Response Cycle

Every behavioral response is the result of an antecedent (trigger) and the internal response (thought or feeling) to that trigger. See the cycle in the following image:

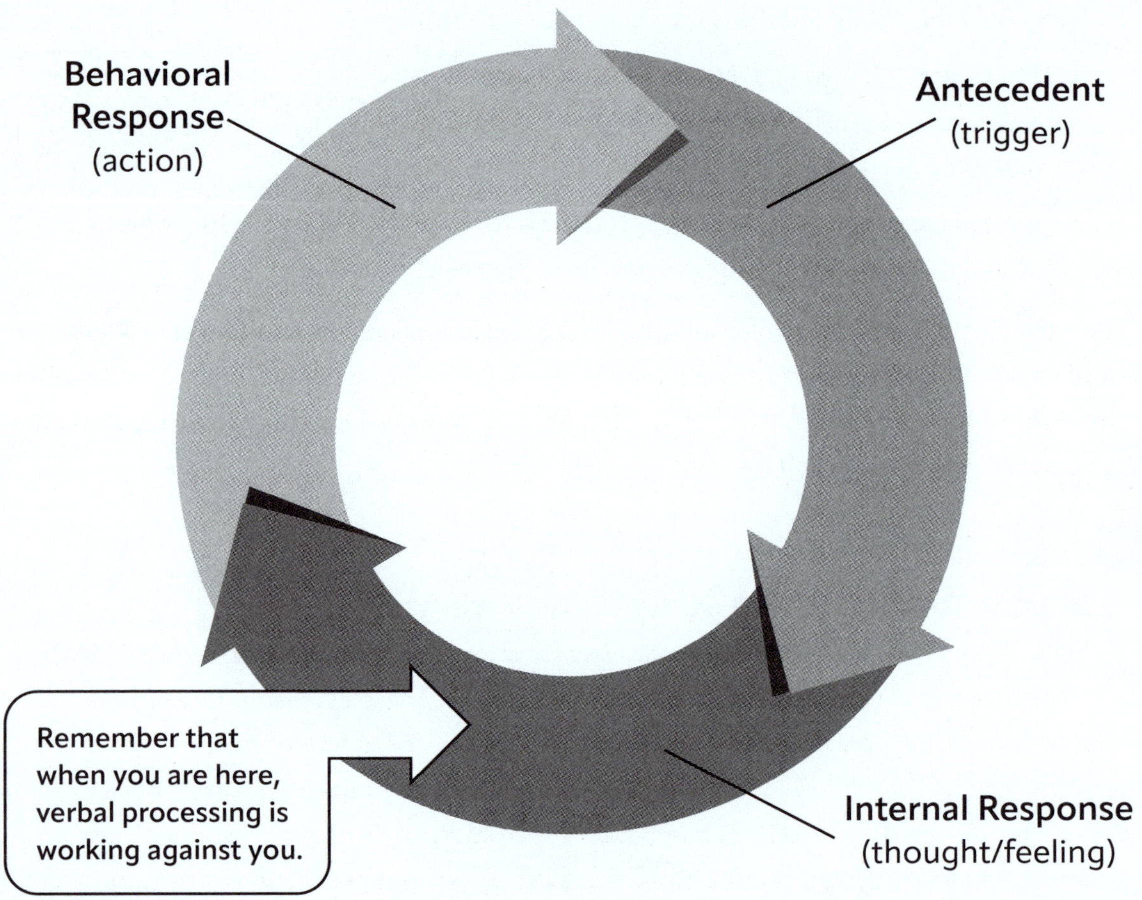

For example:

Antecedent: "You need to wash the dishes right now."

Internal response: Frustration: "I'm busy with something else."

Behavioral response: Refusing the task, arguing, escalating to aggression

Once the cycle begins and the internal response has taken over, verbal processing and other key executive functions have gone "offline" as the child relies on fight, flight, freeze, or fawn to cope until the crisis has passed. Focus should be instead on altering verbal antecedents as a *proactive* tool.

Handout

Altering Verbal Antecedents

1. **Don't ask questions that you already know the answer to.** This can set children up for dishonesty or immediate frustration. Instead of saying, "Have you cleaned your room yet?" (when you know they haven't), perhaps consider saying, "When you are finished watching that show, please remember you need to clean your room." The tone and method of communicating expectations has changed significantly and is more likely to elicit a positive response. This step is especially important for children who are right-hemisphere dominant.

2. **Do not make requests when the child is obviously irritable, agitated, or otherwise involved in an activity.** This often results in a failure to process the verbal expectation. It can also create difficulty in transitioning from one task to another. (See the *Priming the Cognitive Pump* intervention for guidance on functional transitions without behavioral response.)

3. **Do not make long verbal lists for your child to comply with.** This often results in the child's inability to understand and follow through with the expectation. This step is especially important for children who have difficulties with verbal processing and encoding. Remember, using visual lists improves an individual's ability to comprehend and follow through with expectations, as well as retain that information for future application. (See the *Visual Checklist* materials for a review on giving task lists to kids.)

Priming the Cognitive Pump B, N

Therapeutic Rationale:

This intervention is designed to help support kids with ADHD to successfully transition between activities. Transitions are common "pain points" for educators, staff, and caregivers—they waste time giving constant reminders to kids about the transition, all while some kids successfully move on to the next activity and others remain stuck. "Priming the cognitive pump" is rooted in the cognitive shifting research, which tells us that the brain needs (1) *closure* from the first task, (2) a *pause* with no expectations between tasks, and (3) time to *initiate* the next task. This is not unlike pumping water from an outside well: Most often, the first pump causes nothing to happen; on the second pump, a little bit of water flows; and on the third pump, water starts to flow. By taking time to "prime the cognitive pump," you can assist children with internal processing, time management, behavioral organization, and successful completion of step-by-step directives. This exercise promotes EF skills of cognitive flexibility and self-control.

Goals:

- Improve task shifting without increasing agitation or impulsiveness
- Pair visual cueing with verbal prompting

Materials:

- Whiteboard, chalkboard, or other reusable surface
- Painter's tape
- Dry-erase markers and eraser

Directions:

1. Create a visual cue by making three boxes—one to represent each step of the transition—on a space that's clearly visible. In a classroom, you might use painter's tape on the whiteboard at the front of the room; at home or in a therapy office, a portable whiteboard works well.
2. Introduce the exercise (explaining the pump metaphor can be helpful for visualization). Tell the child that you will place a checkmark in one of the boxes as each step of a transition occurs:
    a. **Pump 1 (closure from first task / statement of intent):** Ten minutes *before* the expected transition, find a natural lull or pause in the current task to get the child's attention. State that the transition is coming, wait five seconds, and ask them to paraphrase the expectation back to you (further reinforcing the verbal processing):

        "Hi kiddo, eyes on me for a sec. Thanks. In ten minutes, you will turn off the television and come to the dinner table. [Wait five seconds.] *Please tell me what you will be doing in ten minutes."*

        Put a checkmark in the first box to create a visual cue that the transition has started. The child returns to their activity.

b. **Pump 2 (pause/reminder of the expectation):** Wait five to seven minutes and get the child's attention, repeating the original expectation:

"Hi kiddo, eyes up. Remember, in [three, five, etc.] *minutes, you will turn off the television and come to the dinner table.* [Wait five seconds.] *Please tell me what you will be doing in* [three, five, etc.] *minutes."*

Put a checkmark in the second box to create a visual cue that the transition is in progress. The child returns to their activity.

c. **Pump 3 (initiate transition / follow-through):** When the time is up, get the child's attention and direct them to transition:

"[Name], *eyes on me again. Now is the time to turn off the television and come to the dinner table."*

Put a checkmark in the third box to create a visual cue that the transition is happening *now*.

3. Further reinforce this tool by pairing it with tactile cueing, which is especially helpful for children with rich internal narratives. For example, every time you check one of the three boxes, place a poker chip (or another small token) in the child's hand, where each chip represents a step toward the transition. Be sure not to remove each chip with the new pump, as when the tactile reminder is removed, the sensory reminder is too. When the transition is complete, the child places all three chips back in a designated area, such as a basket.

Note: Instead of checkmarks in each box, consider other ways to show progression, such as coloring in each box, drawing layers of a cake, filling in a progress bar, or building up a mountain.

Tier 1 or 3*

School, Treatment, and Community Settings

Priming the pump is an effective whole-classroom or individual tool for transitions. During each step of the transition, I also like to tell students, "Turn to your neighbor if you need help," which assists in creating a community model of support. It also serves as education for caregivers to bring the activity into different environments for their child. In treatment settings, this tool is effective for closing sessions or moving between therapeutic activities.

Telehealth Application

Using this at the closure of telehealth sessions can help your clients visualize a transition away from structured therapeutic contact. With my younger clients, I use troll dolls with different colored hair, set at the edge of the visual screen; for adolescents, I use sticky notes.

* This intervention is a tier 1 application, but it could also be classified as tier 3 with tactile cueing.

Thoughts Don't Have to Become Behaviors *C, D*

Therapeutic Rationale:

The goal of this intervention is to decrease impulsivity, a hallmark symptom of ADHD that often results in negative consequences at school, at home, and with peer groups. As I say to everyone I work with, "Thoughts are not behaviors, and thoughts do not always have to become behaviors." This mantra gives them permission to reflect and pause before acting. It is also in line with the DBT concept of decisional balance, which helps the child to prevent urges from transitioning into action and to stay present with the moment. By creating space between a thought/urge and a behavior, this tool specifically helps develop the EF skill of self-control, and it is easily incorporated into multiple settings.

Goals:

- Inject a pause in the impulsive thought-to-behavior transition
- Decrease negative impact of impulsive behaviors
- Promote motivation for healthy decision-making

Materials:

- *Impulse Control Decision-Maker* worksheet

Directions:

1. Ask the client to tell you about a time they made a decision too quickly and it resulted in a consequence they didn't like. Perhaps they drove their parents' car alone even though they only had a learner's permit.

2. Help the client to process this thought:

   "Let's take a brief pause with this thought—to weigh whether it should turn into a behavior or it should stay in your head."

3. Help the client write this experience on the *Impulse Control Decision-Maker* worksheet.

   a. The choices may be "do ____" or "don't ____" (e.g., "drive my parents' car" or "don't drive my parents' car") or there may be several different options to list.

   b. Have the client rank the value of each entry from 1–5 on a Likert scale (where 1 is the least important and 5 is the most important).

   c. Tally the results to determine whether the choice should become an active behavior or if it should be refrained from / exchanged due to the environmental consequence.

4. Encourage the client to fill this worksheet out to reflect and pause on a decision before they take any action.

Tier 2

School, Treatment, and Community Settings

Thought-behavior transitioning for students and group members is such a simple tool to promote slowed decision-making and to teach the prioritization of responsibilities and choices. Completing this activity with other peers—especially same-aged peers and mentors, who kids often identify with more than adults—can lend itself to developing insight from social interactions and failures in the past. Reflecting on these choices with another kid teaches them about social observation as well, which can also decrease impulsivity and improve personal self-control in a more generalized fashion.

Worksheet

Impulse Control Decision-Maker

Impulse control, or the ability to create space between your thoughts and actions, helps you avoid behaviors that might cause unintended harm or consequences at school, at home, or in relationships with the people you care about. This worksheet is designed to help you identify any unhelpful urges you may have and weigh the impact of acting on them.

Score each choice by level of importance on a scale of 1–5 (where 5 is "very important" and 1 is "not important at all"). When you have filled out the table, take note of which choice is of higher importance to you in considering the pros and the cons. Use this information to help you make the best decision.

Urge/Thought: I should throw my books down the hallway.

Choices	Pros (What do I gain?)	Importance (1–5)	Cons (What do I lose?)	Importance (1–5)
Throw the books.	I'll make my friends laugh; I'll feel cool.	2	I might get another detention; I'll feel bad later (especially if I hit someone).	(5)
Don't throw the books.	I'll feel proud for making a good choice; I won't be in trouble at home.	(4)	I'll miss a chance to get attention from people.	2

Urge/Thought:

Choices	Pros (What do I gain?)	Importance (1–5)	Cons (What do I lose?)	Importance (1–5)

Urge/Thought:

Choices	Pros (What do I gain?)	Importance (1–5)	Cons (What do I lose?)	Importance (1–5)

5

Autism

Autism populations, with all of their colorful varieties of interests and abilities, are one of the most remarkable groups of neurodivergent individuals to work with, in my opinion. The creative energy invested in growing skill sets from differing perspectives, recognizing opportunity in wide arrays of interests, and navigating sensory and social sensitivities for improved communication is deeply satisfying. Being in a partnership with these individuals as they learn to self-advocate for a shifting mindset from "disability" to "other abled" is a primary goal and a *magical key* for connecting on a genuine level with each individual. Note my use of *individual*—each one with their own nuances and idiosyncrasies, not a consistent and predictable set of symptom presentations like the other populations previously discussed in this text. This requires you to be willing to learn from these individuals about how *they* internally and externally manage experiences, so you can inform mutual treatment goals and expectations.

Of the symptoms of autism spectrum disorder (ASD), differences in the perception, interpretation, and use of social cues are among the most noticeable across home, school, and other settings. Limited in-person interaction during the COVID-19 pandemic further hindered these kids' development, as virtual platforms reduced reliance on physical nonverbal cues. When introducing the notion of social skills training, the observation I hear the most in treatment is "Are you trying to teach me to mask *more*?" Masking, sometimes referred to as camouflaging, is a coping strategy utilized by some autistic individuals to appear neurotypical in order to fit in with others. This energy-sucking coping mechanism uses patterns of mimicking, mirroring, suppressing stimming, and using rigid social scripts to help *other* people be more comfortable, all the while sacrificing what my clients refer to as "my genuine self."

My answer is always "Not at all. Social skills training is helping you create a skill set for communicating and building relationships, and helping you get your own needs met in a more comfortable and consistent way." Social skills, or rather reciprocal skills of communication, serve to improve an individual's social understanding, help them make more intentional choices about social engagement, and foster the growth of mutual relationships with others. This is best achieved in group settings, with a heterogeneous population. If you attempt to train skills of communication in a homogeneous population, you are less likely to see positive responses to interventions or a generalization of skills in multiple settings.

The interventions in this chapter will focus on:

- Developing skills of back-and-forth social communication
- Gaining social and emotional awareness
- Creating a framework for intentional social engagement or disengagement
- Learning how to self-advocate
- Growing acceptance rather than tolerance
- Building scaffolded techniques for growing social expertise
- Improving verbal and nonverbal communication
- Applying interventions to clients based on age (children ages 3 to 8 and youth ages 9 to 18)

Note: This chapter can be used in conjunction with chapters 1, 2, and 4, which provide a variety of tools for self-regulating, managing anxiety, accessing safe support nets, creating and utilizing effective coping skills, using transitional tools, and promoting growth of EF skills.

Key Concept

Differentiating masking and social skills: While social skills reflect authentic communication and connection, children with autism often mask, or suppress, their natural behaviors to fit in with their peers and the people around them.

Case Example

Toby, 7, was referred to me with a provisional diagnosis of early onset schizophrenia due to visual hallucinations (seeing "ghosts") and a delusional narrative of "catching ghosts in boxes to save the world." He has been hospitalized several times and in crisis stabilization placements, been on several different medications, and is often placed outside of the classroom at school because he cannot stop "talking about the ghosts he sees." None of these interventions have resolved the symptoms of psychosis.

His mother reports, "All of his treatment providers says he is hallucinating and has delusions. I don't know what to think, but it's hard to get him to do anything he's supposed to do. He doesn't have any friends, and his behavior and mood are getting worse."

When I meet with Toby, he presents with limited affective expression, persistent waist rocking, monotonous tone and inflection of prosodic speech, avoidance of eye contact, and a love of all things *Ghostbusters*. As I get to know him, he becomes more comfortable in session and his rocking ceases. He draws pictures of ghosts, mechanical packs for capturing spirits, and a very specific 1959 Cadillac Miller-Meteor Sentinel car. He talks nonstop about *Ghostbusters*, sharing even the minute details.

He tells me he has no friends: "The kids at school think I'm weird because I talk too close to them. But they're boring anyway, because no one likes *Ghostbusters*." He also shares that he struggles with meeting the new school guidance counselor, the sound of fire alarms, the smell of school pizza, and wearing school-required shirts because "the tags are scratchy."

Toby has tried to fit in with others by doing his best to keep from talking about *Ghostbusters*, tying himself to his chair with shoelaces so he won't rock, and feigning interest in other kids' topics of conversation, as he learned in treatment at the hospital.

Toby has never been assessed for autism.

No one has taught Toby to:

- Look for nonverbal cues for personal space
- Talk about his interests but also share conversation
- Accurately recognize how he and others around him feel
- Decide who gets to see his genuine self
- Use *Ghostbusters* as a tool for skills training

Autism Key Concept

Differentiating Masking and Social Skills

It's important to understand the difference between social skills and masking in autistic populations. While social skills reflect authentic communication and connection, *masking* often involves suppressing one's natural behaviors to fit in, which can lead to stress, burnout, and a diminished sense of self. Here are some key indicators of when masking is happening versus social skills.

Masking	Social Skills
• Mimicking others; chameleon effect • Avoiding social interactions completely • Restricting stimming behaviors • Covering or minimizing emotions • Forcing physical touch or avoiding it completely • Refraining from speaking in social settings	• Expressing the authentic self • Choosing meaningful engagements intentionally • Self-regulating to increase comfort • Identifying and expressing emotions genuinely • Learning boundaries and effective proxemics • Learning effective tools for social communication

Bull's-Eye for Boundaries **Soc, S**

Therapeutic Rationale:

One of the foundational areas to address when building scaffolded social skills is personal space and boundaries, also known as *proxemics*. Understanding and respecting personal space typically requires reciprocal interaction—such as the use of gestures, body language, and eye contact. It's also important to recognize that proxemics are influenced by the intensity and intimacy of a relationship. Supporting children in distinguishing between different relationship types—such as strangers, acquaintances, new friends, and close family members—helps establish clear parameters for appropriate personal space in various social contexts. This, in turn, provides a structured framework for understanding how personal boundaries can shift over time, fostering greater flexibility and adaptability in navigating social relationships. This intervention aims to do just that; it includes instructions based on age and developmental stage.

Goals:

- Improve back-and-forth recognition of nonverbal communication cues
- Increase awareness of personal boundaries
- Improve generalization of social skills across multiple settings

Materials:

- *Four Kinds of Relationships* handout
- *Bull's Eye for Boundaries* worksheet
- Painter's tape, preferably in four different colors
- Bubbles and bubble wand
- Optional: Carpet remnants or round floor mats in four different sizes, colors, or textures

Directions:

For Older Kids (Ages 8+)

1. Discuss personal space with the client:

   "Let's talk about our personal space. What do you hear about your boundaries from others? Is personal space a struggle for you to understand?"

   [Expect various levels of behavior and insight here: clients who are avoidant, those who are too close too often, those who practice healthy boundaries, and those with no insight at all.]

   "Personal space is about what we are comfortable with and *what the other person is comfortable with. This can be tricky to understand because all relationships are different, and everyone has a different comfort level with being physically close to other people.*

Today we're going to explore four different types of relationships we have with people, and what kind of personal space we should practice."

2. Review the *Four Kinds of Relationships* handout with the client. Ask them to identify people in their lives for each kind, and have them write these examples in the respective areas on the *Bull's-Eye for Boundaries* worksheet.

3. Either ahead of time or with the client, place painter's tape on the floor to recreate the boundaries bull's-eye using the recommended personal space parameters for each of the four relationships (8 to 12 feet for strangers, 4 to 8 feet for acquaintances, 2 to 4 feet for new friends, and 2 or less feet for friends, partners, or close family members).

4. Invite the client to stand in the bull's-eye while you stand in each of the "rings," demonstrating the expected space between the different types of people. Switch places and do it again, or call out different types of people (e.g., the mailperson) and ask them to stand in the appropriate circle.

5. If possible, have the client practice proxemics in public (e.g., grocery store, gym, library) for in vivo learning.

Variation: Use carpet remnants or floor mats to represent the bull's-eye. Have the client take their shoes and socks off to provide tactile engagement. Consider having different textures that get progressively more comfortable closer to the bull's-eye (e.g., scratchy, outdoor carpet or turf for strangers, a soft Berber carpet for inner rings, and fleece or fur for close relationships). Be sure to consider sensory sensitivities. Revisit this exercise as needed as relationships change.

For Younger Kids (Ages 3 to 7)

This age group generally has closer proxemics, so we often use the concept of "the personal bubble."

1. Discuss personal space with the client:

   "We each have a bubble around us, and other people do too. The air in this bubble is where we and others feel comfortable."

2. Provide the client and yourself with a bubble wand. Together, create smaller bubbles and larger bubbles, noting the amount of air in each of those sizes. See if you can catch bubbles together, and show the client that the bubbles can touch, but if they push too hard against one another, they pop.

3. Discuss with the client that everyone has a "personal bubble" that goes all the way around our bodies: hands, feet, arms, legs, and head. Be sure they know that everyone's bubble is different.

4. Role-play blowing up the bubble around your body, and see how the bubble expands in size as you put your arms and legs out around you.

5. Blow up your own bubble, and ask your client to move around the space with their personal bubble and be a visual detective to see if their bubble has pushed too close to yours, is just right, or has space left to get closer.
   a. Role-play nonverbal cues to show that your bubble has been popped (e.g., turning your body away, dropping your face down, covering the middle of your torso with your arms and hands), and challenge the client to communicate what they see. (For more on nonverbal cues, see the *Being an Effective Social Detective* intervention on page 201.)
   b. State, "Uh oh! Your bubble must've popped my bubble. All we have to do is back up and blow our bubbles up again to try one more time."
   c. Allow the client to practice this until they begin to recognize nonverbal cues of overly close proxemics.
6. Encourage the client to take this practice into settings such as family dinners, gym class, the playground, or the park with the prompt: "Let's pay attention to our bubbles."

Tier 1 or 2

School, Treatment, and Community Settings

This technique is useful for students in pre-kindergarten through high school, and even for young adulthood and parent training groups. Remember the ever-important component of *in vivo* or real-life practice in order to generalize personal space and boundaries to different settings.

Telehealth Application

Reflecting on personal boundaries and proxemics in the home as part of telehealth sessions can improve back-and-forth gesturing within family relationships. Telehealth has its difficulties and limitations, with families often attending in very close proxemics in front of one screen, and this is a wonderful opportunity for you to reflect on how they feel when their personal space is infringed upon—and how to make adjustments accordingly. Some ideas to allow for this practice include having the child sit in their own chair (rather than in the caregiver's lap) and placing the screen at a greater distance so the family members can be farther apart from each other while still being visible to the clinician.

Handout

Four Kinds of Relationships

There are different types of relationships in our daily lives. Some relationships already have built-in trust and closeness, while others may be new. We need to be aware of safety and space for the relationship to be comfortable—not just for us, but for the other person as well. We do this by noticing how we are feeling and paying attention to what the other person is telling us through their words and their body language.

While the most comfortable amount of space will be different for each unique person you know, the following guidelines are a good starting point to know about how much space to give someone:

- **Stranger/public:** A person you don't know anything about. You have either just met them for the first time, or you've never interacted with them.
  - Examples: A new student in your class, other shoppers at a grocery store, someone your caregivers work with, people at a park
  - With strangers, keep 8 to 12 feet of space between you and the other person so both of you can feel comfortable.
- **Acquaintance:** A person you have met once or twice, but you do not know much about them.
  - Examples: A classmate you say hi to, a neighbor you wave to, a friend of a friend, a job interviewer
  - With acquaintances, keep 4 to 8 feet of space between you and the other person so both of you can feel comfortable.
- **New friend:** A person you have started getting to know better and you choose to spend time with. You may know what this person is interested in (like playing LEGO or baseball), what they like to eat, or who is in their family.
  - Examples: A classmate you've been playing a lot with at recess, a co-worker you start spending time with outside of work, a teammate you have started to hang out with after games
  - With new friends, keep 2 to 4 feet of space between you and the other person so both of you can feel comfortable.

- **Friend, partner, or close family member (intimate):** A person you have spent a lot of time with and you know a lot about. You trust them and have had long-term positive interactions with them. These are people you might physically touch or allow to touch you, like giving hugs, sitting close, or holding hands.
  - Examples: Your best friend, your boyfriend, your mom, your grandpa
  - With friends, partners, and close family members, you can be within 2 feet of the other person, as long as both of you feel comfortable.

Note: Be aware that relationships with others can change over time. For example, a stranger may become an acquaintance, who might also become a friend some day! It's possible that you may grow apart from others as well. As your relationships change, the safety and appropriate space will change accordingly as well.

Worksheet

Bull's-Eye for Boundaries

Write the names of people that match the relationship in each ring, also including different types of people (e.g., teachers, the mailperson, other shoppers in a store). Review this worksheet often for a reminder of how close you should be when meeting and talking to others.

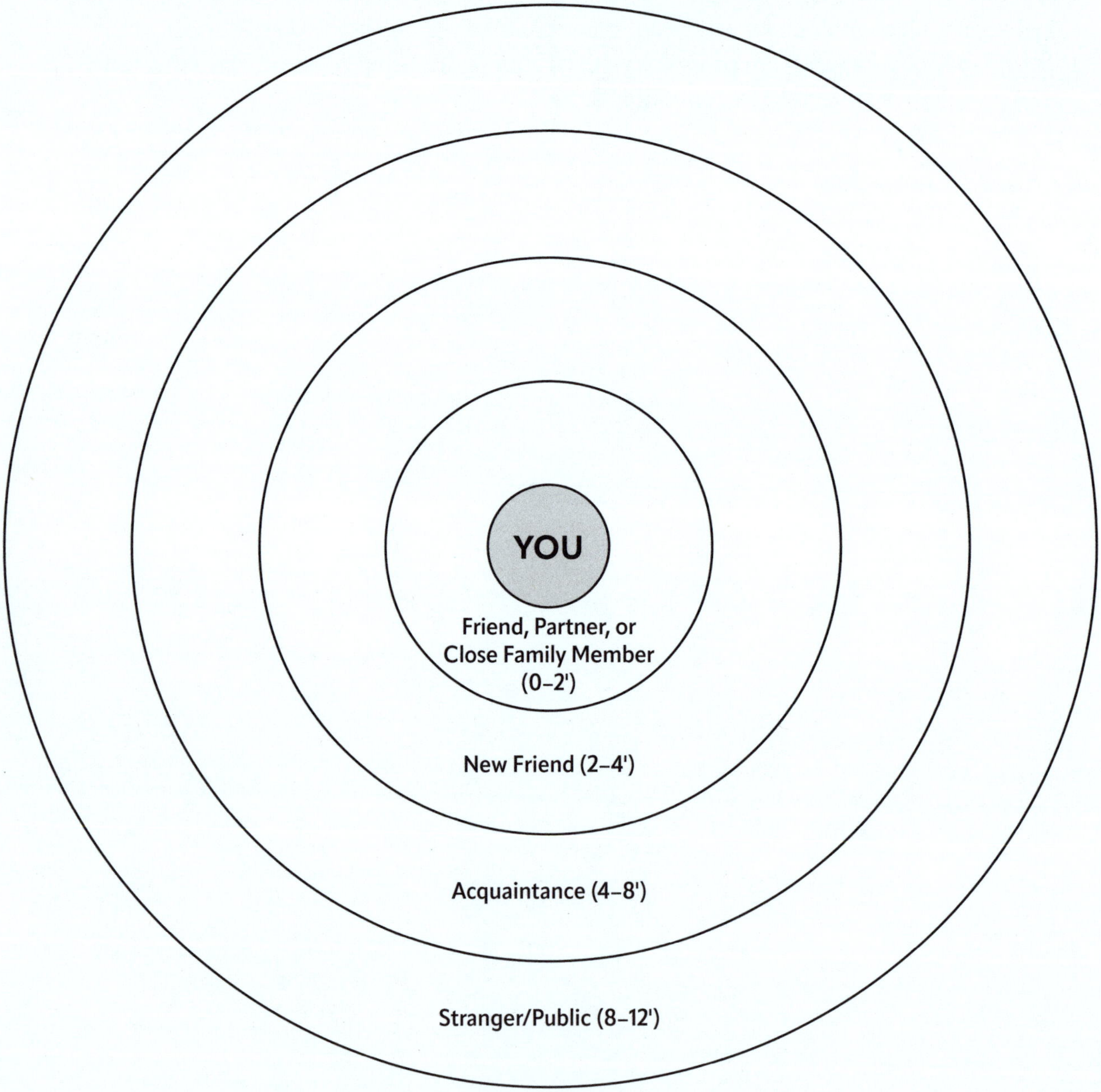

Being an Effective Social Detective

Therapeutic Rationale:

The social communication model emphasizes that individuals in social situations often begin in either a *withdrawn proxemic state* (not actively engaged) or an *overly close proxemic state* (overengagement) when they have not yet learned the rules of space in interpersonal relationships. With appropriate support or gentle challenges—such as prompting someone to sit up straighter or make brief eye contact—they can gradually increase their social engagement and environmental awareness, helping to counter the withdrawal and self-absorption often seen in ASD populations.

As engagement improves, individuals are better able to pick up on nonverbal social cues in their environment, including what Duke and Nowicki (2005) termed *dyssemias*. For example, an individual might learn to understand how others signal that someone is standing too close, and begin to recognize appropriate physical boundaries. This process is crucial not only for the learner (the client) as they build social understanding, but also for others to interpret and respond to their behavior more accurately and compassionately (Altman & Nowicki, 2024; Nowicki & van Buskirk, 2022, Winner & Crooke, 2020). This intervention is designed to teach and enhance these skills.

Goals:

- Improve back-and-forth relational awareness in social situations
- Pay attention to auditory information and nonverbal cues (dyssemias)

Materials:

- *Being an Effective Social Detective* worksheet

Directions:

1. Explain to the client how they can be a "social detective" regarding personal space:

   "Sometimes we have a hard time figuring out where our bodies should and shouldn't be in social situations. When we try to get closer to people, we might hear 'Hey, back it up' and that makes us want to step far away, and then people might say, 'Where are you going?' They might even think you are finished with the conversation and stop paying attention. Personal space can be hard to figure out at first, but the more we practice being social detectives, the better we get at it, and this can help us decide who we want to be close to and who we need more space from."

2. Provide the client with examples of comfortable and uncomfortable verbals and nonverbals.

   a. Comfortable: Smiling, open body posture, leaning in, calm tone, laughter

   b. Uncomfortable: Crossed arms, leaning away, frowning, heavy sighs, loud voice

3. Complete the *Being an Effective Social Detective* worksheet with the client, considering how personal space preferences change based on who you are talking to and what the situation is. Discuss with them that keeping their posture upright and doing visual check-ins can help them be better detectives.
4. If needed, you might role-play moments with the client when they might need *more* information to decide on comfort of proxemics.

Tier 1

School, Treatment, and Community Settings

Teaching all kids how to be more socially aware can improve the milieu of the classroom and decrease the number and intensity of negative social interactions that occur between children. Some kids think everyone is their best friend, while others think no one likes them, and their behaviors tell as much. Allow each child to complete their own *Being an Effective Social Detective* worksheet, and have them compare it with others to improve back-and-forth relational understanding.

Worksheet

Being an Effective Social Detective

When you're learning the "rules of space," you have to strengthen your detective skills and gather clues that help you answer questions about yourself *and* others:

- "Do *I* want to be closer to or farther away from this person?"
- "How is my closeness making *them* feel?"

Let's think about how people communicate with both their words and their bodies. When you pay attention to both, you can make better decisions about whether you need to adjust your own personal space so that everyone feels comfortable.

Can you think of a time when you needed more information before you could make a good choice about how close or far to stand from someone? Can you think of times when *you* tried to show others that you were uncomfortable—maybe by stimming for comfort—but they didn't pick up on your signals?

Now consider how certain nonverbal social cues would tell you a change might be needed in your personal space with four different types of people.

What do you hear with your ears (e.g., yelling, sighing, laughing, growling)?

	Too Close	Too Far	Just Right
Stranger	Heavy sighing	Speaking very loudly	Soft laughter
Acquaintance			
New friend			
Trusted person			

What do you see with your eyes (e.g., postural shifting, arm and hand movements, facial tension, flushing)?

	Too Close	Too Far	Just Right
Stranger			
Acquaintance			
New friend			
Trusted person			

Handshakes, Fist Bumps, and More **Soc, S**

Therapeutic Rationale:

This intervention builds on the previous two—focused on personal touch and nonverbal communication—by teaching kids with symptoms of autism about common touch-based greetings and how the intensity of touch can convey different messages. Understanding appropriate use of touch is particularly important in social interactions, job interviews, and educational settings, and some individuals may need explicit support to navigate this aspect of communication effectively. For school-age children and adolescents, recognizing how various forms of touch are interpreted by others is a key component of social communication and relationship development. As children move into late adolescence and early adulthood, their social interactions often extend to professional environments—such as workplaces or higher-education settings—where expectations around physical greetings, like handshakes, become more nuanced. In these contexts, the quality of a handshake can significantly influence how the individual is perceived: a handshake that is too soft may be interpreted as passive, disengaged, or lacking confidence, whereas one that is overly firm may be seen as aggressive, controlling, or overly assertive. This intervention supports clients in understanding and practicing these subtle yet socially meaningful behaviors to promote more effective interpersonal communication.

Goals:

- Improve the likelihood of occupational placement and academic/social acceptance
- Improve self-awareness in initial contacts with strangers and acquaintances

Materials:

- *Intensity of Touch* handout
- Hand sanitizer (check for allergies and sensory sensitivity)

Directions:

1. Explain to the client how different kinds of touch can send a message:

   "When we talk to other people, we don't just use our words—we also use our bodies to help get our message across. For example, we might give a high-five or shake someone's hand. Today, we're going to learn how to use touch, like high-fives and handshakes, in ways that feel right and respectful for both us and the other person."

2. Guide the client to spend time observing their peers in unstructured times, such as recess, and then discuss the physical contact they see. (You may also do this with the client if possible.) Discuss what they most commonly see when they are with peers.

3. Provide the client with the *Intensity of Touch* handout.

4. Have the client choose a lower-intensity physical contact, such as a high-five, and actively practice with them.
5. Discuss how the intensity of their touch increases with frequency. For instance, giving someone 35 high-fives in a row will make a low-intensity touch become a high-intensity touch. Role-play this with the client.
6. Introduce the "rule of three," which indicates that the client has a total of three uses of a physical touch in a setting (e.g., playground), with one person or up to three different people. The counter will then reset when they transition to a new setting (e.g., hallway before class).
7. Encourage the client to practice their touch communication with trusted people.

Teaching Handshakes

1. Discuss how others may perceive the quality of handshakes, as well as the importance of learning to give an appropriate handshake in occupational or academic settings.
2. Ask the client to shake your hand, noting grip strength, number of shakes, and duration.
3. Directly teach occupationally appropriate handshakes. Guide the client to "follow the leader," meaning:
    a. They should match the person's grip strength.
    b. The person in charge determines the number of shakes.
    c. Watch the other person's shoulder to know when it's time to disengage shaking hands (it will move back).
4. Encourage the client to practice handshakes with multiple individuals in a safe space, asking for feedback.

Tier 1

School, Treatment, and Community Settings

All settings have a different rule about appropriate and inappropriate physical contact between peers. If you allow physical contact in appropriate social activities, you may challenge kids to practice lower-intensity physical touches with low frequency, allowing them to generalize the skills to different locations, such as playgrounds, cafeterias, and sports fields.

Handout

Intensity of Touch

Touch is one way people show feelings—like being friendly, showing care, or needing space. But not all touch feels the same. Touch intensity can be low, medium, or high, and it can feel comfortable (safe, friendly, wanted) or uncomfortable (excessive, too frequent, unexpected, unwanted) depending on how it's done and who it's with. This handout provides a spectrum of how the different intensities of touch can differ.

The Rule of 3
For each setting you are in, you have a total of 3 uses of physical touch. When you transition to a new setting, the counter resets!

High Intensity
What: Close contact, longer, more personal
Who: Friends, close family members
Example: Front hug

Medium Intensity
What: Friendly, a little longer than low intensity
Who: Acquaintances, new friends
Examples: Secret handshake, side hug

Low Intensity
What: Quick, light, and not too close
Who: Acquaintances
Examples: High-five, fist bump

Eye Contact

B, Soc

Therapeutic Rationale:

Appropriate eye contact is a challenging skill to teach and learn because it is highly nuanced and can be especially confusing for children with ASD symptoms. On one hand, eye contact can communicate interest and engagement; on the other, prolonged eye contact—or the expectation to maintain it—can be stressful, interfere with information processing and encoding, and promote masking behaviors. When overly emphasized or forced, eye contact can be counterproductive. Rather than treating eye contact as a requirement, it is more effective to teach it as one of many tools for engagement that support natural, reciprocal conversation. This intervention is designed to do exactly that—helping children understand when and how eye contact can be used meaningfully, without compromising comfort, authenticity, or learning. Further, it encourages self-advocacy by having kids practice communicating their comfort and intention with eye contact.

> **Note:** Cultural sensitivity is essential when implementing this intervention, as eye contact can carry very different meanings across cultures. Be mindful of these differences and consider each individual's cultural background and personal comfort as they work on this skill.

Goals:

- Increase understanding of the appropriate use of eye contact
- Observe and interpret nonverbal cues
- Identify discomfort and communicate personal comfort levels

Materials:

- *Eye Contact Checklist* worksheet
- Video clips of social interactions
- Optional: Access to video recording for direct observation

Directions:

1. Explain to the client that they will be practicing eye contact:

   "Eye contact can be a tricky skill to learn and understand. Looking at someone is one way to show that we are care about them, we are interested in what they are saying, or that we respect them, but looking too intensely or for too long can feel uncomfortable for both people—or it may communicate another message that we don't mean. Today, we're going to learn and practice different ways to use eye contact and notice how it helps us communicate with each other."

2. Start by explaining the difference between direct and indirect eye contact:

   "Direct eye contact is when we look right into someone's eyes and don't look away. [Demonstrate this.] *Indirect eye contact includes looking at a person's face but not directly in their eyes, or briefly looking them in the eye and then glancing away.* [Demonstrate this.] *It's best to use a combination of direct and indirect eye contact when interacting with other people, including friends, family members, and teachers. Let's look at some examples."*

3. Play video clips from shows or movies that show various scenes of social interactions.
   a. Choose a variety of examples: fun and playful, angry or intense, manipulation or lying, a speech.
   b. I recommend those that "break the fourth wall" by looking directly at the camera, such as *The Office* or *Ferris Bueller's Day Off*.

4. Provide the client with the *Eye Contact Checklist* and have them choose one character to watch during the clip. Ask them to reflect on the worksheet what type of eye contact was used and what it conveyed. Repeat for other characters as needed.

5. Transition to real-time practice of appropriate eye contact (both direct and indirect). Engage in two brief conversations with the client: one about a topic the client is interested in, such as an identified special interest, and one about a topic they are less interested in. Compare and contrast the two conversations, noting differences in engagement, comfort, and how eye contact was used to communicate level of connection, interest, and respect in each situation.

6. Brainstorm with the client how they can communicate with others about their comfort level with eye contact or to convey they are paying attention, such as, "I have a little trouble with eye contact, but I am paying attention."

Variation: Obtain consent to video record the real-time skills practice to provide further feedback and reflection.

Tier 2 or 3

School, Treatment, and Community Settings

As you set expectations in your classroom or group, it is important to remember that eye contact is not directly linked to attention or concentration. Using call-and-response cues, such as "One, two, three, eyes on me," can be appropriate; however, keep in mind that many students—particularly those who are neurodivergent—may take breaks from looking at you while still listening and being engaged.

Aim to create an environment where attention, interest, and respect can be demonstrated in many different ways. Encourage students to communicate when maintaining eye contact is difficult for them, and validate alternative forms of engagement that support learning and comfort.

Telehealth Application

If you work with clients that prefer to keep the camera off during session, titrate and challenge them to turn the camera on for brief periods of time and be a "social detective" to your method of communication with and without eye contact. This is an effective opportunity to reflect and model eye contact skills.

Worksheet

Eye Contact Checklist

Show: ______________________________

Character: ______________________________

1. What kind of eye contact did they use? (circle)

Direct	**Indirect**	**Both**

2. What *positive* things did their eye contact make you *think* about them? (circle)

Trustworthy	**Truthful**	**Reliable**	**Worth my attention**
Funny	**Believable**	**Intelligent**	**Makes me want to listen**
Genuine	**Calm**	**Friendly**	

3. What *negative* things did their eye contact make you *think* about them? (circle)

Dishonest	**Unreliable**	**Scary**	**Intimidating**
Manipulative	**Aggressive**	**Cold**	**Fake**
Unfriendly	**Disruptive**	**Anxious**	

5. In general, would you like to have a relationship with someone who regularly uses this type of eye contact? (circle)

Yes	**No**

Why or why not?

____

____

____

____

Tone, Tempo, Volume, and Inflection for Prosodic Speech

B, Soc

Therapeutic Rationale:

As we advance to the next stage of scaffolded skill development, we will focus on prosodic speech production and its role in effective social communication. Many kids with ASD-related symptoms struggle to regulate prosody, which conveys *emotion* and *intent*. The most common pattern is monotone speech with occasional abrupt emphasis, though other presentations may include:

- Excessive loudness or high pitch
- Sharply articulated consonants
- Echolalia with stuttering
- Consistently low volume with limited inflection

For effective communication, children must develop the ability to produce *and* perceive emotional and intentional cues in speech. Difficulties interpreting tone, tempo, volume, and inflection (TTVI) can hinder understanding during interactions. When teaching prosody, clinicians should use neutral phrases to model variation, as emotionally loaded language may add unnecessary cues for the intention of the sentence. Audiological factors also warrant attention: Similar prosodic patterns may appear in individuals who are deaf or hard of hearing, so comprehensive hearing screening should be part of the case history and evaluation.

Goals:

- Produce and perceive variations in prosodic speech to convey intention and emotion
- Provide psychoeducation surrounding TTVI
- Improve accurate interpretation in social communications

Materials:

- *Emotions List* handout (which can be made into laminated slips to be drawn from a bag)

Directions:

1. Explain to the client how tone can change meaning when we speak:

   "Sometimes the way we talk can be misunderstood by others, just like we sometimes misinterpret what others are saying too. For example, you might say to your teacher, 'I'm coming in a second,' but your volume might be too loud, so they see it as disrespectful. Your mom might say, 'It's time for dinner,' but she says it so quickly that you might think she's worried or upset with you."

2. Educate the client on the four areas of prosodic speech that they have control over:
    a. **Tone:** Pitch (high or low)
    b. **Tempo:** Speed (fast or slow)
    c. **Volume:** Degree of loudness (loud or soft)
    d. **Inflection:** Stress/intonation (emphasizing words/syllables)
3. Select a neutral phrase (e.g., "Take out your book") and repeat it to the client several times, demonstrating different levels of TTVI in speech to convey different emotional states.
4. Have the client choose an emotion from the *Emotions List* handout.
    a. You may also choose to write each emotion on separate slips of paper (laminating is optional) so they can choose one at random.
    b. Ask them to practice using their TTVI to convey that emotion while saying another neutral phrase (e.g., "The sky is blue today").
    c. Take turns with the client demonstrating and guessing the emotion.

Tier 1

School, Treatment, and Community Settings

This intervention can be readily used in classrooms or other group settings. If you are doing this exercise with a group, have one person choose an emotion and challenge the group to guess what is being portrayed. Have the group members name what specifically conveyed (or did not convey) that emotion. After reflection, allow the person to shift their delivery as needed before the next group member's turn. For added skill practice, invite additional staff to participate—for example, by having an administrator briefly pop in with an announcement. Prosody occurs everywhere!

Handout

Emotions List

Emotion	Intensity: Low	Medium	High
Happy	Glad Content Comfortable Pleased	Cheerful Upbeat Optimistic Delighted	Excited Overjoyed Thrilled Elated
Sad	Unhappy Blue Disappointed Hurt	Tearful Upset Distressed Sorrowful	Depressed Dejected Hopeless Crushed
Angry	Annoyed Perturbed Put out Irritated	Upset Mad Dismayed Frustrated	Furious Enraged Outraged Seething
Confused	Unsure Puzzled Unclear Hesitant	Baffled Unsettled Mixed up Perplexed	Bewildered Lost Flustered Disoriented
Afraid	Uneasy Nervous Worried Concerned	Scared Frightened Threatened Insecure	Terrified Horrified Fearful Panicked
Guilty	Uneasy Regretful Apologetic Sheepish	Sorrowful Remorseful Embarrassed Ashamed	Devastated Unworthy Anguished Tormented

Gestures and Posture

B, Soc

Therapeutic Rationale:

Advancing toward greater clarity in social communication, we turn to gesture and posture. These nonverbal behaviors act as "long-distance communicators," signaling engagement, interest, and presence. As noted earlier, upright posture and brief eye contact form the foundation for establishing connection. Building on these, we now consider how intentional body use supports communication.

For many kids—including those with ASD-related symptoms—gesturing and postural regulation are challenging skills. Targeted intervention is therefore needed to strengthen effective gesture and posture use. These skills enhance message clarity, complement prosodic speech, and align with proxemics, ultimately improving overall social communicative competence.

Goals:

- Increase communicative competence
- Improve perception of nonverbal body cues in social interactions

Materials:

- *Message Cards* template
- *Body Parts* template
- Optional: Mirror or access to video recording for direct observation

Directions:

1. Explain to the client that they can use their body to communicate:

   "Sometimes, people don't fully understand what we mean if we only use our voice. That's because our bodies help tell the story too! The way we stand, move our hands, or look at someone adds extra clues that make our message clearer."

2. Model types of posture and gestures that can be misinterpreted as disinterest or disengagement (e.g., slouched posture, limited use of hands and arms, chin dropping) to the client.

3. Either ahead of time or with the client, cut out the pieces from the *Body Parts* and *Message Cards* templates; spread the pieces out across the floor or a table with the words/images face-up.

4. Select (or have the client select) appropriate combinations of a message and a body part. Invite them to use their own body parts to convey the message.

   a. Encourage them to use only gestures without adding any verbalizations (e.g., sighing, squeaking) to convey the message.

   b. You may also have the client practice shifting gestures to demonstrate both "sides" of the message (e.g., "I'm confused" and also "I understand").

Variation: Obtain consent to video record the client's practice to provide further feedback and reflection. The client can also watch themselves in a mirror as they act out their message.

Tier 1

School, Treatment, and Community Settings

This intervention works the same way in group settings, except you can use peer feedback in addition to using a mirror or video.

Template

Body Parts

Arms

Hands

Shoulders

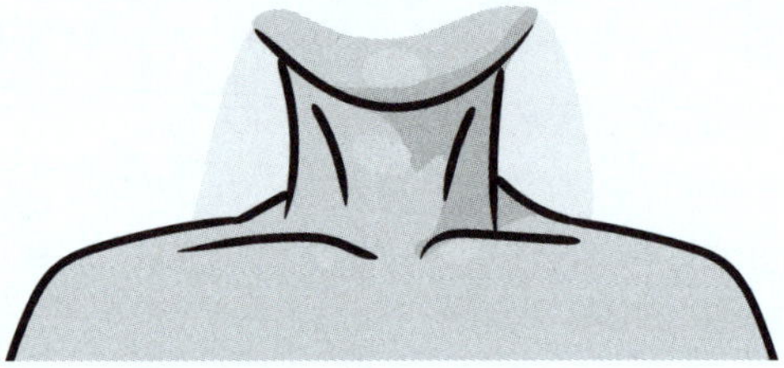

Eyes and Eyebrows

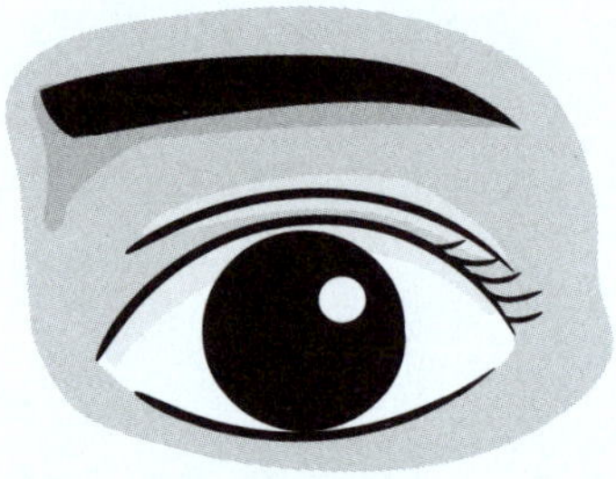

Mouth

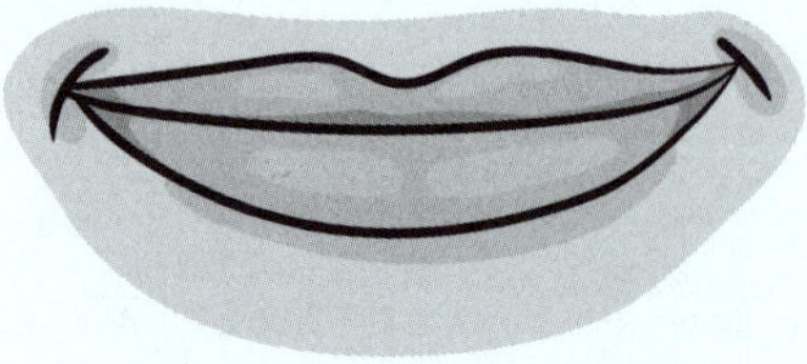

Legs

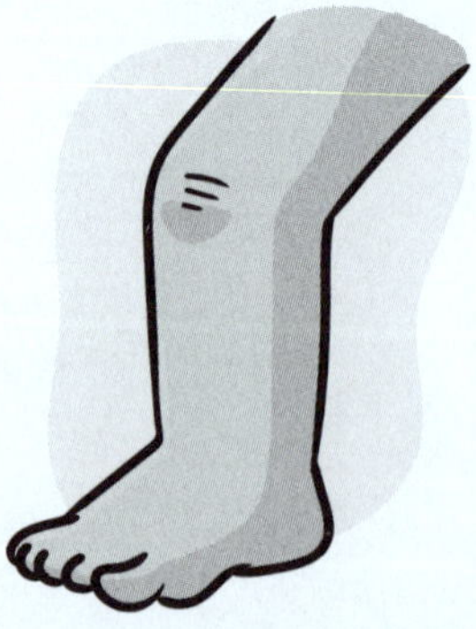

Template

Message Cards

Hello	Goodbye
I'm bored	I'm interested
I'm frustrated	I'm confident
I'm confused	I understand
I'm sad	I'm happy
Be quiet	Speak up
I'm overwhelmed	I'm comfortable
Come here	Go away
I'm tired	I have lots of energy
I need a minute	I'm ready to start
I'm hungry	I'm full
I'm serious	I feel silly
I want to be alone	I want to be with friends
I'm hurt	I'm okay

Sharing the Conversation **B, Soc, S**

Therapeutic Rationale:

Now that we have addressed physical and verbal aspects of social communication, we turn to the skill of effective conversational shifting and shared speaking time. For many kids with autism, one of the most challenging skills to learn is how to transition to topics outside of their interest and allow others space to speak. Social scripts can teach what to say and to whom, but they often fail to prepare learners for moments when a conversation naturally shifts or ends. This can lead to embarrassment, frustration, and reduced willingness to initiate future interactions. This intervention provides three activities designed to address this gap.

Goals:

- Increase social awareness in conversations
- Practice conversational shifting and sharing of time to speak
- Create a skill set for social-communication flexibility

Materials:

- Sand timers (one to two minutes for younger kids; three to five minutes for older children)
- Talking object (e.g., talking stick, ball, feather boa)
- Playing cards

Directions:

1. The three iterations of this intervention share a common objective, but each offers specific advantages. You may adapt, combine, or modify components from any version to suit your particular population and setting.
2. Explain to the client that they will be practicing shared speaking time:

   "It can be hard for us to have a conversation if it's not about what we are interested in. Other people feel the same way about their interests, and they can start to show boredom if we go on too long about our topic. Part of being in conversations is more than just listening for when we can talk about what we want to again, but also listening to what others are saying. We are going to practice ways of giving everyone in a conversation time to share."

Timer:

A sand timer provides visual cues to reinforce the client's awareness of the linear fashion of time as it dissipates, a concept that is quite abstract in nature and difficult for concrete and literal thinkers.

1. After setting the timer, one person speaks about a topic for the duration.

2. Whoever is *not* speaking about their topic is expected to ask who/what/when/where/why questions or provide commentary related to the current topic only.

3. When time is up, pass the timer to the next person to share.

Talking Object:

Use an object like a talking stick, ball, or my personal favorite, a colorful feather boa. Making the object a little silly or fun infuses some humor, which soothes the amygdala and sets a nice tone for the activity.

1. Whoever has the object is the speaker, and the other people must serve as active listeners (with their eyes and ears). Consistent eye contact is not required, but checking in with eye contact is a good way to show engagement.

2. Direct the children when to pass the object to the next person, or use a sand timer to visually show the end of each person's turn.

Playing Cards:

In this iteration, the playing cards serve as both visual and tactile cues to represent how many opportunities each person has to speak. A standard 52-card deck is great here; add some fun with Uno and include reverse or wild card opportunities.

1. Deal out the same number of cards to everyone who is participating (four or five cards is a good start).

2. After a person contributes to the conversation, they must place a card down, creating a growing pile as the conversation progresses.

3. If someone runs out of cards, they engage in listening to the people who still have cards remaining.

Tier 1

School, Treatment, and Community Settings

In addition to social skills development with ASD populations, this intervention can be beneficial for high-stakes or emotionally volatile conversations among groups, families, and even staff.

The Actors' Faces **B, N, Soc**

Therapeutic Rationale:

The next area of scaffolded skills training involves strengthening limbic system functioning to support accurate identification and labeling of emotions. This focus is particularly relevant in addressing alexithymia, a difficulty frequently reported by individuals with ASD symptoms that involves challenges in recognizing, expressing, sourcing, and describing emotions. Alexithymia may be associated with an underdevelopment of the limbic system—the neurological system central to emotional processing. This underdevelopment is often compounded by early social-emotional learning that restricts emotional vocabulary to a limited set of categories (e.g., mad, sad, and glad). Such oversimplification fails to capture the full spectrum and varying intensity of emotions, which can lead to incongruent or mismatched emotional responses to environmental cues. This intervention seeks to expand children's "emotional glossary" by providing opportunities to practice expressing and interpreting emotions across a range of intensities. This approach aims to improve emotion recognition, increase expressive accuracy, and reduce confusion or emotional incongruence in social interactions.

Goals:

- Develop the limbic system by labeling and recreating mirrored emotions
- Expand the limbic system glossary to include emotions of varying intensity
- Improve perception and expression of varied emotions
- Create congruent emotional responses through active self-monitoring

Materials:

- Pictures of human faces depicting emotions of varying intensity
- Optional: Mirror

Directions:

1. Explain to the client that they will be practicing their facial expressions:

   "We show other people how we feel by using our faces. Sometimes the feelings are hard to get out, unless they're the biggies—anger, joy, and excitement—but we have lots of different feelings inside of us. Some of those feelings are high energy and easier to spot, while others are lower energy and a bit more confusing to figure out, like boredom, disappointment, and calmness. Practicing how to show a feeling and recognize a feeling on someone else's face can help us grow our feelings expression skills when we choose to."

2. Lay out the pictures of the faces and invite the client to focus on one at a time. Photographs of real humans, preferably children, are best. Aim to have a wide array of cultural representations. For an even more concrete approach, use photos of real people the client knows, such as caregivers, educators, or siblings. For each one, ask the client to write down the emotions that

they are seeing in the picture (use the *Emotions List* handout on page 213 if needed) while you do the same.

3. Compare notes on what you each observed. (Typically, your list will have a wider range of emotions.) Discuss why and how you chose the emotions you did; encourage the client to look at the whole face and head (e.g., eyes convey the intensity of a smile).
4. Allow the client to sit in front of a mirror and use their own face to express the emotion they see (creating congruent connection in the limbic system). Make corrections to their expression by exhibiting the corrections on your own face and allowing the client to review in the mirror.

Note: Many individuals are uncomfortable looking into a mirror. Use clinical judgment to determine whether this is an appropriate step to the intervention.

5. Return to each picture and ask the client the following questions:
    a. "Is this a high-, medium-, or low-intensity feeling?"
    b. "What clues can we look for to see how much energy is being used on the feeling?"

Tier 1 or 2

School, Treatment, and Community Settings

This intervention is helpful for all kids, but it is particularly effective in upper elementary and middle school (kids ages 8 to 13). During this stage of development, many believe others are watching, judging, and paying attention to them, sometimes called the "personal fable" or "imaginary audience."

Emotion Charades

B, N, Soc

Therapeutic Rationale:

Building on skills of emotional recognition, expression, and limbic system congruence, we can integrate emotional awareness and authentic expression through the use of *social stories*. Carol Gray's (2021) work highlights the effectiveness of assessing and evaluating social experiences while also preparing individuals for expected emotional and social responses. Emotion charades is an extension of social stories specific to certain scenarios to promote cognitive flexibility when kids encounter changes in their environment, reducing emotional misinterpretation and social confusion and supporting more successful engagement in interactions with others (Como et al., 2023).

Goals:

- Increase awareness of internal emotional responses to social interactions
- Respond with authentic self when engaged in social communication
- Further advance identification, internal experience, and expanding limbic system function

Materials:

- *Emotion Charades* template
- *Emotions List* handout

Directions:

1. Explain to the client that they can use more than just their voice to show their feelings:

   "Let's play charades! This is a game that helps you use your face, body, and voice to show *someone how you're feeling, and you get to guess how other people feel too. We are going to choose some everyday experiences and see how we can show our inside feelings to others."*

2. Introduce the *Emotion Charades* template. For each square, have the client read it to themselves, and ask them, "In this scenario, what are you feeling and thinking on the inside, and what are you showing on the outside?" Have them act it out without speaking so you (or the group members) can guess what is happening. There are many ways you can use the template:

   a. Flip a coin onto the form and read the square it lands on.

   b. Cut out the squares from the template and pull them out of a bag or hat.

   c. Cut out the squares from the template, flip them over (text-side down), and have the client choose one at random.

   d. Cover each square with a scrap of paper and have the client uncover them.

   e. Include blank squares to add actual social experiences from the client's life (especially with concrete thinkers).

3. Then challenge the client to think of any secondary internal thoughts and emotions: "Were you thinking or feeling anything else when you picked this item?" They can refer to the *Emotions List* handout on page 213 if needed.

4. Repeat as needed for skills practice, adding new scenarios if possible.

Tier 1 or 2*

School, Treatment, and Community Settings

When doing this activity in schools and treatment settings, it is okay to use specific examples on your emotion charades card. Placing both "positive" and "negative" interactions within the classroom, hallways, the gym, cafeteria, playground, school bus, living room, grocery store, and sports activities can help generalize recognition of emotion and thought when in those varied situations. Reflecting on responses as a group can improve a child's ability to be their authentic self in terms of emotional responses, and this can further promote peer acceptance.

* The use of this tool in these settings is considered tier 1, but it can also be a tier 2 application with small-group work.

Template

Emotion Charades

Your teacher is gone for the day and you have an unexpected substitute.	You look in the mirror and like your outfit.	You get a failing grade on an assignment.	You overhear someone talking badly about you.
You hit the game-winning home run.	You have to say goodbye to a friend after a really fun time together.	The teacher tells you there are five minutes left to finish a test.	You hear that your favorite food is on the menu for lunch.
You pass your driver's test the first time.	You find out you are not invited to a classmate's party.	You lose a video game race at the last second.	You hear your parents are going to separate.

Chronemics: Time Blindness **B, Soc, S**

Therapeutic Rationale:

Another area to address with children diagnosed with ASD (or ADHD) is the notion of "time blindness," or difficulty understanding linear time and how time passes when completing activities or focusing on preoccupational interests. Common issues are showing up significantly late for scheduled activities (e.g., school, appointments, extracurriculars) and becoming so absorbed in a preoccupational interest that the passing of time is lost altogether. So how can we help kids to develop independent living skills and adjust to schedules that are outside of their routine?

For young children, understanding how much time has passed during activities can be problematic. For example, being told they need to wait five minutes before they can ask a question—but not being able to conceptualize internally how long five minutes lasts—can result in agitation and meltdowns in classroom or home settings. These kids have limited references for time duration, which to some degree is developmentally appropriate; however, it can cause social difficulties due to interruption and dysregulation. Therefore, understanding the rules of chronemics and time is a vital social skill to master.

Goals:

- Improve chronological and linear time awareness
- Decrease feelings of frustration and difficulty coping with unexpected transitions and routine

Materials:

- *Understanding Time* worksheet
- Timer (preferably a sand timer for visual reinforcement)
- Watch (with auditory beeps)

Directions:

1. Explain to the client that you will be practicing measuring time:

   "Sometimes it's hard to figure out time. It can feel like it goes by very fast or very slow, making it hard for our brains to realize that all time is the same; it just feels *like it changes when we are doing something we like don't like. Having a way to measure time with our bodies and activities can help our brains get regulated and keep us from being late or feeling rushed."*

2. Fill out the *Understanding Time* worksheet with the client:

   a. **Part 1:** Set a timer and sit in silence. Ask the client, "How long do you think has passed?" in increments of:

      i. 10 seconds

    ii. 30 seconds
    iii. 60 seconds
    iv. 5 minutes

b. **Part 2:** Create a list of physical cues to determine time duration.
    i. How long can the client stand in line before they feel like they want to move?
    ii. How long can they raise their hand before their arm gets tired?
    iii. How long can they chew a piece of gum before the taste goes away? (Check for allergies or food sensitivities.)
    iv. How long can they write before their hand gets tired or tight?

c. **Part 3:** Help the client create a resource list of auditory and visual time references. For example:
    i. "I sing *Twinkle Twinkle Little Star* and the ABC song once each, and then I know my hands are clean."
    ii. "The timer on my watch lets me know that I have [*time limit*] to finish using the bathroom."
    iii. "I heard the cues from my teacher that it is almost time to clean up: The second box has been checked; I have two poker chips in my hand." (See the *Priming the Cognitive Pump* intervention on page 184.)
    iv. "My one-minute sand timer has almost run out."

3. Help the client recognize that these exercises are helpful for them to pay attention to exactly how much time has passed so they can be ready for changes.

4. Challenge them during times of task persistence to determine how long they have spent on an activity by referencing physical, auditory, visual, and silent time reference measures.

Tier 3

School, Treatment, and Community Settings

Creating time references in classroom and group settings can decrease significant issues with agitation, dysregulation, and argumentativeness. Incorporate this into your daily instruction or group leadership by identifying the specific types of external and internal cues that are most effective for recognizing time delineation.

Worksheet

Understanding Time

Time is a funny thing. It can happen very *quickly*. Sometimes it seems to fly by when you're doing something fun or rushing to finish a test. But it can also happen *slowly*—like when you have to stand in a line or wait for your turn playing a video game.

1. Let's see if you can figure out how much time has gone by. Sit in silence while an adult sets a timer for a certain amount of time. When they say *Stop!* write down how long you think it has been. Then compare this to how long it has actually been.
   a. How long you think it was: ___________ How long it actually was: ___________
   b. How long you think it was: ___________ How long it actually was: ___________
   c. How long you think it was: ___________ How long it actually was: ___________
   d. How long you think it was: ___________ How long it actually was: ___________
2. Now let's ask your body some questions about time.
   a. How long can you stand in line before your body wants to move? ___________
   b. How long can you raise your hand before your arm gets tired? ___________
   c. How long can you chew a piece of gum before the taste goes away? ___________
   d. How long can you write before your hand gets tired or tight? ___________
3. Sometimes you might *forget* how long it takes to do things. You can use *sounds* to help you remember how long you have been there:
   a. **Hand washing:** Sing *Twinkle, Twinkle Little Star* and the ABC song one time each.
   b. **Using the bathroom:** Set a timer on your watch or phone, so you only stay for five minutes. Sometimes, you may need to set two timers so you don't forget or get distracted.
   c. **Waiting your turn:** For things like waiting for the water fountain or turning in work, count to 10, then count to 10 again.
   d. Name other activities where you lose track of time while you're doing them.

   ____

Chronemics: How Long Do I Wait? *B, Soc*

Therapeutic Rationale:

Not only is it important to develop a conceptualization of time, but it is also crucial for kids to apply that knowledge to real-life situations, such as arriving punctually for appointments. In many contexts—medical, therapeutic, or psychiatric—there is a clear expectation that clients arrive on time, or even early. However, appointment times are not always exact; clients may present on time but then need to wait for an extended period (hours, even) before being seen, without recognizing that the provider may be running behind schedule due to emergencies or other factors. In response, these clients may arrive late for subsequent appointments, assuming the same flexibility applies to them. This often results in being marked as a no-show or a missed appointment. Such experiences can be highly frustrating, particularly for kids who rely on concrete or literal thinking and who depend heavily on established routines. This intervention provides education around this.

Goals:

- Improve chronological and linear time awareness
- Create a dialogue for self-advocacy
- Decrease feelings of frustration and difficulty coping with unexpected transitions and routine

Materials:

- *How Long Do I Wait?* handout

Directions:

1. Explain to the client that in certain situations, they may have to wait:

   "Sometimes the importance of the person we are seeing means that we will need to wait longer to meet with them. They are providing a service to us that we cannot do by ourselves, and they have the training and education necessary to fill that need for us."

2. Provide the client with the *How Long Do I Wait?* handout, explaining that a provider's status and power impact the amount of time the client is expected to wait. Status is determined by a provider's level of education, the fulfillment of a specialty need, and a limited access to this need.

3. Practice verbal engagements with the client so they can learn to self-advocate. You may find it beneficial to role-play as if the client is speaking to a receptionist or other staff member. For instance:

   a. "I am checking in for my appointment at [*time*]."

   b. "Do you know if they are running behind?"

   c. "Do you have an estimated time that I might be seen?"

d. If the estimated time has passed: "Do you know how much longer I might be waiting? I have other responsibilities today."

e. "Would it be better if I rescheduled or planned a telehealth session?"

4. Encourage the client to be on time for their next appointment, following the same self-advocacy communication pattern.

Tier 2

School, Treatment, and Community Settings

Preparing students for time awareness and unexpected moments are important parts of transition planning for them to be successful in young adulthood. This helps promote tolerance for timelines outside of rigid expectation, a useful skill for those entering higher education, where there are also rules about how long to wait for an educator or other professional.

Handout

How Long Do I Wait?

You may need to wait longer if the person:

- Has a higher level of education
- Provides a service
- Is necessary in meeting a need

Highest Status/Power

Doctors, dentists, teachers, counselors

Moderate Status/Power

Grocery checkout, bank tellers, bus drivers

Low Status/Power

Siblings, friends

How can you advocate for yourself when you are waiting?

- "I am checking in for my appointment at _____."
- "Do you know if they are running behind?"
- "Do you have an estimated time that I might be seen?"
- "Do you know how much longer I might be waiting? I have other responsibilities today."
- "Would it be better if I rescheduled or planned a telehealth session?"

Cheat Sheets for Difficult Interactions *B, C, Soc*

Therapeutic Rationale:

Although the primary goal is to foster self-initiated communication and in-the-moment adaptability, some kids with ASD encounter repetitive interactions that become persistent social hurdles. After skills in proxemics, TTVI, and gesturing and posturing have been mastered, we may introduce scripting as a communication tool. Earlier forms of scripting focused on "What can another person do to help me feel better?" but *preventive* scripting reframes the approach toward "What can I do to change or improve this interaction?" This shift promotes greater ownership of communication while reinforcing the reciprocal gestures and social awareness emphasized throughout this chapter.

Goals:

- Create verbal references for recurrent communication blocks
- Increase the variety of scripted responses and problem-solving to combat rigid thinking
- Improve verbal and visual references in problematic social interactions

Materials:

- *Tricky Situations Cheat Sheet* worksheet

Directions:

1. Explain prepared scripts to the client:

   "Even if we've worked extremely hard to gain communication skills, conversations with other people can still cause trouble and frustration for us. When these situations repeat often, it is okay to have a plan of action for improving communication with a prepared script. When we learn the best approach, we will be less dependent on the script over time and become more empowered to handle the interaction as it is happening."

2. Ask the client to think of an interaction with a person (e.g., educator, sibling, friend) where they used all their skills of verbal and nonverbal communication and it just didn't seem to work. Provide them with the *Tricky Situations Cheat Sheet* worksheet and add the scenario to the top.

3. First, have the client consider how the other person could do things differently to help the situation. Have them write these in the top half of the worksheet.

4. Then assist the client in brainstorming several different options for how *they* could approach this hurdle of social communication differently, filling in the bottom half of the worksheet. In this section, the client might:

   a. Communicate what they need differently

   b. Ask how they can help the other person understand what they're needing

   c. Be willing to compromise on a part of their expectation, but not all of it

5. Discuss the different options, and help the client choose the top *two* choices for addressing the issue. Encourage them to bring the hard copy of options with them and practice before initiating the conversation.
6. If these two strategies do not work for the client, troubleshoot and come up with some new options. If needed, the client can ask for help from a trusted adult from their support net.

Tier 3

School, Treatment, and Community Settings

Creating direct reference sheets for problematic and recurring difficulties in social interactions should be considered a last course of action for children with symptoms of ASD. This can cause them to fall back on former masking behaviors, but it can also be a necessary tool to use for moving past a rigid sticking point in social communication in classroom settings, group participation, or interactions with peers. Remember that using this tool in a heterogeneous group setting can aid in social modeling of novel solutions to communication gaps.

Telehealth Application

Using this worksheet for persistent communication issues in homes can be helpful in telehealth settings, and keeping digital copy of handouts can help illustrate the progression of social-communication skills over time.

Worksheet

Tricky Situations Cheat Sheet

What happened? ______________________________

The old way of doing things . . .

"It would be fine between ____________________ and me if *they* would . . ."

- ______________________________
- ______________________________
- ______________________________
- ______________________________

How has expecting the other person to fix the communication worked so far?

____

A new way to try . . .

"It would be fine between ____________________ and me if *I* would . . ."

- ______________________________
- ______________________________
- ______________________________
- ______________________________

How does this change the problem in your eyes?

____

What can *you* control to help the relationship?

____

How might *you* start the change?

____

What You Like to Talk About **B, C, Soc**

Therapeutic Rationale:

Professionals can use an autistic client's preoccupational interests as a starting point for building social skills. Because these interests are highly diverse and deeply personalized, they provide a powerful opportunity to connect with the person's passion. Kids with strong preoccupational interests are often told—sometimes quite bluntly—"Don't talk about your interest." Yet restricting someone from discussing a preferred topic can create a negative internal feedback loop, resulting in withdrawal, increased perseveration, avoidance behaviors, and distractibility—patterns that can be challenging to reverse.

A more effective approach is to allow discussion of these interests while using visual cues to set clear time limits. Even a brief, structured opportunity to share a preferred topic can help redirect cognitive energy toward developing social-communication skills.

Because many preoccupational interests are thematic, they naturally support structural and social exploration. For instance, zombie-themed movies and games often illustrate community-based survival, with roles such as leader, hunter, gatherer, healer, protector, organizer, teacher, and nurturer. Using this lens, children with ASD-related symptoms can examine collaboration, interdependence, and community roles, identifying the role they most connect with and assigning roles to people in their lives. This intervention builds on that process and offers additional reframing strategies for common thematic preoccupational interests within the ASD community.

Goals:

- Improve the client's awareness of social constructs embedded in most preoccupational sets
- Disrupt the negative feedback loop associated with restricting the client from discussing preoccupational focus

Materials:

- *What You Like to Talk About* worksheet
- *Making Bigger Connections with Preoccupational Interests* worksheet

Directions:

1. Explain to the client how they can use their interests to build their skills:

   "I know you like to talk and think a lot about [interest]. *It is okay to think about your very favorite thing, but I'm going to work with you on how to think about it with a different twist. We are going to find ways to use* [interest] *to help you work on social skills, recognizing feelings, the importance of relationships with other people, and more—instead of getting lost inside of yourself alone and thinking about* [interest]."

2. Provide the client with the *What I Like to Talk About* worksheet. Let them choose one specific area of preoccupational interest to practice with.

3. As the client describes to you why they like this topic, assist them in breaking down the preoccupational interest, reflecting on how categories or themes could support them in their day-to-day life.

4. Outside of session, you can further reflect on social interactions, social skills, or EF skills for future skill-building. Use the *Making Bigger Connections with Preoccupational Interests* worksheet to brainstorm your ideas. Some examples are included here.

	Themes	Examples	Skills
Ghostbusters	• Teamwork and team roles • Turn-taking and communication • Problem-solving together • Emotions and reactions • Community and helping others • Humor and social connection • Relationships	• Egon is smart • Ray is excitable • Peter is social • Winston is practical • Talking and planning before opening the ghost trap; coordinated efforts against the Stay-Puft Marshmallow Man • Is crossing the streams worth the risk? • Fear, frustration, excitement, pride • Saving New York City, even though they don't believe in them right away • Bonding through jokes and playfulness • Janine and Egon's "cat and mouse"; Janine's nonverbals showing interest, Egon's initial lack of awareness or reciprocity	• Self-awareness, valuing differences, team roles • Turn-taking, clear communication, listening • Collaborative problem-solving, flexible thinking • Reading facial expressions and emotions in others • Understanding interdependence, community roles • Social reciprocity, shared enjoyment • Nonverbal communication, reciprocity
Thomas the Tank Engine	• Teamwork and team roles • Turn-taking and cooperation • Problem-solving together • Emotions and perspective-taking • Community and helping others	• Thomas is an eager helper • Percy is a loyal friend • Gordon is strong • James is proud • Engines often need to take turns on tracks or share tasks (like pulling coaches)	• Recognizing personal strengths, understanding group roles • Turn-taking, waiting, cooperative play • Flexible thinking, asking for help • Emotion recognition, empathy

	Themes	Examples	Skills
Thomas the Tank Engine (continued)	• Friendship and apologies	• Engine making a mistake (e.g., getting stuck, being boastful) and then finding a solution with help from friends • Engines show clear faces and emotions (e.g., sad, happy, angry, proud) • The trains' main job is helping on Sodor (e.g., delivering goods, carrying passengers) • Many episodes show conflict (boasting, not listening), followed by saying sorry and making up	• Understanding interdependence, community contribution • Conflict resolution, repairing relationships
Dinosaurs	• Chronological time / linear order • Negative impact of a "critical event," recovery and rebuilding	• Conceptualizing time periods, such as Triassic, Jurassic, and Cretaceous periods; linear order of evolution of dinosaurs over the Mesozoic period • Asteroid wipes out everything, causing social interactions, community losses, and other major environmental stresses	• Time awareness, linear progression • Self-regulation, social reciprocity, conflict resolution

Tier 3

School, Treatment, and Community Settings

In order for you to have more time dedicated to instruction, helping kids recognize social themes can help you turn preoccupational interests into opportunities for engagement. For example, you might tell a student who loves Thomas the Tank Engine, "In my classroom, I'm like Sir Topham Hat because I am the leader. Now is the time we listen to the leader and do the assigned job, and when it's time to pass out papers, you can be like Thomas and be my helper."

Worksheet

What You Like to Talk About

What is your favorite topic to talk about, do research on, or think about often?

____

What are your favorite things about this topic?

1. ____
2. ____
3. ____
4. ____
5. ____

What lessons and skills can you learn from this topic that could support you in other areas of your life (e.g., at school, with friends, at home, when you feel anxious, when you feel bored, when you need to communicate a need)? Use your answers from the previous question to help you get started!

What You Like About This Topic	Lesson or Skill

What You Like About This Topic	Lesson or Skill

Therapist Worksheet

Making Bigger Connections with Preoccupational Interests

Using your client's favorite preoccupational interest, consider themes, characters, and other information from this topic that you could extend into therapeutic work. Use the *What I Like to Talk About* worksheet that you and your client filled out to get started.

Client's interest: ____________________

Themes	Examples	Skills

Client's interest: ____________________

Themes	Examples	Skills

6

Behavior Management

Kids and teens who display challenging behaviors—arguing, defiance, lying, tantrums, disrespect, skepticism, and even aggression—are often among the most frustrating populations to work with. They also happen to be among the most rewarding. Largely misunderstood for much of their lives, these young people are some of the smartest, most creative, adaptive, funny, and deeply sensitive individuals you will meet. Once you begin to understand the *why* behind their behavior, all of that becomes visible—and when they know you see them as a person and not a problem, they feel safe enough to share themselves with you. Consider yourself lucky. That's a well-guarded, vulnerable side of them that they're allowing you to be a part of!

Schools often use an FBA to identify the function of a student's behavior and guide an intervention—that is, to determine what purpose the behavior serves for the student. This is a useful starting point. As an attachment-informed clinician, I prefer to replace the idea of "function" or "purpose" with "need." Kids who cannot effectively verbalize their needs will often *show* them instead. This subtle shift changes the conversation from "Why is the child acting like this?" to "What need is the child trying to meet through this behavior?"

We may excel at interpreting verbal language, but we are not always skilled behavioral listeners. If a child exhibits repetitive behavioral patterns in a particular environment and has been "resistant" to intervention there, this is a strong indicator that we have not accurately identified the need that the behavior is fulfilling. Misidentifying these needs can cause the persistence of challenging behaviors.

Ultimately, many challenges associated with behavioral disorders are not rooted in anger or contempt but in a misunderstanding of what is missing in the child's environment to help them feel safe, supported, and securely attached. Recognizing and meeting these needs is often the key to meaningful and lasting behavioral change.

In previous chapters, we have addressed critical skills for behavioral populations—such as self-regulating, preventing escalation cycles, building self-efficacy, and developing EF and social skills. These scaffolded techniques are particularly important for children with diagnoses such as oppositional defiant disorder and conduct disorder.

This chapter will strive to shift your mindset to create goals and expectations that are realistic, meeting individuals where *they* are to grow more functional skill sets, subtly altering the milieu to promote opportunity for growth, to be better listeners of nonverbal communication of unmet needs, and to communicate more effectively with these growing brains.

We will be returning to the multimodal approach to seamlessly improve positive behaviors quickly, process information accurately, and problem-solve effectively and efficiently. This requires you to be willing to think about the function of behaviors differently, and have adaptive and flexible approaches to interacting with these individuals.

The interventions in this chapter will focus on:

- Gaining self-awareness, communicating needs, and slowing the internal system
- Growing skills of cognitive flexibility and compromise
- Establishing physical and emotional boundaries
- Promoting whole-brain problem-solving
- Decreasing the negative impact of aggressive media
- Promoting delayed gratification

Key Concepts

Realistic intervention timelines: When response times for expected change are realistic, you can better evaluate the effectiveness in real time; in this time you can also gauge more successfully whether a child's needs have been accurately identified.

Consequences: Any consequence or connection to an originating behavior should be action-oriented and something that you are doing to heal the relationship or improve the community environment.

Case Example

Joe, 15, was referred to me as a condition of release from a juvenile detention facility. With multiple charges pending, including assault, harassment, and a history of running away from home, he has "agreed" to see me only because of the diversion agreement with the court, which requires twelve months of outpatient counseling. In our first session, Joe opens with, "I'm here, but I'm not gonna do anything you say . . . why bother anyway? This is so fucking stupid."

Joe's school and clinical records indicate a long history of verbal aggression, refusal to complete tasks, threatening others for touching his things or looking at him wrong, becoming explosive "for no reason," damaging books and other school property, and making fun of younger peers with special needs. The collective message from school staff is that his behavior is attention-seeking and purposeful, that he can listen "when he wants to," and that he has the intelligence to do better academically if he only put forth more effort. Indeed, recent educational assessments indicate Joe's full-scale IQ is 125 despite extremely low academic performance.

His mother, a single parent of four children, expresses hopelessness and exhaustion, stating, "I love him, but sometimes I can't be around him because he makes me feel scared. I can't get him off the video games without him throwing things. I've tried every parenting skill, but it never works for long, so he pretty much runs the house."

When I meet with Joe, I notice that when he speaks, he uses words that are related but out of context to the topic of conversation. He also seems to have difficulty accurately interpreting verbal statements and directions. When I gently ask him about this, he says he gets frustrated and gives up when he "can't think of the word he wants."

Joe needs:

- An assessment of behavior function and need (i.e., an FBA)
- A receptive/expressive language assessment
- Consistency at home and school
- Skills of deescalation
- Improved boundaries
- A sense of purpose

Behavior Management Key Concept

Realistic Intervention Timelines

Intervention teams in schools and clinical settings often emphasize the importance of *consistency* with a new behavior intervention—and that's absolutely true. However, what that same group of people is often missing is a collective understanding of a *realistic timeline for change* and an acceptance, recognition, and expectation that there will be fluctuations in response from the child whose behavior is changing. Without context, these fluctuations are often the point where the team misinterprets the intervention as no longer effective ("It stopped working"), which often results in a lack of fidelity in implementation going forward, inevitable frustration and diminished commitment to the plan, and even abandonment of the intervention altogether.

When clear expectations aren't established from the start, even well-designed, needs-focused interventions can appear to "fail." Even worse, this gap often fuels harmful narratives like "Nothing works with this child." This creates a significant disservice to the child, their family, and the professionals working to support them.

A broad understanding of expected response times to intervention allows teams to evaluate effectiveness in real time. Just as importantly, it encourages meaningful discussion on whether a child's needs have been accurately identified, whether environmental factors are being considered, and whether the goals for skill mastery are realistic.

The following graphic summarizes a young person's expected trajectory of change in a school or clinic-based program over a six-week period of time. Note that their progress does not improve in a completely linear fashion—we'll explore this in the next sections.

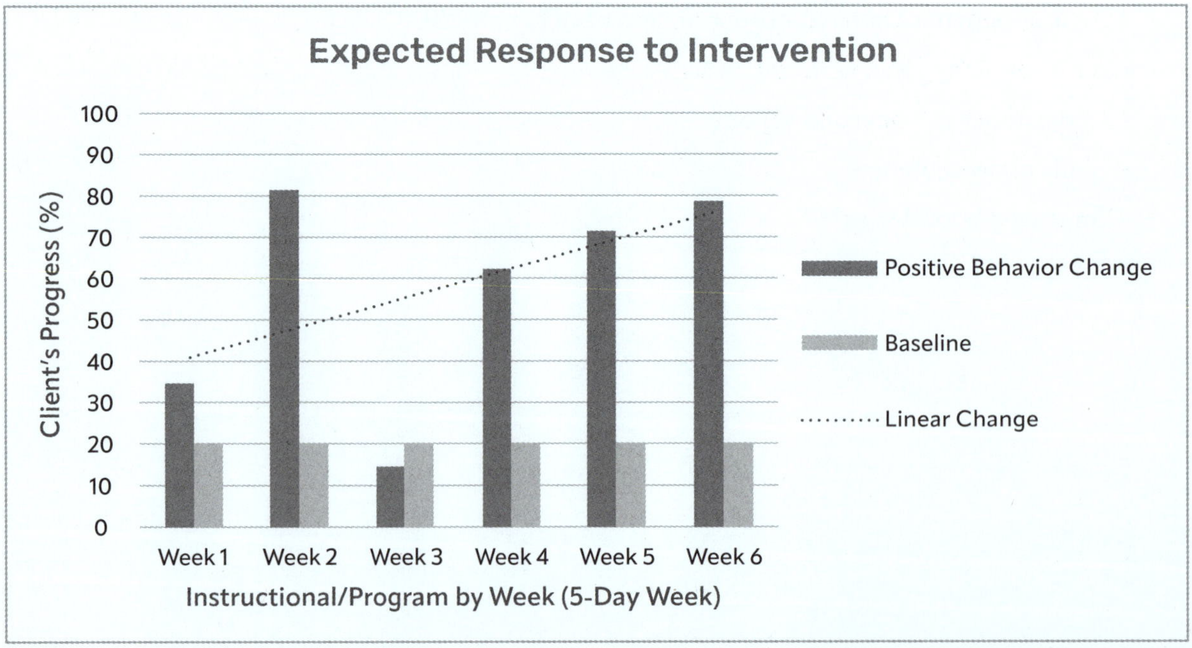

The Honeymoon Period

The first 7 to 10 days post-intervention introduction are often referred to as the *honeymoon period*, as there is often a significant improvement in behavior. However, it's too soon to tell if this improvement is in response to the intervention or simply the novelty of something new being introduced. After all, adding anything new to an environment can have the same effect.

Test-the-Limits Period

Directly following the honeymoon period, at the end of week two or the beginning of week three, is the testing-of-limits phase, referred to in the behavior analysis world as a *response burst*—a sudden yet predictable drop in progress, sometimes even regressing to pre-baseline behaviors.

This challenging period is when most educators, caregivers, clinicians, and other staff members give up because they believe the tool is no longer working. In reality, this period is the most important time to stay consistent with delivery of the intervention. This is where the change happens. What may look like failure is actually growth in disguise—the child is displaying the very behaviors we want to change. It's often the moment when a child builds new skills by stretching beyond their comfort zone. When staff can anticipate these challenging periods and respond with strategies like planned ignoring, the child ends up learning and growing more, not less.

Recovery and Plateau Period

Given consistent delivery of the intervention, the test-the-limits phase lasts from about day 10 and into week 4, followed by a trajectory of forward progress that plateaus around 70–80 percent in weeks 5, 6, and beyond, where it is expected to maintain with slight variability for the duration. Sustained plateaued success for an *additional* 30 days (60 instructional days in total) is considered mastery of a functional skill.

Reassessment

Unfortunately, most intervention teams review intervention plans every 12 to 36 months, when they *should* strive to review intervention plans every six weeks (30 instructional days) to identify and address flaws in the intervention itself. The most common areas for adjustments are the following:

- **There is no behavior change at all:** This usually means the function of the behavior was misidentified at the start and needs to be adjusted.
- **Behavior does not improve as expected after the response burst:** This is usually because there was a drop in consistency during the burst, and the staff working with the child may need more support.
- **The plan does not continue after skills mastery:** In 30 days, the child succeeds in mastery of the functional skill, continuing another 30-day period after that. However, no additional skill sets are introduced and the plan sits idle.

This gives professionals a total timeline of just *60 days* for the following steps:

30 Days

1. Introduce a new intervention.
2. Review progress at 30 days to determine if changes need to be made.
3. Adapt the intervention type, reassess function, or introduce support for team consistency.
4. Identify the achievement of a progress plateau with realistic expectations.

60 Days

1. Perform plateau maintenance—with small fluctuations—for the remaining 30 days.
2. Identify when the child has mastered the skill set.
3. Introduce a new behavioral goal, and start the process again.

Behavior Management Key Concept

Consequences

While proactive and preventive models of intervention are generally the preferred approach to addressing behavior disorders, consequences as a response to behaviors are still necessary and a crucial piece of behavior management. Learning theory tells us that allowing natural consequences to occur, having logical consequences connected to a behavior, and emphasizing restorative justice and action-oriented intervention works best in improving behavioral issues.

When working in treatment, we make it clear that consequences are "earned," not "given." When completing behavior intervention plans with schools and treatment facilities, we clearly communicate what types of consequences are to be expected should a positive alternative behavior not be chosen or performed. Consequences should only be created when the adult is not experiencing a high level of emotional response, so that the adult is better able to choose consequences that are meaningful and realistic (i.e., not something like "You're grounded for two years").

Natural Consequences

Natural consequences are directly related to the action and do not require intervention by an adult. They are generally quite effective due to the immediacy of the consequence. Examples include:

- The child falls off the kitchen counter and gets a bruise because they climbed on it.
- Peers change their seats after the child hisses like a cat in class.
- The child feels cold because they refused to wear a coat.
- A toy falls off the balcony because the child played with it outside even though they were instructed to do differently.

Note: Always intervene when safety is at risk; some natural consequences can be dangerous and should not be allowed in the name of learning. Safety always comes first.

Logical Consequences

Logical consequences are directly tied to the target behavior; they usually require some intervention from adults. Examples include:

- The child repairs their sister's toy because they broke it.
- The child sweeps up pieces of the plate that they dropped on the floor.
- The child apologizes after using unkind words toward someone.

Counterproductive Consequences

Counterproductive consequences are ineffective and may not lead to real change. Examples include:

- The adult puts the child in isolation.
- The adult limits the child's personal care.
- The adult offers no opportunity for correction, repair, or an exchange behavior.
- The adult's consequence is exaggerated or unrealistic (e.g., "You're grounded for two years!").
- The adult delivers the consequence with anger or high emotions.

In the same vein of logical consequences are restorative justice corrections, which are especially important with conduct populations and juvenile justice and court systems. Restorative justice is a relational approach to conflict resolution, whereas retributive justice focuses mainly on the crime committed, and less on the individual with potential for rehabilitation. Restorative justice is not a specific program, but a philosophical approach to responding differently to behaviors in institutions. The emphasis on restorative justice is to *heal* the victims and to create peaceful and collaborative ways to change our communities. Not only should the restorative justice consequence be utilized to heal the relationship, but it should also be action-oriented in nature. In our home we say, "Don't say you're sorry, be sorry."

Differences Between Retributive and Restorative Justice

Retributive Justice	Restorative Justice
Behavior is an act against the institution.	Behavior is an act against the individual/community.
The institution controls the behavior.	Behavior control lies in the milieu.
Accountability is defined by punishment.	Accountability is defined by responsibility.
Victims are peripheral.	Victims are central.

These distinctions fall directly in line with efforts to shift mentality from punitive models of intervention to growth- or reward-based models of goal setting and achievement. We must find an individual's point of entry to affect real change, and in doing so, we meet them where they are at in the process of growth and transformation. With consistency and conscious effort, we create opportunity for individuals who have been ostracized and vilified, sometimes with reason, to see that rehabilitation is a possibility. This also aids us, the treatment and academic providers, in having a new mindset for approaching behavioral disorders in all arenas.

Examples of Restorative Justice Corrections

The child punches a classmate.	They walk the classmate to the nurse to get medical care.
The child throws food in the cafeteria.	They stay and sweep up and mop at the end of lunch.
The child tells someone their outfit is stupid.	They compliment the other person on a characteristic they like about them.
The child interrupts the group leader when they are talking.	The child must remain quiet until the time for questions arises.
The child tells their parents they hate them.	The child spends the evening with their parents watching a show of their choice.

Life Skills Resume B

Therapeutic Rationale:

Some kids might think, "Well, I reached my goal. It's not on my treatment/intervention plan anymore. Now I'm working on something else." But this checkbox approach can cause issues with behavioral regression, and it also removes the opportunity for the child to realize that this new skill is now part of their permanent life skills "toolbox." This intervention encourages kids to continue using their skills while fostering a sense of pride in their accomplishments.

Goals:

- Create a visual representation of positive growth and change
- Create a reference to return and remind of mastered skills

Materials:

- *My Life Skills Resume* worksheet
- Optional: Blank wooden chips / coins that can be written on
- Writing utensil

Directions:

1. Explain how learning new skills isn't a "one-and-done" process:

   "When we are working on goals and making big changes in our lives, we sometimes forget that we aren't just working on goals to check a box and reach a finish line. What we are doing is learning new ways of living that become a part of who we are forever. When we are a master of a new life skill, it is important to create a reminder to come back to, especially on the days that test us and make us want to go back to the 'old way.' On these days, we know we already have a better skill in our life toolbox that gets us better results and helps us feel confident."

2. Introduce *My Life Skills Resume* to the client and guide them to fill in the skills they have accomplished so far. They can continue to fill out this worksheet as time goes on.

3. For older youth who have achieved mastery level on a goal, I state, "You are a master of [*skill*], and this is yours forever. You can do it all the time, even without reminders."

4. Guide the client to look back at their resume often as a reminder that these skills are part of their life toolbox or resume now.

Optional: For younger ages and stages, consider a "life skills toolbox" metaphor: Write the skills they have learned on wooden chips or coins and place them in a decorated "treasure box" or toolbox.

Worksheet

My Life Skills Resume

A resume is something we write to show others our expertise, but it can also be used as a visual reminder of our successes in growing and building new skills all the time. When we learn something new and practice it on the regular, it's important to recognize the work we've put into becoming "masters" (experts) at something new. Use this worksheet to craft a life skills resume, and be sure you add new things as they become a part of who you are.

Name: ____________________

Skills:

Communication:

(Examples: Using "I" statements, walking away from an argument)

Skill: ____________________ Date I achieved mastery: __________

Skill: ____________________ Date I achieved mastery: __________

Skill: ____________________ Date I achieved mastery: __________

Skill: ____________________ Date I achieved mastery: __________

Self-Regulation:

(Examples: Breathing/imagery tools, self-monitoring)

Skill: ____________________ Date I achieved mastery: __________

Skill: ____________________ Date I achieved mastery: __________

Skill: ____________________ Date I achieved mastery: __________

Skill: ____________________ Date I achieved mastery: __________

Problem-Solving:

(Examples: Whole-brain problem-solving, using my support net)

Skill: ____________________ Date I achieved mastery: __________

Skill: ____________________ Date I achieved mastery: __________

Skill: ____________________ Date I achieved mastery: __________

Skill: ____________________ Date I achieved mastery: __________

Decision-Making:

(Examples: Pros and cons, wise mind, knowing when to ask for help)

Skill: ______________________ Date I achieved mastery: ______________

Skill: ______________________ Date I achieved mastery: ______________

Skill: ______________________ Date I achieved mastery: ______________

Skill: ______________________ Date I achieved mastery: ______________

Self-Control:

(Examples: ACCEPTS, using coping skills to prevent explosion)

Skill: ______________________ Date I achieved mastery: ______________

Skill: ______________________ Date I achieved mastery: ______________

Skill: ______________________ Date I achieved mastery: ______________

Skill: ______________________ Date I achieved mastery: ______________

Self-Concept Cake B, C, T

Therapeutic Rationale:

This intervention serves as an assessment tool for identifying the functional need behind a behavior. Traditional FBAs rely heavily on qualitative data drawn from the external environment, which can lead to guesswork, slow progress, and a significant gap in "information" coming directly from the child. This intervention helps close that gap by assessing the child's needs through the lens of their self-concept. By creating an *external* representation of their self-concept, we can start to identify how the child's behavior communicates an *internal* need—and help them develop healthier ways to communicate it. This also gives educators, staff, and family members insight into how their own interactions impact the child's self-concept, relationships, and behavior.

Goals:

- Create a visual representation of negative self-perception associated with stratified social environments
- Communicate functional needs that are not being met or identified
- Visually represent and document nontangible incentives
- Assess and improve self-concept
- Compare functional needs and meaningful nontangible reinforcements

Materials:

- *Self-Concept Cake* worksheet (parts 1 and 2)
- *Self-Concept Cake* examples
- Variety of writing utensils (in at least five different colors)

Directions:

1. Explain the meaning of self-concept to the client:

   "This activity explores your self-concept, which is your belief about who you are, based on your interactions with your world."

2. Using the *Self-Concept Cake Part 1* worksheet, ask the client to consider the following question: "What do you hear about who you are from . . . ?" Have the client answer the question for each layer of the cake (immediate family, extended family, educators, peers, and counselors/support staff). Many clients like to use a different color writing utensil for each layer. Show them the included *Self-Concept Cake Part 1* example handout as needed.

3. On the *Self-Concept Cake Part 2* worksheet, follow the same instructions but with the prompt: "What would you *like* to hear about who you are from . . . ?"
    a. The strength of the intervention lies in this step, when the client identifies what they would *like* to hear about themselves. This insight creates a valuable opportunity for targeted, meaningful intervention based on the qualities they hope to develop or be recognized for, which can be transformed into nontangible reinforcers.
4. Let the client know the importance of this intervention:

    "It seems like some people may be confused about what you really need and what helps you see you are being successful. I'd like to share this information with your support team, so we can stop wasting your time on what isn't working and what seems to get you more negativity. Can I do that for you?"

5. Use the completed worksheets as a tool to communicate with and advocate for the client—using their perspective (qualitative data)—with their support team. For example:
    a. "Cake 1 tells us that we may not have correctly identified the function or need of this client's behavior because they are telling us something different." (e.g., "We thought attention but they say control and autonomy")
    b. "Cake 2 is telling us exactly the type of nontangible incentives this client finds meaningful, and it's something we can immediately incorporate into reinforcement contingencies for behavioral change." (e.g., "They'd like to hear that someone is proud of them and that they are accepted")

Tier 2 or 3

School, Treatment, and Community Settings

This technique can be used in whole-group, small-group, or individual settings. As a whole-group activity, this can improve community validation of negative self-perception in the group space, which is especially impactful for adolescent populations. Each layer of the cake can be filled on separate days, or it can be completed as a one-and-done activity. In psychiatric settings, this tool can assist support staff and clinicians to rapidly recognize what requires their focus and adaptation for improving immediate stability, as well as aftercare planning.

Worksheet

Self-Concept Cake Part 1

What do you hear about who you are?

Counselors/Support Staff

Peers

Teachers

Extended Family

Immediate Family

Worksheet

Self-Concept Cake Part 2

What would you *like* to hear about who you are?

Counselors/Support Staff

Peers

Teachers

Extended Family

Immediate Family

Example Worksheet

Self-Concept Cake Part 1

What do you hear about who you are?

Needs are NOT being met

Counselors/Support Staff

Broken, flawed, a problem

Peers

Weird, crazy, annoying, different

Teachers

Not worth the time, rejectable, lazy, slow, frustrating

Extended Family

An embarrassment, not welcome, exhausting, too complicated

Immediate Family

Bad, a burden, too much to handle, frustrating, defiant, lazy, just like my mother, confusing, impossible

Example Worksheet

Self-Concept Cake Part 2

What would you *like* to hear about who you are?

Self-identified nontangible reinforcements

Others

Capable, learning

Peers

Cool

Teachers

Smart, capable, a hard worker, worth my time, a part of this class

Extended Family

Welcome, accepted, my own person, funny, included

Immediate Family

Loved, proud of you, important, a priority, valued, a part of this family, worth it

Punishment vs. Growth-Based Models of Intervention

B, C

Therapeutic Rationale:

While most interventions in this book focus on tools to use directly with clients, this zooms out to a systems level to address the professionals who work with them every day: educators, paraprofessionals, case managers, direct care staff, caregivers, and families. It aims to shift the collective perspective of behavior management from punishment-based to growth-based, in order to make real progress toward goals and long-term change.

Punishment may work in the moment, but it requires ongoing effort, repeated intervention, and often a rigid, black-and-white view of progress. Traditionally, punishment involves delivering a consequence for a behavior (e.g., a student swears at a teacher and receives detention or loses a privilege). In the context of this work, however, it can also include failing to meet an (often unrealistic) performance threshold (e.g., a student does not meet their required IEP goal of staying on task 90 percent of the time and therefore receives reinforcement). Punitive models often set exceedingly high expectations that few can meet, and they ultimately foster hopelessness, worthlessness, and defensiveness. Punishment teaches clients to behave in ways that avoid consequences rather than cultivating skills and emotional growth toward empathy, remorse, and personal responsibility.

A *growth-based model* offers a flexible approach that meets clients at their current level of skill or insight (reality) and adapts as those levels improve. It uses successive approximation, or shaping—a technique that breaks a goal into smaller, achievable steps, reinforces each step as it more closely resembles the target behavior, and gradually increases expectations as the person becomes more skilled. This approach is strength-based and fluid, accounting for personal and environmental factors that may affect progress, such as the death of an attachment figure, a move to a new home, custody changes, or permanency planning. Within a growth-based model, defensiveness is greatly reduced, allowing clients to build functional skills like accountability, accepting support, empathy, and self-compassion.

This intervention includes information, handouts, and examples of how adults who work with children can shift their mentalities to create a bigger impact in a more functional way.

Goals:

- Replace punitive-based models of intervention with growth-based models
- Improve awareness of environmental stressors on behavioral progress
- Promote appropriate expectations and corresponding reinforcements to improve behavioral change
- Increase the effective use of nontangible reinforcements

Materials:

- *Punishments vs. Growth-Based Interventions* example worksheet
- *Punishments vs. Growth-Based Interventions* worksheet

Directions:

1. Explain the effectiveness of a growth-based approach to the adult:

   "As caregivers and professionals, we ask ourselves often, 'Why is this not working?' 'What am I doing wrong?' 'Why is this kid so difficult?' These are all valid questions, and they're usually an indication that we need to take a step back and rethink our approach to challenging behaviors. Continuing what we are doing unsuccessfully only repeats the pattern, creating frustration and disengagement by you and the kids we are trying to help. A great place to start is by exploring and reflecting on whether we are using a punishment-based approach or a growth-based approach."

2. Introduce the *Punishment vs. Growth-Based Interventions* example worksheet and walk the adult through the concept, explaining the difference between the models if needed.

3. Starting with the punishment-based model on the *top half* of the page, explain how this approach can result in resistance and defensiveness from the start, specifically the large discrepancy between the child's current ability and the goal.

   a. First, discuss the child's perspective on their goal: What types of thoughts do they have? What kinds of feelings do they have? (Include both thoughts *and* feelings to create whole-brain connections.) How do those thoughts and feelings have an impact on behavioral change?

   b. Identify that the child continues to work at 25 percent (failing at their goal), with limited change and movement.

   c. Given this failure, discuss the perspective of the adult: What types of thoughts do they have? What types of feelings do they have? (Include both thoughts and feelings to create whole-brain connections.) How do those thoughts and feelings have an impact on the child's behavior?

   d. Reflect on how this model perpetuates failure, creates combative relationships, and reinforces already negative thoughts and feelings. Make note of feelings of hopelessness and worthlessness specifically, as they are both contributors to increased prevalence of suicidal ideation and self-injury.

4. Then transition to the *bottom half* of the page, the growth-based model, which starts at the last line and works up. Note that the goal has moved to at or just slightly below the current level of performance. Walk the adult through the same process as with the punishment-based version:
    a. The identified goal is now based in reality of ability with a *range of functioning*, not a finite point of success.
    b. Identify that the child is likely to quickly meet or exceed their goal, which increases the likelihood of repeated behavior and improvement.
    c. This time, after seeing some positive behavioral movement, first discuss the adult's perspective on the goal: What types of thoughts and feelings do they have now? How are those thoughts and feelings likely to impact the behavioral change? Does this change the way they interact with the child? Does it improve the collaborative relationship? Emphasize here the power of intangible incentives, (e.g., "I'm proud of you," "We are doing this together," "You are doing a good job"), which are now real experiences and genuinely stated, rather than just words the adult is supposed to say.
    d. Given this success, discuss the perspective of the child: What types of thoughts and feelings do they have now? Do those different thoughts and feelings change the way they view themselves and their abilities? Does this shift help them believe that the nontangible reinforcers are true?
    e. Reflect on how this model promotes success, creates collaborative relationships, and builds new neuropathways for *everyone* related to confidence, worthiness, and hope for the future.
    f. Note here that the outcome (noted by the bar on the arrow) in both scenarios is the same (the child works at 25 percent) but the *trajectory* is markedly different. The long-term goal for the child—learn to communicate appropriately—hasn't changed. The change is that instead of asking the child to take one enormous step without any tools or skills, the adult is asking the child to take smaller steps, collecting tools and skills along the way.
5. From here, tailor your discussion to the people involved and the setting, encouraging reflection on their own approach. Provide the adult with the blank *Punishments vs. Growth-Based Interventions* worksheet so they can work with their own scenario with your assistance. Decide together where changes can be made and what steps they can take to get there, revisiting the example as needed.

Worksheet

Punishments vs. Growth-Based Interventions

PUNISHMENT

Goal:
Current level:

★ Child is working at _____ (failing each day)

Adult

Thoughts:
Feelings:
Behavior:

Child

Thoughts:
Feelings:
Behavior:

- ✕ No progress; risk of regression
- ✕ Combative relationships ("child vs. me")
- ✕ Reinforced negative thoughts and feelings for child

- ✓ Smaller steps; immediate success
- ✓ Collaborative relationships ("we")
- ✓ Intangible, genuine reinforcement for child and adults

★ Adjust goal incrementally based on skills and ability.

GROWTH

Child

Thoughts:
Feelings:
Behavior:

Adult

Thoughts:
Feelings:
Behavior:

★ Child is working at _____ (meets goal!)

Goal:
Current level:

Example Worksheet

Punishments vs. Growth-Based Interventions

PUNISHMENT

★ **Goal:** Child will have appropriate communication 90 percent of the time.
Current level: 25 percent

★ Child is working at 25% (failing each day)

Adult

Thoughts: "They're not working hard enough," "I'm doing a bad job," "I'm a terrible parent"
Feelings: Overwhelmed, frustrated, resentful, angry, disappointed
Behavior: Gives up, disengages from child, gives further consequences, blames child

Child

Thoughts: "There's no way I can do this," "This is impossible," "I suck," "Why bother?"
Feelings: Hopeless, worthless, unlovable
Behavior: Continues working at same level or below

✗ No progress; risk of regression
✗ Combative relationships ("child vs. me")
✗ Reinforced negative thoughts and feelings for child

GROWTH

✓ Smaller steps; immediate success
✓ Collaborative relationships ("we")
✓ Intangible, genuine reinforcement for child and adults

★ Adjust goal incrementally based on skills and ability.

Child

Thoughts: "That seems doable," "I can do this," "This is possible"
Feelings: Capable, supported, proud, loved, successful, hopeful
Behavior: Puts forth effort, quickly meets or exceeds goal

Adult

Thoughts: "We are doing it," "This is working," "Things can get better"
Feelings: Successful, proud, relieved, happy, hopeful, confident
Behavior: Engages with child, provides intangible incentives (e.g., "I'm proud of you," "You can do this"), wants to keep helping

★ Child is working at 25% (meets goal!)

★ **Goal:** Child will have appropriate communication 20–25 percent of the time
Current level: 25 percent

Breath Training for Self-Regulation C, D, N, S

Therapeutic Rationale:

Regulated breathing, the gold standard for proactive agitation prevention, efficiently and effectively engages parasympathetic initiation to decrease escalated responses to environmental cues (recall the description of the autonomic nervous system from page 25). Paced and controlled breathing has a positive impact on smooth muscle tissue tension control (i.e., heart, lungs, and gastrointestinal), which can relieve secondary anxiety cognitions, such as negative rumination, obsessive thoughts, and catastrophic thinking. Breath training also increases oxygenation to the brain, improving concentration, the processing of novel tasks and instructions, and the encoding of information to long-term memory.

The majority of traditional breath training focuses on "breathing in through the nose and out through the mouth," and many clients benefit from this instruction. But there is always a percentage of clients who are easily sensitized or triggered through traditional models of training. This is most prevalent with high level comorbid anxiety presentation, trauma-exposed clients, and medical or environmental issues. These kids benefit from self-paced breathing with physical comfort, which decreases "overfocused breath" and triggered escalation.

With younger children, the 4/7/8 pacing can also be difficult, as they may have issues counting high enough, trouble perseverating while holding their breath, or limited core development. For some kids, shorter initial tempo should be considered, like 3/5/6 pacing, which promotes awareness of the need for a breath without unintentionally triggering the sympathetic nervous system response. A helpful addition to all breath training tools is practicing crossing of the midline of the brain. For example, the child might cross their legs; cross their arms and place their hands on the opposite biceps; or extend their arms in front of their body, cross their wrists, and weave their fingers together. This promotes bilateral engagement and decreases the amount of time needed for breathing techniques.

Goals:

- Improve self-regulation through directed breath training
- Improve self-monitoring of breath as a component of persistent agitation

Materials:

- Bubbles
- Candles or tea lights
- "Trick" cake candles
- Facial tissues or tissue paper squares
- Balloons

Directions:

Bubble Breath

1. Provide yourself and the client with bubbles and a bubble wand.
2. Model a slow consistent breath until the bubbles in your wand are depleted.
3. Ask the client to show you how they can do the same.
4. Model fast breath expulsion by blowing little bubbles. Then ask the client to do the same.
5. Model regulated/even breath with slow pacing to "grow" big bubbles. Ask the client to do the same.
6. Have the client blow "little bubbles" for one trial, and then "big bubbles" for three trials.
7. Encourage them to try this exercise five (or more!) times a day until you see them next.
8. Replenish their bubbles if they return with an empty or low container. You can also adjust the density of the bubble by adding extra dish detergent to the solution, making breath training more challenging.

Candle Breath

1. Light a candle or tea light.
2. Have the client stand three feet from the candle and try to blow out the flame.
3. Have the client step back one foot and try to blow out the flame again.
4. Challenge them to continue distance blowing, moving back one foot every time, until the flame no longer wavers or flickers when they blow.
5. This begins to grow breath endurance, which is especially important for children with limited core strength. They can practice on their own by pretending their fingertip is a candle they are blowing out.

Trick Candle Breath

1. Light a trick restarter candle.
2. Ask the client to blow out the candle; it is designed to relight after going out.
3. Say, "Oh, that was unexpected! I wonder how many blows it will take to put out *this* candle?"
4. Have the client count after every breath until they are able to blow it out. Model the blowing and counting before you let them try.
5. Let them rest for 20 seconds.
6. Ask them how their body feels after that exercise. Give examples if needed, such as hot, sweaty, or a fast heartbeat.
7. Tell the client they will now try the same exercise on a regular candle. Let them guess how many times they will need to blow on it.
8. Let them rest for 10 seconds.
9. Ask them to compare how their body feels after resting and breathing more slowly versus when they were blowing and breathing quickly.

Tissue/Balloon off the Ground Breath

1. Tell the client their goal is to see how long they can keep a tissue or balloon from hitting the ground, but they can only use their breath.
2. For the first round, guide them to try with fast puffs of breath. Model rapid breathing while exaggerating shoulder lifting.
3. In the second round, guide them to try with slow breaths. Model slow exhalation while exaggerating your hand on your belly.
4. Bring the client's attention to the fact that they could keep the balloon up longer when they used their slower breath.

Standard 4/7/8 Paced Breath

1. Introduce the client to the 4/7/8 model, which they can use to calm themselves down when their breathing gets short and fast. Remind them that the tip of their tongue should rest on the gum line just behind the front teeth. If you work with children with a shortened frenulum, they can push their tongue to the bottom of the mouth.
2. Guide them to close their mouth and inhale slowly through their nose while you count to four (one second per count).
3. Instruct them to hold their breath while you count to seven.
4. Guide them to blow the air out of their mouth while you count to eight, and tell them to make it noisy!
5. Do this exercise three more times for a total of four.

Note: You may need to adjust the pacing of this exercise based on need and ability, such as children with asthma or cystic fibrosis. There are several other paced breathing techniques available through online apps; kids and their families should try several to find ones that suit them best.

Tier 1

School, Treatment, and Community Settings

Breath practice is one of the simplest tools to incorporate into academic and group treatment settings. Remember the importance of practicing at least five times a day for proactive prevention of ANS sensitivity. For example, you may start the morning with a breathing activity, repeat after lunch or unstructured activities, and repeat again before leaving at the end of the day. Effective breathing practice takes less than two minutes and is a worthy investment of six total minutes in the instructional day to prevent dysregulation.

Music for Stress Reduction C, N, S

Therapeutic Rationale:

Integrating music into daily routines can reduce limbic system reactivity, lessen ruminative worry, and ease the physical symptoms of anxiety and stress. Music activates the auditory cortex, improving information processing and supporting neural plasticity and long-term memory formation. This intervention is designed to teach children how music influences their brain and body so they can choose the types of music that help them feel calm and avoid acting out in response to internal distress.

Goals:

- Decrease feelings of agitation with music
- Create proactive coping skills

Materials:

- *How to Check Your Heart Rate* handout
- *Your Calming Music* worksheet
- Selections of music (chosen by the client)
- Earbuds or headphones

Directions:

1. Explain to the client how music can be a coping skill:

   "Music can be great for helping us feel less agitated, but it can also make it worse, so choosing the right music is important. Just because we like a certain song doesn't mean it's helping our brain and body calm down. We are going to learn how to do that together today, so you can take it with you everywhere."

2. Teach the client how to check their heart rate, explaining that it can tell them when their body and brain are calm and chill (lower rate) or anxious, happy, or scared (higher rate). Before checking their pulse, breathe with the client and "relax" for about three minutes to get them close to their resting heart rate.

3. Provide the client with the *How to Check Your Heart Rate* handout, going through each step with them and demonstrating the steps.

4. Document the client's resting heart rate and record it on the first arrow on the *Your Calming Music* worksheet under song 1.

5. Have the client select four songs. Write in the first of their songs and invite them to listen to it (in earbuds or aloud). Record their heart rate on the "New HR" arrow.

6. Ask them to compare their new heart rate with their resting heart rate. Did it stay the same, decrease, or increase?
   a. If it stayed the same or decreased, they can mark "Yes," which indicates they can use this song as a calming technique.
   b. If their heart rate increased, mark "No." Remind them that just because their HR went up, it does not mean they can't listen to that song. They can use this song for moments like doing homework, exercising, or doing chores, but not for calming themselves down.
   c. In either scenario, have the client decide on a time when it might be beneficial to listen to this song. They can write it down on the final arrow for song 1.
7. Have the client do this for three more songs, recording their findings on the *Your Calming Music* worksheet.
8. Encourage the client to use the songs that calm them on a regular basis, and they can also do the experiment with more songs to build their calming skills toolbox.

Tier 3

School, Treatment, and Community Settings

Although students are rarely allowed to use their phones during the school day, incorporating access to agitation-reducing music into their daily routine is a quiet and nondisruptive tool to prevent acting out, and it can be one of the five recommended self-regulation tools incorporated into your routine.

Handout

How to Check Your Heart Rate

Your pulse tells you a lot about how you're feeling. When you feel relaxed and calm, your pulse is usually slower. When you are agitated or angry, your pulse rate is usually much faster. However, a faster pulse rate does not always mean something is wrong—it could also mean you are playing, exercising, or feeling happy or excited! This handout describes how to check your heart rate by feeling your pulse in your wrist.

1. Press your pointer finger and middle finger on the side of your wrist, under your thumb.
2. Once you can feel a steady beat, count how many beats you feel in 30 seconds.
3. Multiply that number by 2, and you have your heart rate, which is described as _____ beats per minute.

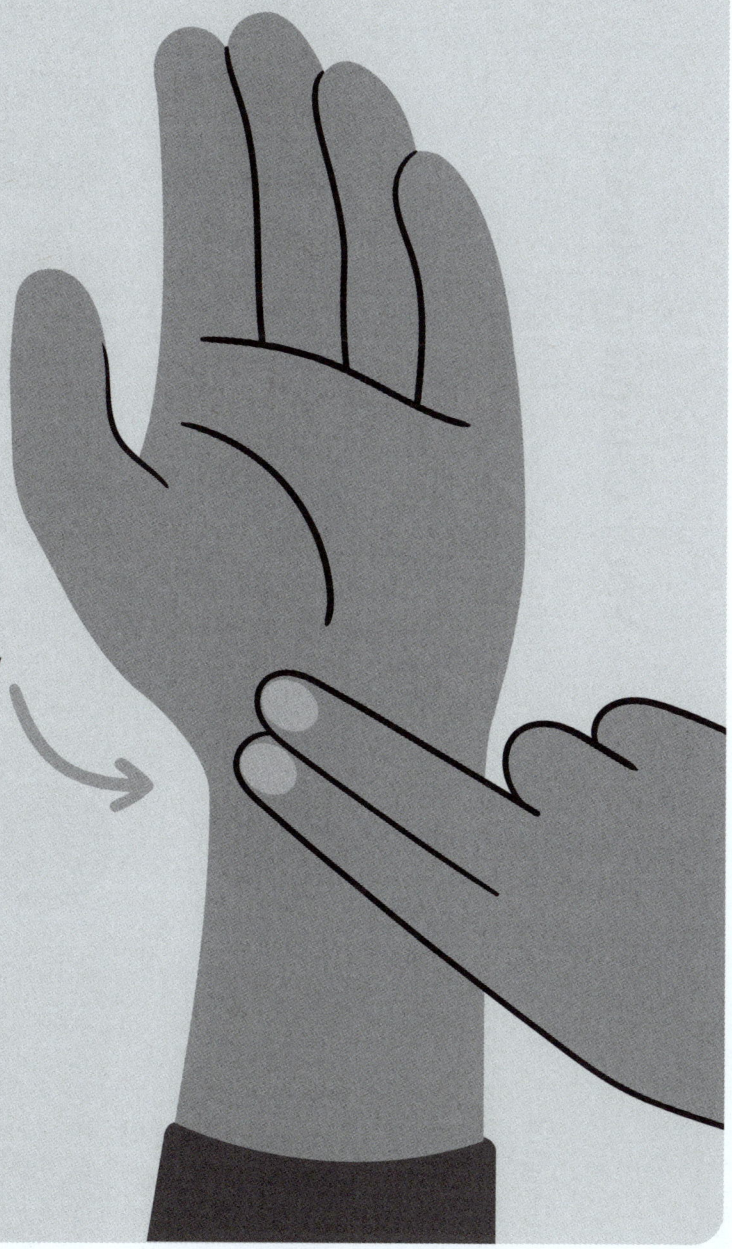

Worksheet

Your Calming Music

Finding the right music to help your body and brain get—and stay—calm can be a fun discovery. Not all music is meant to calm us, and that's okay. It just means some music works better for different activities. Together, we're going to explore and find the music that can help you calm down when your emotions run high.

Song 1:

Resting Heart Rate ________ → Song → New Heart Rate ________ → Calming Song: Yes / No → Where to Use This Song

Song 2:

Resting Heart Rate ________ → Song → New Heart Rate ________ → Calming Song: Yes / No → Where to Use This Song

Song 3:

Resting Heart Rate ________ → Song → New Heart Rate ________ → Calming Song: Yes / No → Where to Use This Song

Song 4:

Resting Heart Rate ________ → Song → New Heart Rate ________ → Calming Song: Yes / No → Where to Use This Song

The Anger Volcano **B, C, N**

Therapeutic Rationale:

Most interventions labeled "anger management" are designed to use *after* an outburst and rely on a reactive approach. Proactive interventions, however, focus on helping kids recognize the subtle cues that signal early stages of escalation. When they can identify these sooner, they're better able to use coping strategies when they can think more clearly and engage their bodies in ways that help prevent escalation.

The metaphor of the anger volcano pairs verbal and experiential activities to deepen the intervention, helping kids recognize a signal of escalation and pair it with a coping skill. Through this process of pairing, they are better able to slow the internal system of escalation and *prevent* explosion and acting out.

Goals:

- Develop self-awareness of early escalation behaviors
- Create empathy for the effects of behaviors
- Access a person in the client's support net to prevent the negative impact of melting down

Materials:

- *The Anger Volcano* handout
- Play dough
- Small figurines to represent people, buildings, and activities
- Variety of art supplies (e.g., colored pencils, crayons)
- 3×5 note cards
- Optional: Sand tray, video of volcano eruption

Directions:

1. Explain to the client how they can notice anger cues before explosion:

   "Anger is a feeling we all have that is perfectly normal and okay, but it becomes a problem when it turns into aggressive words and behaviors. Sometimes it feels like we can't control our behavior when we're that mad, because it seems like it comes out of nowhere. The thing is, anger is a lot like a volcano. A volcano seems like it erupts out of nowhere, but if we pay closer attention, there are clues it's getting ready to blow. Our bodies work the same way."

2. Provide the client with play dough, and have them create a volcano that represents them. Discuss how volcanoes are dormant, or *sleeping, calm, and cool*, a lot of the time. People even live near volcanoes because they feel safe.

3. Have the client place sand tray toys or figurines near the play dough volcano scene (or in a sand tray). The objects should represent people, places, or situations in their life. Guide them to put the objects most important to them nearest to the volcano.

4. Discuss that when volcanoes erupt suddenly, they spew lava and ash high into the air and down the sides of the volcano to the ground below.

Optional: Show the client a video clip depicting a volcano eruption to add another sensory experience (great for older children).

   a. Allow the child to play out and observe the eruption and the impact of the lava and ash on the things around the base of their volcano.
   b. "Survey the scene" with the client, identifying the ways people and places were impacted by the eruption, including how it will take a long time to recover from its destruction because no one knew the early warning signs that the eruption was coming.
   c. Discuss how helpful it would have been if the people had known what to look for, like an early alarm system. Help the child brainstorm what cues might have told the people the volcano was going to erupt so they could get to safety (e.g., rumbling, shaking ground, smoke rising, temperature getting hotter).

5. Introduce the client to *The Anger Volcano* handout. Discuss how anger is like a volcano, and review the low, medium, and high warning signs of explosion. Explore with the client what their early alarm system is like: What are the cues from their body that they are working up to an eruption of anger?

6. On a 3×5 note card, have the client draw or write the cues that represent what they look like before they "erupt." For younger kids, draw a simple outline of a body and have them color or draw their cues as they experience them.

7. Discuss how volcanoes sometimes *look* like they are going to erupt, but instead of a full eruption, it simply lets off some steam and then settles back to dormant again. Pair this concept with the idea of using coping skills to prevent an explosion.

8. On the back of the 3×5 card, have the client write or draw a coping skill (see the *Active Coping Skills* handout on page 37 or the *Passive Coping Skills* handout on page 38) that will help them let off steam instead of erupting. Reiterate as needed: "This is how you can slow down your volcano from erupting every time, and you can avoid the damage that comes afterward."

9. Encourage the client to share their card with their support net to help build awareness of their cues of escalation. Supportive adults can intervene (e.g., "Now seems like a good time to get a cold drink of water. Let's do that together") while also helping build the client's self-awareness of their escalation cues.

Tier 1

School, Treatment, and Community Settings

The anger volcano is a valuable group activity for normalizing anger and brainstorming individually effective coping strategies.

Handout

The Anger Volcano

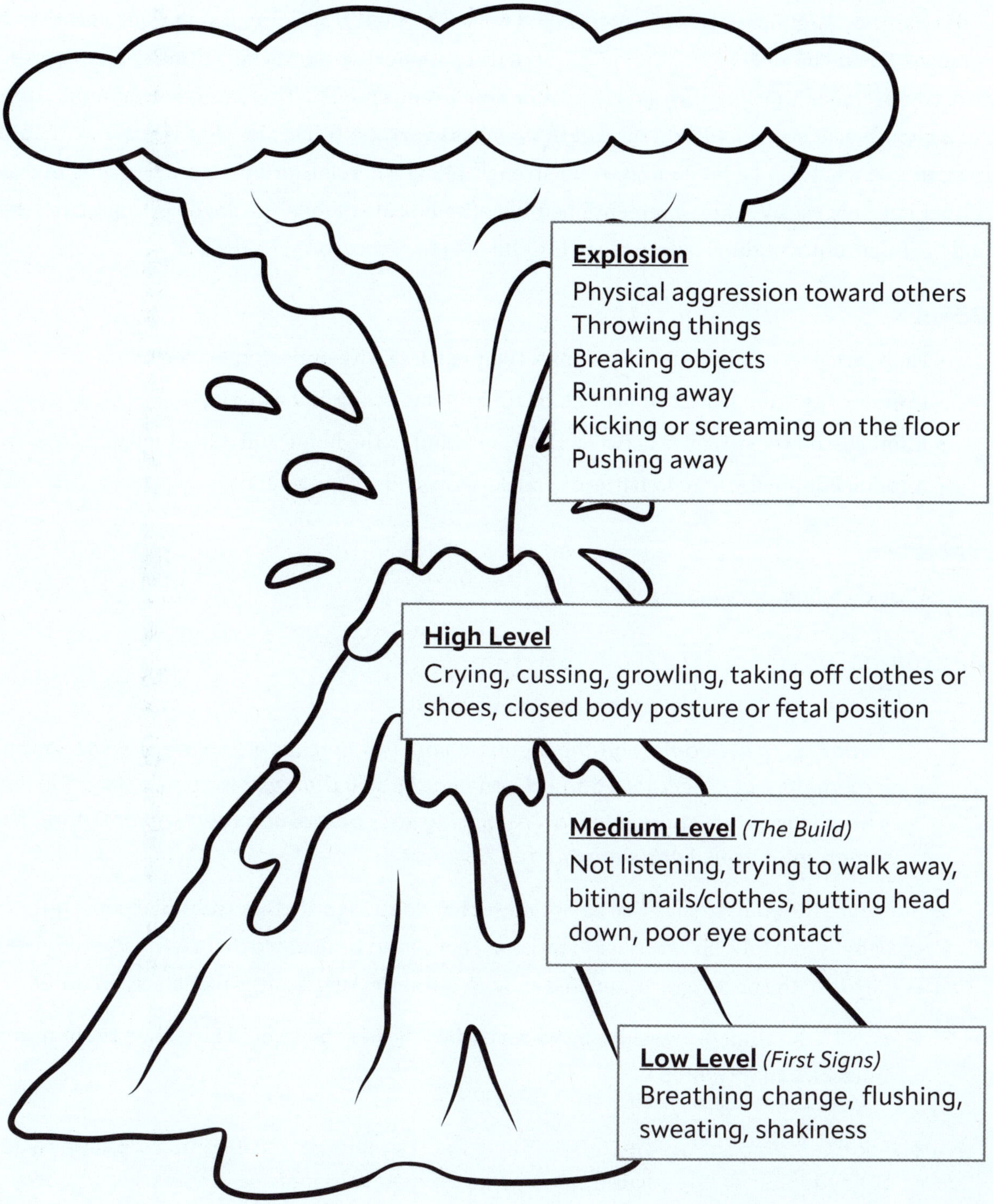

What are the signs that you are getting ready to blow?
What do you look like when you are getting angry?

Wise Compromises B, C

Therapeutic Rationale:

Kids who show argumentative or oppositional behavior often resist compromise because they believe it means "giving in" or "losing." Caregivers and other supportive adults may think something similar—that compromising means they aren't firm or consistent enough. This intervention aims to reframe compromise as a *smart and healthy skill* that allows everyone to decide what is truly worth standing firm on and what can be let go in favor of strengthening the relationship and well-being of everyone. Adults not only receive the aforementioned benefits but also model willingness, cognitive flexibility, and the importance of the relationship to the children they care for.

Goals:

- Help caregivers and professionals "pick their battles" with oppositional behaviors
- Promote the growth of flexible thinking through modeling and experience
- Eliminate power struggles between child and adult in the home and school settings
- Alter dichotomous thought patterns and develop skills of abstraction

Materials:

- *Wise Compromises* worksheet

Directions:

1. Explain the importance of compromise to the adult:

   "It may seem like compromising means losing, yielding, or letting the child get away with something, but it's actually a smart and healthy skill *that has two parts: choosing what is worth investing your energy in (i.e., picking your battle) and then implementing the compromise itself. Let's start with the first part."*

2. Introduce the adult to the *Wise Compromises* handout. Identify the issues that come up repeatedly and take up excessive emotional energy and time. Have them write five of these down at the top of the page (e.g., arguments about bedtime, eating healthy foods, screen time).

3. Work with the adult on considering which of these issues they would be willing to compromise on and which they wouldn't.

Note: Reiterate to caregivers and other adults that they should *never* compromise on issues of safety or anything that is regulated by law (e.g., drug and alcohol use, underage sex, curfew).

4. Have them choose an issue they are willing to compromise on—this is usually a compromise that gives both parties at least *some* of what they want. Walk through the three "Steps to Compromise" questions of the worksheet for that specific argument. For example:
   - What does the child want? *Not to drink milk at dinner.*
   - What do you want? *I want my child to drink one glass (8 ounces) of milk at dinner*.
   - What's the middle ground? *Drinking half a glass (4 ounces) of milk at dinner.*
5. Guide the adult and child to verbalize their understanding of the agreement to each other as they shake hands: *I understand this agreement means you are / I am going to drink half a glass of milk at dinner.* Encourage them to create a visual reference to the agreement so they can remember it when it occurs; in this example, the child and adult may create a drawing of a half-glass of milk to display at dinner time.

Tier 3

School, Treatment, and Community Settings

Compromise can be a highly effective tool for oppositional students, especially when supporting class participation and managing course workload. When a student has an accommodation, such as an adjusted courseload, I often recommend that educators avoid premodifying the assignment. Instead, provide the full assignment and negotiate in real time as the student works. For example, if a worksheet contains 20 math problems and the student is required to complete only 10, present all 20 and say, "For each problem you get correct at the beginning, I'll cross one off at the end." When reinforcement is used effectively, students typically complete the required number of problems—and often view the agreement as a beneficial trade for themselves. Strategies like this commonly increase adjusted-courseload performance from 40–50 percent to 70–80 percent, as students build momentum and require less removal of items.

This same approach can be useful in therapeutic groups. Rather than expecting full participation, you might say, "You don't have to talk for the entire group, but we agree that you'll participate in about half." You might also set a specific, manageable target like answering four questions. This balance of structure and flexibility supports engagement while still honoring the client's needs.

Telehealth Application

If you are working with children with behavioral issues in the more severe range, participation in telehealth services is often quite tedious, and the use of compromise as part of participation for treatment can easily be applied. For instance, you might say, "For every minute you participate in treatment, we will cut off one minute at the end of our time together."

Worksheet

Wise Compromises

Identify some of the issues that come up repeatedly between you and the child.

1. ______________________________

____

2. ______________________________

____

3. ______________________________

____

4. ______________________________

____

5. ______________________________

____

Now cross out the ones you are unwilling to compromise on and put a check next to the ones you are willing to work on.

"I've noticed that we've been spending a lot of time and emotional energy arguing about things that, if we took the time to meet in the middle on, may have not even grown into an argument. I want to suggest we try something new: a compromise. When two people compromise, one person gets some of what *they* want and the other person gets some of what *they* want. We meet in the middle. Neither person gets everything they want or nothing that they want, which means it's a win-win."

Steps to Compromise

1. What does the child want?
2. What does the adult want?
3. What is the "middle ground" between what both people want?

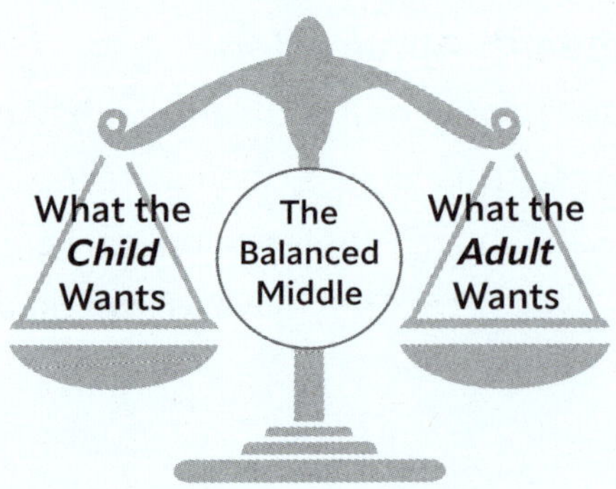

Choose one of the issues you listed as "willing to work on" and answer these questions:

1. What does the child want?

   ____

   ____

2. What does the adult want?

   ____

   ____

3. What is the "middle ground" between what both people want?

   ____

   ____

When an agreement is made, verbalize an understanding of the agreement to each other while shaking hands. You may also create a visual reference to the agreement so you and the child can remember it when it occurs.

Remember:

- Think long and hard about your side of the compromise, because once you choose, you cannot change your mind.
- Always start with what the child wants first. It helps them feel heard and "locks in" their response, allowing you to provide a measured counter response.
- Not everything is up for compromise. (You are still the adult, after all.) However, the more you can compromise, the better.
- Never compromise on issues of safety or anything that is regulated by law (e.g., drug and alcohol use, underage sex, curfew).
- You can always walk away from the discussion and return later. This models impulse control and that it's okay to think a decision through before agreeing.
- Keep age and maturity in mind, especially for topics like bedtime, understanding that your position will likely change in the future (e.g., give the child a "win" of 10 extra minutes at bedtime because it won't always be an issue as they get older).

Boundary Word or Phrase *B, C, N*

Therapeutic Rationale:

Kids with behavioral disorders often have trouble conceptualizing emotional and physical boundaries. These are kids who have significant difficulty play fighting, joking, or teasing without it escalating into a more significant behavioral event; often they just don't get it when they have "gone too far." These types of persistent difficulties tell us that these kids need better training on "when I have hurt someone's body, feelings, or property." The Cloud and Townsend (2017) research on boundaries discusses three specific types of boundaries: (1) rigid, (2) permeable, and (3) nonexistent (Cloud, 2023). Some children with behavioral disorders simply do not recognize that boundaries exist at all. After a play fighting incident that has escalated significantly, resulting in a disciplinary action, they might say, "I don't know why *I* am the one that's in trouble, since they started it. It's not my fault they have a broken arm." The same is true with sibling and caregiver interactions, in that they seem to "push everyone's buttons." Therefore, this intervention develops effective boundaries to start promoting the skills of empathy, remorse, and personal responsibility.

Goals:

- Define and establish emotional and physical boundaries with language and visual cueing
- Improve skills of empathy, remorse, and personal responsibility
- Improve confidence and competence of asking for support
- Prevent escalation of benign interactions

Materials:

- *Boundary Word or Phrase* handout
- Paper cut into slips
- Hat or bag

Directions:

1. Explain the importance of boundaries to the client:

   "Sometimes we have a hard time telling when things have gone too far, and we don't understand that when someone says, 'Ouch, stop! You're hurting me,' that means we have stepped over their boundary for safety and need to stop whatever we are doing at that moment. Those words have lost their power to tell you a wall has been broken down, so we need to create a new language to tell other people they have gone too far, or for others to tell us the same thing."

2. Introduce the client to the *Boundary Word or Phrase* handout. Using the rules on this sheet, everyone in the client's family (or group) gets to pick a word or phrase to add to the drawing hat. The word must be:
    a. Humorous (which soothes the amygdala)
    b. Outside the context of normal conversation
3. Place the words in a hat or bag and randomly select the new boundary word/phrase.
4. Identify this word as a "power" word—a word that helps tell others that your body, feelings, or property are at risk of being seriously harmed.
5. Identify that the word is for use with everyone, and it means they must immediately stop what they are doing. (You can layer in an apology later as empathy is growing, but it is not necessary at first, as there is a nonverbal cue of apology in the stopping itself.)
6. Remind the client that the word cannot be abused, or it will lose its power. They cannot use it to manipulate or intimidate someone else, and they must follow others' boundary requests.
    a. If the word is abused, an adult should remind the child of the power of the word (usually after the first 7 to 10 days).
    b. If it is abused again (10 to 30 days), the family or group will choose a second word or phrase (only after the testing-of-limits phase, and following the same rules for word selection).
    c. If the second word continues to be abused (30 days), this intervention may not be appropriate for the family or group. (In my experience, this has been the case less than 2 percent of the time.)

Tier 1 or 2

School, Treatment, and Community Settings

This is an excellent technique for group treatment and classroom settings, as the use of the word is not considered a "reminder" unless it requires adult intervention. Positive peer pressure and modeling can be used to your advantage with this technique, and it also helps children set limits with others when they are feeling agitated or overwhelmed. Some self-contained units even create their own boundary word as smaller groups, separate from the whole-school word, so when they are out at field trips or other public events they have a tool to use quickly without creating shame responses from students.

For younger children (pre-K through first grade), I often use a word paired with a visual cue. Most often, I use the word "ladybug," as it is a familiar image and is red. Kids can carry this image with them on the backside of a break-away lanyard to all the places boundary testing occurs: hallways, playgrounds, restrooms, buses, and cafeterias. If a child is unable to quickly access the language of "ladybug," they can simply turn over the image to tell others to stop their behavior.

Handout

Boundary Word or Phrase

A boundary word is a way to tell or show someone that they have hurt your body, feelings, or property before you feel like you are going to blow up.

Rules of the Boundary Word/Phrase

When creating a new boundary word or phrase:

1. The word must be humorous.
2. The word must be outside the context of normal conversation.
3. The word cannot be abused, or it loses its power.

How to Handle Word Abuse

If someone abuses the boundary word or phrase:

- First abuse (in the first 7 to 10 days): Remind the child of the power of the word.
- Second abuse (10 to 30 days): Identify a new boundary word or phrase.
- Third abuse (30 days): A boundary word or phrase may not be the right intervention.

Remember, you can use a visual representation of the word or phrase too!

Processing Aggressive Media Content **B, C, N**

Therapeutic Rationale:

As discussed in chapter 1, technology use among young people has increased significantly (6 to 8 hours on weekdays and 10 to 12 hours on weekend days) and with it, the exposure to content that is aggressive or violent. There remains an inaccurate belief that exposure to *any* aggressive content increases the likelihood a child will behave aggressively ("It's the video games!"), but research offers more nuance. Specifically, there is a significant difference in neurological response during exposure to a video game as compared to content showing real human beings engaging in emotional or physical aggression; it seems the brain can differentiate between the two (though the rise of artificial intelligence and advances in computer-generated imagery are beginning to blur the lines here).

When a child views "real" content of an aggressive nature, hypothalamic mirrored aggressive neurons are triggered (the *fight* of fight/flight/freeze/fawn) and can be hardwired into the brain structure as a result. Given the ubiquitous nature of this content—reality TV, social media, mainstream news, and aggression in schools and treatment centers—and the average age for viewers becoming younger and younger, interventions to reverse the negative impact on the brain are crucial.

This intervention utilizes two-step processing, starting with addressing the perpetrator's experience (frontal/prefrontal cortex), and finishing with connecting this to emotion (limbic system)—in essence, always connecting thought and behavior with feelings. Many techniques of the past have focused only on the perpetrator role and have not made effort to expand limbic system processing to aggressive material, which is necessary to develop empathy and remorse. By repetitively following this processing component on a daily basis, we actually see a *decrease* in aggressive behavioral responses.

Goals:

- Create fantasy and reality distinction and cause-and-effect connections in the frontal/prefrontal cortex
- Improve recognition of consequences for aggressive behaviors
- Develop accurate emotional responses to aggression

Materials:

- *Processing Aggressive Media* worksheet
- Direct examples of any television program, video game, or internet exposure to violence or aggression (physical or emotional)
- Optional: *Emotions List* handout

Directions:

1. Explain to the client how aggressive content can affect the brain:

   "Sometimes when we see or play games with violence, it can change our brains and make us more aggressive, which can result in us having more consequences. It's important to help our brains to see when something is real or not, to know that our behaviors can affect others, and to learn that feelings are connected to behaviors. We are going to start asking questions after watching these things so we can see how our brains are doing."

2. Have the client think of a video game they've played or a TV show they've watched in the last few days. Introduce the client to the *Processing Aggressive Media* worksheet, where they will process *both* sides of the aggressive content: perpetrator (step 1) and victim (step 2).

3. Show the client a video clip of the game or show so you can reference a specific sequence of emotional or physical violence or aggression. (You can also have them tell you something that happened while they were playing and use this example to work from).

4. Discuss with the client what might happen in "real life" if they were the perpetrator in this scenario:

   a. Ask the client, "If this were real life, what might happen to you if you [*smashed into someone's car, stole someone's purse, etc.*]?"

   b. Take a nonjudgmental stance, because the goal of this step is to process fantasy and reality separation; you are simply making a cause-and-effect connection in the prefrontal cortex. When the client gives you an answer—for example, "If I took the purse, I'd have more cash!"—do *not* say something like, "Well, you wouldn't want that kind of money because that's stealing." *Do* say, "Well, that's something that can happen."

5. Next, discuss with the client what it might feel like if they were the victim in the scenario:

   a. Ask the client, "What would it feel like if someone [*hit your car, stole something from you in public, etc.*]?"

   b. This step of processing has a goal of connecting emotion to thought and behavior, which engages the limbic system.

   c. Kids with more severe conduct symptoms are less likely to engage meaningfully in this step of this process. They may offer fantasy responses to prompts, such as, "They wouldn't hit my car, because I would just jump up and over it in hyper speed" or "I don't care if they steal from me because I don't have any money." An adjustment to this step is to give some distance to the example and say something like, "How would it feel if someone stole your friend's money?"

   d. Some kids also have a tendency to use foul language instead of accurately labeling limbic system emotions, and they may benefit from a word bank of feelings to promote expansion. (See the *Emotions List* handout on page 213.)

6. Complete this worksheet again and again with the client over time, addressing different types of aggressive media exposure. Repeating the exercise *daily* is effective for aggressive behavioral responses.
   a. In time, clients will sigh and say, "I know, it would make me feel frustrated," but the goal is to create emotional recognition, not just an impulsive thought-behavior response.

Tier 1 or 2

School, Treatment, and Community Settings

This technique can be used as a whole-classroom or a small-group activity, as most students are playing the same games, watching the same shows, and viewing the same videos on social media. Taking the time daily to do the dual processing with a class or group will result in decreased impulsive aggressive responses to environmental stimuli.

Worksheet

Processing Aggressive Media

Think of shows, video games, or other media you have seen or played in the last few days. Did anything happen that was violent? Did the characters or actors seem violent, scary, angry, aggressive, or threatening? Did they harm anyone else's body, feelings, or property?

Describe the scenario:

____

____

____

If this were real life, and you were the **perpetrator** (i.e., the person who carries out a harmful act), what might happen to you after you did this?

____

____

____

If this were real life, and you were the **victim** (i.e., the person who is harmed), what would it feel like if this happened to you?

____

____

____

How would you feel if this happened to someone you know (e.g., your friend or caregiver)?

____

____

____

Advanced Processing and Whole-Brain Problem-Solving

B, C, N, S

Therapeutic Rationale:

Now that we have prepared these brains for early recognition of escalatory cues and processing aggressive media, we are ready to start working on problem-solving. Remember that "a thought is not a behavior." For behavioral populations who also have impulsivity issues, taking the time to *slow* the internal process of problem-solving will aid in recognizing that "just because I think it, doesn't mean I have to do it." This is also in the arena of the EF skill of self-control.

Kids often internally and cognitively limit themselves to one solution as the only possibility to resolve an issue, which is not actually a choice but an *initial impulse*. Therefore, we can help them discover that there are several opportunities for problem-solving within a single incident. This intervention uses the old-school concept of a "choose-your-own-adventure" book, in which a reader reaches a choice in the story, makes their decision and turns to a certain page, and receives a consequence to their choice (i.e., a reaction from the environment). Sometimes these choices work out and the story progresses, and other times the choices result in the story ending. This concept is not unlike children who have issues with "one-and-done" problem-solving, which significantly limits neural growth and processing capabilities.

Whole-brain problem-solving addresses a variety of difficulties beyond only problem-solving. It also assists in the following:

- Chronological and linear ordering for cause-and-effect training
- Whole-brain connection with thought, behavior, and emotion
- Realignment of serial chains of behavior in the brain

Serial Chains

A serial chain is a behavior an individual has practiced so frequently that they no longer think about all of the steps it takes to get to the final result. For example, driving a car has become second nature to most of us because it is a cognitive habit, and we don't have to think about turning the key, putting our foot on the brake, or moving the car into drive. It's *neurologically habituated*.

Kids with behavioral issues have what are called *negative serial chains* of behavior. These are behaviors that are so well-practiced that they have become neurologically hardwired for them, and they essentially put them on the "wrong track," often resulting in statements like, "I blacked out" or "I don't remember." Part of the processing in this activity is to back up in chronological order and find an opportunity for retraining a *positive serial chain* of behavior ***before*** the event happens, and then incorporating reinforcement contingency into shaping—or the successive approximation of—a positive behavioral response. In time, this can become directly connected to problem-solving and develops a preventive mindset and skill set rather than responsive ones.

Note: As an advanced intervention, the following intervention should be practiced by clinical staff with appropriate training in behavioral health.

Goals:

- Convert negative serial chains of behavior into positive serial chains
- Incorporate chronological order and linear timelines into problem-solving
- Slow impulsivity and offer other options for decisions in a deescalated state
- Improve skills of self-control
- Create a tactile and visual cue for preventive problem-solving of specific behavioral difficulties

Materials:

- *Choose Your Own Adventure* worksheet
- *Choose Your Own Adventure* example worksheet
- Optional: Blank paper, variety of art supplies

Directions:

1. Explain to the client that their initial reaction to something is not always the best option:

   "Sometimes, when things don't go our way or something unexpected happens, our brains move really fast and make decisions that hurt us or result in a consequence. If we could help our brain slow down and think about different options before we act, *we could solve our problems without arguing, feeling bad, or getting a consequence. Let's take some time to change the way your brain works before feelings are hot or messy."*

2. Introduce the *Choose Your Own Adventure* example worksheet and walk through it together, introducing the example of: "My sister ate the last waffle, so I told her I was going to chop her head off, and I lost my PlayStation for six weeks."

3. Discuss with the client that in this scenario, there are three different "adventures" (choices) to the problem. In each adventure column, the client will explore:
   a. The likely consequence to making that choice
   b. How that consequence would make them feel

4. Discuss with the client how to choose which adventure is the best choice. Guide them to reflect on which problem-solving choice gets them the best result from the environment, and which makes them feel the best.

5. Now ask the client to identify a specific behavior of theirs that resulted in a consequence recently, writing (or drawing) the details on the blank *Choose Your Own Adventure* worksheet. Be sure to validate and reinforce their answers as you go.

Optional: You can also offer them blank paper and a variety of art supplies to create their own flow chart.

6. The first adventure listed should be the choice that the client actually made in real life.
   a. They should already know the consequence, and they can reflect on how it made them feel.
   b. Since they know how this adventure ends, invite them to talk through another choice/adventure, teaching them that their first thought doesn't have to become a behavior.
7. Complete adventures 2 and 3 with the client, helping them come up with ideas if needed.
   a. It's common to hear "I don't know" in this step (especially in the third column), which is where the intervention comes to life.
   b. In this instance, guide the client to go through the day in *reverse* chronological order to find an earlier place to initiate a positive serial chain. Review adventure 3 on the *Choose Your Own Adventure* example worksheet again to show how to do this.
8. After the client has filled out their three adventures, assist them in choosing the best option by filling in the checkboxes at the bottom of each column.
9. You can cut the "winning" column from the worksheet and send it home with the client as a visual and tactile reminder for using the choice in preventive problem-solving.
10. Remind the client that even if they make their new choice, there is no guarantee that they will get exactly what they want. Challenge them to be a detective and gather all of the information before problem-solving to prevent unneeded explosions and negative behaviors from occurring.

Tier 2 or 3

School, Treatment, and Community Settings

Use these worksheets for problem-solving specific incidents in classrooms and group settings. This can help adults remain focused on the problem-solving component and retraining negative serial chains instead of their own frustration and negative emotion connected to a repetitive behavioral incident. When children focus on several options to make an informed selection, you encourage growth of positive serial chains of behavior, which will decrease necessity for adult intervention in this setting in the future.

Worksheet

Choose Your Own Adventure

Problem:		
Adventure 1:	**Adventure 2:**	**Adventure 3:**
What does the choice get you?	What does the choice get you?	What does the choice get you?
How does this make you feel?	How does this make you feel?	How does this make you feel?
Is this the path you choose? ❒ **Yes** ❒ **No**	Is this the path you choose? ❒ **Yes** ❒ **No**	Is this the path you choose? ❒ **Yes** ❒ **No**

Example Worksheet

Choose Your Own Adventure

Problem: My sister ate the last waffle.

Adventure 1:	**Adventure 2:**	**Adventure 3:**
I threaten her.	I ask my mom to make pancakes instead.	I wake up earlier so I can get the waffles before my sister does.
What does the choice get you? I lose my PlayStation.	What does the choice get you? I get pancakes but not waffles.	What does the choice get you? I get to eat waffles.
How does this make you feel? Frustrated, sad	How does this make you feel? A little disappointed but okay	How does this make you feel? Smart, happy
Is this the path you choose? ☐ Yes ☒ No	Is this the path you choose? ☐ Yes ☒ No	Is this the path you choose? ☒ Yes ☐ No

Praise/Correct/Praise **B, C, N**

Therapeutic Rationale:

Praise/correct/praise (PCP) is a successive approximation technique that uses positive, intangible reinforcement to encourage desired or on-task behavior. Children with behavioral challenges often receive feedback focused on what they're doing wrong; even when meant to be helpful, it can feel mostly critical. PCP, a strategy adapted from martial arts, takes a different approach by highlighting what the child is already doing well, offering a small correction or adjustment, and then giving immediate praise for making that improvement.

Goals:

- Improve successive approximations for task completion
- Develop neural connections for shaping of tasks

Materials:

- None

Directions:

1. **Praise:** Highlight what the client is already doing well.
2. **Correct:** Offer a small adjustment to be made; ask a question that prompts the next step.
    a. Keep the adjustments small and doable so the child can experience *success* and will want to do it again.
    b. Empower and challenge the client to come up with solutions to solve the adjustment; this develops problem-solving skills.
    c. Resist jumping in and doing the task for the child. A child who doesn't learn to do tasks develops into a teen who doesn't know how to do tasks. Work alongside them, but not for them.
3. **Praise:** Immediately reinforce the adjustment the client is making.
    a. Encourage the behavior to repeat, with specific emphasis on nontangible reward.

Example: A young child cleans her room by stuffing all her belongings in her closet.

1. **Praise:** "Wow, this is the cleanest room I have ever seen! You worked hard."
2. **Correct:** "I see all your stuff is in your closet. Where are all your books supposed to go?" Perhaps she says, "On my bookshelf." You can state, "That's right. Now you can put your books on the shelf."
3. **Praise:** "Great job putting the books on the shelf."
4. Return to the closet to identify the next bite-size adjustment (e.g., blankets go on the bed, toys in the box, stuffed animals in the chair) and continue the process to shape the overarching goal of cleaning the child's room.
5. Once all successive approximations are completed, provide reinforcement through a nontangible reward (*not* a cookie, sticker, token, etc.). For a young child whose developmental task is to become more independent, it might sound like "Oh my gosh, look at this room! It is so clean. And now you can do this all by yourself!"

Tier 1 or 3

School, Treatment, and Community Settings

This technique is especially useful for early childhood to complete tasks such as cleaning up work areas, organizing materials, hand raising, and waiting in line. Small PCPs can be used with whole groups or individuals and are not time-consuming as part of instruction.

Get Out of Trouble Free Passes **B, C**

Therapeutic Rationale:

Children with behavioral challenges often struggle with dishonesty or taking responsibility for their actions, largely because of how their environments have responded to them in the past. These are kids who tend to make noticeable mistakes, and the typical response has often been disciplinary—loss of privileges, restrictions, or punishment. As a result, even when they make a small mistake, they may be less likely to admit it, which limits the ability to guide them toward positive behavioral change. Teaching kids that mistakes are not occasions for punishment but rather *opportunities for change* shifts the entire tone of conversations about behavior.

This intervention is designed to provide kids with the opportunity to take responsibility for and correct their behavior, think critically about their choices, and experience relief from unnecessary consequences that can derail their whole day.

> **Note:** This intervention is applicable for *minor* behavior problems that can be used as opportunities for learning, such as accidentally saying a bad word or bumping into someone on the playground. More serious offenses, like hurting someone's body, feelings, or property, should not be included in this intervention. For repetitive or persevering behaviors, particularly when there doesn't appear to be any effort toward trading the mistake for the exchange behavior, I recommend a three-passes-you're-out policy, after which a pass is no longer an option for that behavior and they need to accept the consequence.

Goals:

- Improve recognition of what behaviors warrant either teaching or consequence
- Increase ability to take personal responsibility for behaviors
- Decrease intensity of intervention when unnecessary
- Improve self-regulation in times of perceived failure or error

Materials:

- *Get Out of Trouble Free Passes* template

Directions:

1. Explain to the client the importance of learning from mistakes:

    "Sometimes, when we've had a lot of behavior challenges and people at home or school have spent a lot of time focusing on what we're doing wrong, it can start to feel like we can't make even the tiniest mistake without getting in trouble. That can make us feel like we've already failed or that the whole day is ruined. When that happens, it can be really tempting to hide what we did or even lie about it, but everyone needs a little grace sometimes. Mistakes shouldn't make us feel ashamed—they should help us learn and

grow. The best way to do that is to see mistakes as chances to make a change. That's exactly what these passes are for."

2. Introduce the client to the get out of trouble free passes. Walk through the directions and prompts about what passes can and cannot be used for:
    a. The client can use them for small mistakes to get a "pass" on the consequence for that choice.
    b. To use one, they must catch themselves making a mistake, and explain—and try—what they could do differently next time.
    c. Once they use a pass, the mistake won't be held against them or brought up again.
    d. They get to choose when to use and save their passes. If they make a mistake and decide *not* to use a pass, it means they're choosing to accept the consequence for their action.
3. Help identify behaviors that would be small and worthy of using a pass, and behaviors that a pass can never be used for. (If you've used the *Boundary Word or Phrase* intervention on page 278, include "not responding / ignoring our boundary word" as a non-pass behavior.) Encourage the client to give some examples as well so you know they understand.
4. Determine how many passes to offer for a specific time period. This will depend on your setting and population; here are some general guidelines:
    a. **Pre-K to first grade:** Two passes per day
    b. **First grade to sixth grade:** Five passes per week
    c. **Middle school:** One pass per week
    d. **High school:** One pass per quarter

Note: There will inevitably be kids who choose to stockpile their passes for a later time, such as the end of the semester or school year. This is okay; they are still engaged in prioritization, adjustment of behavior, and accepting consequences. Do be ready for rapid-fire use of the passes at some point, though!

Tier 1

School, Treatment, and Community Settings

Administrators have long been fans of this technique, as it increases the opportunity for them to do proactive intervention and problem-solving with students in their office, decreasing the amount of time dedicated to documenting benign behaviors. Some have transitioned this tool into a punch-card system, and each kid in their school receives a punch card at the beginning of each semester. If they are sent to the office for behavior that is determined to be sub-threshold for consequence and the student is able to share their exchange behavior, the punch card is marked, and this small behavior no longer warrants conversation or excessive processing.

Handout

Get Out of Trouble Free Passes

These are your get out of trouble free passes. You can use them for small mistakes to get a "pass" on the consequence for that choice. To use one, catch yourself making a mistake, and explain—or try—what you could do differently next time. That's it! Once you use a pass, the mistake won't be held against you or brought up again. You get to choose when to use your passes and when to save them. If you make a mistake and decide *not* to use a pass, it means you're choosing to accept the consequence for your action.

Delayed Gratification **B, C, N**

Therapeutic Rationale:

Delayed gratification is difficult for most people. In a world where we get quick rewards, instant information, and constant dopamine hits, it's no wonder kids struggle with waiting. For children with behavioral disorders, this challenge is even greater. They face the same difficulty as all kids—it's hard to wait—but they've also learned that big behaviors often lead to immediate responses from adults. This unintentionally reinforces interrupting, nagging, yelling, screaming, or acting out, and can cause a simple request or task to quickly escalate into a significant behavioral episode. The therapeutic objective of this intervention is two-fold: educate adults about how to stop reinforcing negative behavior, and increase self-awareness and tolerance of delayed gratification for clients who are exhibiting the negative behavior.

Goals:

- Decrease negative impact of reinforced immediate gratification
- Increase self-awareness and delays in decision-making
- Improve patience and turn-taking in social interactions

Materials:

- *Delayed Gratification* worksheet

Directions:

1. Explain to the client that they will be practicing how to wait:

   "Sometimes it's hard to wait. Our brains say, 'I want this right now' or 'I might forget my question.' Unfortunately, other people have jobs and things to do that make it hard to get to us right away. This can make us feel frustrated or angry, but it doesn't mean they will never help us. It just means we need to pause for a little bit until they can get to us. It means we need to learn how to wait."

2. Ask the client to consider how the world responds to interruption or nagging, and how this translates into a positive, negative, or neutral *feeling*.

3. Provide the client with the *Delayed Gratification* worksheet. Help them brainstorm times that they were unable to wait for something or wanted immediate attention but didn't get it.

4. Help the client brainstorm ways to pause before interrupting. Separate ideas into low-importance strategies (rating of 1–5) and high-importance strategies (rating of 6–10). Some examples could be the following:

   a. Count to a certain number.

   b. Doodle or free write.

c. Ask yourself, "Do I need this right now or can I wait?"

d. Check the clock or set a timer (if you know the amount of time you need to wait).

5. Practice these pausing techniques with the client and encourage them to use their favorites the next time they need to wait for something or someone.

Tier 1

School, Treatment, and Community Settings

Creating a system of delayed gratification in your instructional and therapeutic settings is vital to allowing children the opportunity to pause and problem-solve on their own, as well as identify when they actually need help. If you have a clock in your classroom or therapy space, consider adding colored "pie pieces," which can be a wonderful visual cue to show distinct "listening times" and "speaking/sharing times." You may also pair this intervention with the *Sharing the Conversation* intervention on page 218, which helps children to practice pausing and letting others speak.

Worksheet

Delayed Gratification

Waiting can be hard to do. Your brain might sometimes tell you:

1. You should get what you want *right now*.
2. What other people want doesn't matter.
3. If you keep asking, get loud, or act out, you might get what you want quicker!

Then you end up with consequences you don't want. Maybe you should have just waited! Think of a time you felt impatient waiting for someone or interrupted someone while they were busy with something else. What happened?

____

____

____

____

On a scale of 1–10 (where 1 is "not important at all" and 10 is "very important"), how important was the thing you were waiting for or wanted? ______________

If your score is between 1–5, what are some strategies you could use to practice patience?

1. ____
2. ____
3. ____

If your score is between 6–10, what are some strategies you could use to appropriately get what you need?

1. ____
2. ____
3. ____

Let's practice these together!

Assigned Participation Tasks **B, C**

Therapeutic Rationale:

Refusal to participate or engage in tasks can be problematic with behavioral populations. This warrants a conversation regarding comorbidity of behavioral disorders and mood disturbance. In fact, behavioral populations are at a much higher risk for comorbid mood disturbance, which typically gets framed as part of their behavioral presentation rather than indicative of difficulties with depression or anxiety. Kids with comorbid depression have difficulties with motivation, lethargy, and task initiation; this can manifest in behavioral populations as "refusal to work" or "resistance to engage in tasks." Comorbid anxiety also manifests in behavioral populations, especially as symptoms of perfectionism, where children become overwhelmed before even trying or start a task and then refuse to finish it.

Both of these sets of presentations inform addressing not just the behavioral component but also the mood-related symptoms associated with it. This group intervention engages individuals in a task, improving task initiation and working toward task completion.

Goals:

- Improve task initiation, task persistence, and task completion
- Incorporate group/family model interventions to transition responsibility within a compartmentalized task

Materials:

- A heterogeneous group or family system to include normative, behavioral, and mood-related individuals
- A classroom, therapeutic, or home task, broken into several pieces to be distributed equally among the participants

Directions:

1. Explain to the group that we can get things done when we share responsibility:

   "Sometimes getting a job started and finished can be hard, but when we share the responsibility with others, we feel connected and confident."

2. Introduce the group to a participation activity that will be broken into several steps. Let them know that each person in the group will complete only a *part* of the assignment, like a relay race.

3. The chore or task the group chooses will depend on the environment and the age of the children involved. You may also need to break the tasks down further if there are more people participating. For example, in a task to do the dishes as a family, the task distribution may be as follows:

   a. Child 1 clears the dishes from the table.

   b. Caregiver 1 scrapes the food from the dishes into the trash.

c. Child 2 washes the dishes in warm, soapy water.

d. Child 3 rinses the dishes.

e. Caregiver 2 dries and puts the dishes away.

4. Each person will complete their part and pass to the next, not unlike passing the baton.

5. In the next three to five days, invite the group to decrease the number of participants and increase the percentage of the assignment to be completed by each person. For example, this could be the change over a period of a few weeks:

    a. Five participants at 20 percent each

    b. Four participants at 25 percent each

    c. Three participants at 33 percent each

    d. Two participants at 50 percent each

    e. One participant at 100 percent (keeping in mind that 100 percent is an unrealistic expectation for final completion)

Tier 2 or 3

School, Treatment, and Community Settings

By actively practicing this in classrooms and therapeutic settings, you will see an increase in ability and a desire to initiate tasks and persist as part of a hand-to-hand transition for task completion. In my experience, a student that normally completes 30–35 percent of an assignment will successfully complete 65–70 percent in just two weeks. Even if change does not occur this quickly, making small adjustments as you go will help the child move in the direction of full task completion.

References

Altman, H. P., & Nowicki, S. (2024). The role of posture in the formation of social relationships. In D. Chadee & A. Kostić (Eds.), *Body language communication* (pp. 129–150). Springer Nature Switzerland.

Brodersen, K., Hammami, N., & Katapally, T. R. (2022). Smartphone use and mental health among youth: It is time to develop smartphone-specific screen time guidelines. *Youth, 2*(1), 23–38. https://doi.org/10.3390/youth2010003

Cloud, H. (2023). *Trust: Knowing when to give it, when to withhold it, how to earn it, and how to fix it when it gets broken.* Worthy Publishing.

Cloud, H., & Townsend, J. (2017). *Boundaries: When to say yes, how to say no to take control of your life* (Rev. ed.). Zondervan.

Como, D. H., Goodfellow, M., Hudak, D., & Cermak, S. A. (2023). A scoping review: Social stories supporting behavior change for individuals with autism. *Journal of Occupational Therapy, Schools, & Early Intervention, 17*(1), 154–175. https://doi.org/10.1080/19411243.2023.2168824

Di Salvo, G., Perotti, C., Filippo, L., Garrone, C., Rosso, G., & Maina, G. (2024). Assessing suicidality in adult ADHD patients: Prevalence and related factors: Suicidality in adult ADHD patients. *Annals of General Psychiatry, 23*(1), 42. https://doi.org/10.1186/s12991-024-00528-8

Duke, M., & Nowicki, S. (2005). The Emory dyssemia index. In V. L. Manusov (Ed.), *The sourcebook of nonverbal measures* (pp. 35–46). Psychology Press.

Gath, M., Horwood, L. J., Gillon, G., McNeill, B., & Woodward, L. J. (2026). Longitudinal associations between screen time and children's language, early educational skills, and peer social functioning. *Developmental Psychology, 62*(3), 638–652. https://doi.org/10.1037/dev0001907

Gentzke, A. S., Wang, T. W., Cornelius, M., Park-Lee, E., Ren, C., Sawdey, M. D., Cullen, K. A., Loretan, C., Jamal, A., & Homa, D. M. (2022). Tobacco product use and associated factors among middle and high school students — National Youth Tobacco Survey, United States, 2021. *Morbidity and Mortality Weekly Report, 71*(SS-5), 1–29. http://dx.doi.org/10.15585/mmwr.ss7105a1

Gray, C. (2021). Social stories™. In N. Grove (Ed.), *Storytelling, special needs and disabilities* (2nd ed., pp. 152–158). Routledge.

Kar, S. S., Dube, R., Goud, B. K. M., Gibrata, Q. S., El-Balbissi, A. A., Al Salim, T. A., & Fatayerji, R. N. M. A. K. (2025). Impact of screen time on development of children. *Children, 12*(10), 1297. https://doi.org/10.3390/children12101297

Morgan, A., & Jacobson, E. (2019). Autism spectrum disorders. In V. F. Carrión & J. Rettger (Eds.), *Applied mindfulness: Approaches in mental health for children and adolescents.* https://doi.org/10.1176/appi.books.9781615379255.lg09

National Sleep Foundation. (2025, November 17). *How much sleep do you really need?* https://www.thensf.org/how-many-hours-of-sleep-do-you-really-need

Nowicki, S., & van Buskirk, A. (2022). Non-verbal communication: From good endings to better beginnings. In R. J. Sternberg & A. Kostić (Eds.), *Nonverbal communication in close relationships* (pp. 277–305). Palgrave Macmillan.

Srichawla, B. S., Telles, C. C., Schweitzer, M., & Darwish, B. (2022) Attention deficit hyperactivity disorder and substance use disorder: A narrative review. *Cureus, 14*(4), Article e24068. https://doi.org/10.7759/cureus.24068

Winner, M. G., & Crooke, P. (2020). *You are a social detective! Explaining social thinking to kids* (2nd ed.). Think Social Publishing.

Acknowledgments

I would be remiss not to extend my thanks for every single individual that has entrusted me with their mental health and journey of healing, for without them I would not have grown as a clinician (and person) and stayed hungry for knowledge, compassion, and humility.

To:

- My husband, David, who is forever my greatest cheerleader, advocate, and rump-kicker.
- My child, Ruth M., whose creativity, worldview, humor, and resilience is awe-inspiring.
- PESI, who 23 years ago took a risk on a bold and outspoken young clinician and helped her see the country one city and conference room at a time, and Kate Sample, who stumbled through this publishing process with me and gave me the space to share my voice and ideas.
- All of my friends and family who have unconditionally loved me through the arduous process of going to the cabin in the mountains to get this book out of my head . . . finally . . .
- And especially, for those who have challenged my way of thinking about expectations in a truly transformative way: LeAnn, Court, Tracy, Dave, Melissa, Marc, Geraldine, the Stanleys, and Amanda/Squirt.

> "Think not about if your glass is half full or half empty, but rather, am I still thirsty or has my thirst been quenched? In the reality of your experience, you will discover . . . perspective." —JWD

About the Author

Jen L. Wilke-Deaton, MA, LPA, has more than 27 years of experience providing therapy, consultation, and psychological testing for kids, teens, and families across multiple settings, including inpatient treatment, outpatient clinics, schools, and the judicial system. She currently works in a private practice in central Kentucky, specializing in crisis management, ADHD, child abuse, PTSD, DBT, behavioral disorders, anxiety, ASD, and attachment. A nationally recognized trainer, consultant, and keynote speaker, Jen has traveled to all 50 states, providing education to foster care organizations, social services, schools, psychiatric hospitals, juvenile detention facilities, early intervention programs, in-home therapy, colleges and universities, and case management services. She is a tireless and passionate advocate for children and families, and her authenticity shines through, often coupled with humor, storytelling, and a genuine commitment to helping others.

She has developed a parent training program recognized by the Governor's Commission for the Treatment of Children & Families and Kentucky's Child Protective Services and helped develop a regional children's crisis stabilization unit, a children's advocacy center, and an intensive after-school program for behaviorally challenged youth.

Jen regularly speaks on mental health issues and child abuse for Morehead State University, Eastern Kentucky University, Kentucky Child Protective Services, and National Public Radio; serves as the psychometrician for college athletes through the Center for Academic and Tutoring Services (CATS) at the University of Kentucky; and provides psychological evaluations and therapeutic support services for the Department of Disability Determinations and the Office of Vocational Rehabilitation.

She has also published *Creative Parenting Skills, Parenting Better Children, Awareness in Focus: Modern Guided Imagery Techniques for Immediate Practice* (audio CD), *Awareness in Focus by Kids for Kids* (audio CD), and *The Mandala Workbook: Activities Across the Lifespan.*

Jen earned her undergraduate degree in psychology from Northern Illinois University, with research focus in trauma-informed care and EMDR. She earned her master's degree in clinical psychology from Morehead State University, with emphasis in areas of neuropsychology, trust, betrayal, and trauma.

A Chicagoland native, Jen has resided in central Kentucky for the last 30 years with her profoundly patient and supportive husband and their child, a precocious and talented pianist and composer. She is a supporter of the arts and the local community mission garden and acts as a prop-mom for the MCHS marching band. (Yes, she welds and builds!)